BY WALTER KERR

How Not to Write a Play

PIECES at EIGHT

by

Walter Kerr

SIMON AND SCHUSTER   NEW YORK

1957

FIRST PRINTING

LIBRARY OF CONGRESS CATALOG CARD NUMBER 56-6682

MANUFACTURED IN THE UNITED STATES OF AMERICA

BY AMERICAN BOOK–STRATFORD PRESS, INC., NEW YORK

for my mother

ACKNOWLEDGMENTS

For permission to reprint the pieces that follow, the author wishes to thank the editors of The New York Herald Tribune, The Commonweal, Harper's Magazine, Harper's Bazaar, Theater Annual, and World Theater.

CONTENTS

Contents

∽ ONE ∾

Dress Rehearsal

∽ *1* ∾

LATE AUGUST is a fine time of year in the theater. The first handful of shows is just slipping into rehearsal. People with jobs are lounging around stage doors, chattering happily. People without jobs are still going to get jobs. Everything is starting all over again, and the season is going to be wonderful.

Five or six of the most beautiful plays ever written are being read aloud on cool, darkened stages. The stages may not actually be cool, and the assistant stage manager may be running out for cartons of Cokes pretty regularly, but they seem cool. It's dawn on Broadway at the moment and no vulgar statistics about the heat, the chances of success, or anything else are going to diminish the universal, confident glow.

Never have there been cleaner, firmer scripts to turn in the hand. Looking at such magnificently typed prose, with nary an unkind cut on it yet, you know that anything so perfectly formed, so lyrically literate, so impeccably punctuated is bound to fall like honey from the lips. This is molten gold, this script; and everybody is in love with it.

The first week of rehearsals is like the beginning of time, before the universe has been soiled by dirty commerce, despicable critics, or benefit audiences. Lifelong friendships are formed lasting right into Boston. Actors speak to authors; actors' agents speak to authors' agents. Warm little groups cluster in the auditorium and chuckle appreciatively over each new piece of stage business. Members of the production staff actually lunch with one another, a common vision of burgeoning beauty binding them into a mutually admiring brotherhood.

Appreciation runs high. The director has but to crinkle his eyes boyishly and chance some such sally as "Well, are we all here?" to get a trill of merry laughter from the bright-eyed folk in freshly laundered dungarees. Off in a corner a player with forty-six sides (a big part) is ardently telling a player with six sides (a small part) that he really has the much better role. "You're not on long, but when you're on, you count" is the choked-up phrase. "Do you really think so?" asks the six-side recruit just up from the summer theaters, clutching his magic little half-sheets of paper a bit tighter and pushing far, far to the back of his mind the absolute certainty that all six will be eliminated in New Haven. When the assistant stage manager, who is ready to take over the directorial reins should the director fall ill, snaps a knowing "Take ten," there is a great proffering of cigarettes on the sidewalk while somebody produces a Brownie and takes pictures of everybody else.

The second week is, shall we say, more businesslike. Everyone wears glasses now, and hair-dos tend to become more severe. The director, who has promised himself that he will keep to a pack a day, now has three half-filled, nervously rumpled packages of cigarettes at his elbow at all times. Somebody has done a little unnecessary tinkering with the script; and somebody else is going to have to do a lot more to get it back where it was. A backer has been reported in the auditorium, but no one is able to find out whether he said anything before he left.

The author, who formerly liked to sit in the second row so that he might be available for quick consultation with the director, now sits in the rear, close to his agent. When author and agent are ready to leave, they no longer climb, beaming, over the rickety stairs to the stage and pass chummily through the company; they slip out through the double-doors at the back and are heard in soft, urgent conversation in the lobby. The actors have begun to eye one another's agents speculatively, wondering whether they ought to switch ("After all, if she can do so much for that clunk, what mightn't she do for me?"). Toward the end of the week the play is run through, roughly, from beginning to end, after which the company is solemnly dismissed while the staff, poker-faced, goes into a huddle. Half the company is very slow to get out of rehearsal clothes, hovering on the fringes in the hope of overhearing something; the other half is very quick to go, in obvious fear that they might.

The third week of rehearsal is merely confusing. Now that the play is ready to be put together, all the actors disappear. Should anyone be foolish enough to inquire where they have gone, he will learn that they are, one and all, at the costumer's being fitted. Fitting comes in very handy at this time; it keeps everyone's mind off the play, which must soon open. During this trying period the author goes to a great many cocktail parties, where he fastens eagerly onto anyone who will ask him the key question: "What are they doing to your play?" The director is busy with the scene designer, being reassured that a 48 x 22 setting will actually go onto a 36 x 12 stage. He nods sagely as the mechanics of this feat are explained to him, and holds the ground plan up to the light in a very professional fashion.

The lighting expert gets the director on the telephone to point out that it will be impossible for the company to rehearse in New

Haven because it will take three days to mount and focus the necessary electrical equipment. The company, back from Capezio's and now shod as well as sequined, are heard to express mild concern about the shape of the play, of which they have retained some dim memory. They are promptly assured that the first out-of-town performance counts for no more than "a dress rehearsal" and that "we'll have plenty of time to fix." Forgotten for the moment is the fact that this "dress rehearsal" is likely to be reviewed; forgotten also is the blind panic which sets in in the lounge of the bar across the street immediately afterward. Hope is with them and the world is young and all scamper blithely to the company manager to find out about train accommodations. Two of the younger members of the company miss the train next morning and arrive in New Haven, ashen with despair, just in time to hear the electrician threaten to quit because the director wants to rehearse. The neatly fitted costumes arrive in stages: one third for the first performance, one third immediately after the first performance, and one third in time for the Saturday matinee.

By that time the first reviews are out. Either the local press is good and *Variety* bad, or *Variety* is good and the local press is bad. In any case, there's something for everybody, and all can go to work with a will. All that remains to do is rewrite, recast, redirect, and, heaven forbid, refinance the show. The actors now rehearse by day and play by night until they are sufficiently exhausted to be seen in New York.

⤳ 2 ⤶

THE PEOPLE who empty wastebaskets in New Haven have a terrible time of it during these early weeks. With a whole squadron of productions hurling themselves at the out-of-town firing lines, hoping to survive for what always looks like a lush October in New York, the period of cutting and hacking and wholesale rewriting begins.

Into the trash cans of Philadelphia and Boston go entire scenes, once cherished characters, long speeches the author truly loved, and thousands of odd snippets that have—under the chillingly accurate eye of an actual audience—become spectacularly superfluous. Subordinate figures that were written as males turn, in the twist of a typewriter, into females; where two noble souls once threaded their ways through the labyrinth of an author's plotting, one composite soul now strides the stage on sturdier, or perhaps wobblier, legs; an ingénue who has spent her rehearsal time finding true love in the arms of a swarthy juvenile discovers, after the first week's run, that her heart was quite misplaced and that the curtain is hereafter going to come down on her passionate acceptance of the elderly roué who was so funny in the first and second acts. Life is malleable in the theatrical suburbs.

This paste-pot revision of what were thought to be eternal values, so characteristic of the American theater during its warming-up exercises, is something of an open scandal to other nations. The British, for instance, are candidly appalled at the transpositions that are wrought on the American road. One recent complaint by a distinguished British dramatist describes the whole untidy business as nothing more than "hasty improvisation" and registers outright horror at production methods "that allow a leading character to have a cancer in Boston but only a touch of arthritis on 42nd St."

5

And absurdity is very often the result of those frantic late-night decisions in cluttered hotel rooms, decisions arrived at under the pressure of mounting financial losses, the increasing tremors of a star facing disaster in New York, and the joint bafflement of authors, directors, and producers who had imagined they were creating one kind of play and are now being told by intelligent customers that they have hatched quite another. The British have it rather better than we do: since it is still possible to make money on a provincial tour before daring London, the inevitable pruning and patching can be done in an atmosphere of relative calm, relative rationality, and relative confidence. Even obvious successes, doing capacity business on the journey into town, are apt to take weekly losses here. The costs of repainting a piece of furniture that a backer's wife doesn't like, relighting an alcove that the star's agent doesn't like, and restaging a scene that even the author's mother doesn't like are so high that possible profits are quickly gobbled up in the desperate determination to make a going thing go better. The rumble of thunder is always overhead.

I doubt, though, that much real harm is done. When a show comes into New York with the leading character suffering from sunstroke rather than her original sinus condition, or with the principal comedian doing his old vaude routine to make up for a certain lack in the second act, the chances are about a thousand to one that the enterprise wasn't exactly a pip to begin with. I am reliably informed that a musical to which we were treated not long ago was actually worse when it opened on Broadway than it had been six weeks earlier and a thousand miles away; but since it seems to have had only about a forty per cent protein content when it first saw the light of night, the reduction to thirty was not a serious loss. It is the transparently failing show that is likely to make the most frantic forays into left field.

A show that has a chance acts as a quick stimulus on all connected with it. *Guys and Dolls,* which might have relaxed on its Philadelphia raves, managed to add the "Floating Crap Game" chant and "Take Back Your Mink" before catching the train to New

York. Even a "sensitive" play may become more sensitive under pressure: *The Chalk Garden* seems to have done exactly that. If we have three or four versions of one of Shakespeare's most popular plays our puzzlement may be partly due to the fact that the management loved the thing and never tired of trying to brighten it up.

The pressure itself, exhausting as it is to the folk who are fretting under it, sometimes serves as a supercharge. Complacency is less productive than concern. And, in the end, we've always got to remember that the theater is, for good or ill, a social situation. If the paying guests don't respond as a writer meant them to respond, they can't really be told to stand in a corner and hang their heads. The writer has simply got to trot out something to keep the party going, whether it is an improved soliloquy or a passel of dancing girls.

What is going into those September wastebaskets, then, is an audience's boredom. And what comes coiling out of those hot New Haven typewriters is—sometimes—inspiration.

∽ 3 ∾

WE DON'T HEAR only from our British cousins about the mayhem we visit on scripts. We hear, occasionally, from our own playwrights, too. A young man named Harry Essex, for instance, has devoted an entire novel, *I Put My Right Foot In*, to the matter.

Mr. Essex appears to have started out in life as a playwright. His first play, like so many other first plays, failed. The story he tells in his book is that of a young playwright whose first play has failed, and failed for very specific reasons: it was destroyed in production by the manager, the director, the actors and—Mr. Essex doesn't say this, but I'm sure it's a mere oversight—the bill posters.

In the cold and gloomy theatrical world of the author's experience and/or imagination, a corrupt manager helps scuttle the author's beautiful script by asking for tasteless changes in it. A vain and hysterical director batters it into still worse shape by putting a couple of Hollywood hacks to work rewriting it. The acting company, apparently an assortment of drunks and nymphomaniacs, apply their subhuman intelligences to the lines of the play and satisfactorily complete the wrecking job. The playwright's lot is a sorry one.

The book is not all self-pity, and the playwriting hero is assigned some of the blame for the debacle. As he cuts his way through this creative jungle he becomes greedy, disloyal, intellectually dishonest. He too is corrupt. But since it is the production process that has corrupted him, the theater—or at least our kind of theater—remains the principal villain.

I'm sure that a convocation of playwrights could substantiate, in one detail or another, each of Mr. Essex' gaudy charges. I guess you could find a manager without taste if you went looking for one. As for directors, Maxwell Anderson has long since pointed out that the masterpiece was never written that could stand up under the staging of a really inspired bonehead. Mr. Anderson is right; you have only to look at Shakespeare's plays in production to be sure of it. And everybody knows what actors are. Actors are people who clamber over the footlights during rehearsal and shamble up the aisle toward the author with grieved countenances and the plaintive question: "Say, are you really in love with this line?"

I once knew an author who used to hide in the balcony where the principal actor couldn't find him. The day came, though, when he heard the soft pad of familiar feet stumbling up the balcony stairs in the dark, and the jig was up.

But if Mr. Essex' little chamber of horrors were to be authenticated in its every nuance, its final effect would still, I think, be false. Worse yet, for the young playwright who took its fiction for warning fact, it would be seriously misleading.

Mr. Essex is, whether intentionally or not, perpetuating some lamentable legends. One of these, of course, is that of the brilliant first play that has been butchered during its out-of-town tryout, wrenched out of shape by panic-stricken professionals terrified of losing their investment.

No doubt there have been such mishaps, in which cases the play, if it is any good, has probably turned up three years later in an off-Broadway production and become a sensational success. But most plays are not butchered out of town; most plays are saved out of town—by the use of scissors, stilettos, and clouts on the head. Most plays are not sand-bagged by selfish actors; most plays are conscientiously performed and many are given more dimension than they deserve by personable players. Most plays are not subtly but irretrievably ruined by managerial suggestions for revision; most plays are slowly teased into shape by careful managers, practical directors, and even inspired scene designers. (I know of two enormous successes in recent years that took their final structural shape from the imaginations of the men responsible for mounting them.)

I'm not concerned, however, with singing a little song of praise to helpful professionals. I'm mostly concerned with the psychological effect of this sort of thing on the young playwright.

The green young man with the green young play is, quite naturally, in love with it. His critical faculties, especially where his first love is concerned, are apt to be slightly underdeveloped. He has, furthermore, conducted his flirtation with the muse in the favorable air of the study; he has very little intimacy with that sharp-eyed, quick-witted, terribly discerning group called the audience.

Having heard all the legends, though, and being morally certain that there is a theater-wide conspiracy against the integrity of his work, he goes into battle clad in armor. His spine is firm, his manner wary. Better to stand on his rights, and not cut that comma, than run the risk of distortion. When he gets into trouble in Philadelphia, he sets his jaw, clutches the pristine script to his breast, and waits for vindication in New York—or thereafter. At the time when his mind needs to be most supple, it is most suspicious.

9

The legend hurts him in another way. Should the play fail—and most first plays have a fairish chance of failing—he has dozens of people to blame it on. The managers mauled it, the director misunderstood it, the actors vulgarized it. He has horrifying stories to tell his friends, and the legend supports him down the line. The likeliest eventuality is that he will now go back to his typewriter, his inexperience intact, to bang out another beautiful dud.

A playwright does need tenacity, and a certain measure of self-respect. But in the earliest stages of his career he also needs what the philosophers used to call docility: a capacity for being taught. He needs to listen to an audience and be able to hear what it is coughing. He needs to be able to listen to a suggestion as though it were not necessarily a cunning trap.

When he is very rich and very famous he will have plenty of time to be intractable. Everybody will be afraid of him then, and he will get his own way with ease. (It will be interesting to see what he does with it. The most successful playwrights, suddenly in trouble in Philadelphia, are the first to grab a phone and badger their acquaintances into hurrying down to give them a "tough opinion." They may not really want a tough opinion; but they have learned to ask for it.)

At the moment, the beginning playwright wants an infinite flexibility, and a slowness to wrath. It's no simple matter to be self-critical after a failure. But it's probably the only way of preventing the next one.

✌ 4 ✌

BLACK MAGIC may not be indispensable to success in the theater, but it's handy to have a few incantations around while producers are putting their new shows through the agonies of an Eastern exposure and beginning to wonder whether the scripts they loved so dearly a month ago are what New York needs after all.

Tryout time is a trying time. Intelligence, energy, taste and cold cash have gone into the preliminary stages of getting a show together. But now that all sorts of unpredictable things have happened during rehearsal and the out-of-town audience is behaving in an exceedingly curious fashion, all pretense to sophistication must be abandoned. The rabbit's foot, the witch's forelock, and the cheerful aphorism learned at mother's knee are swiftly rushed into the breach.

Somewhere these September evenings—high up in the Ritz or deep in the Touraine—one pair of bloodshot eyes is looking into another.

"Well, we know one thing—we've got an audience show."

This means that the reviews have been bad. "Audience show" is an old Druid phrase originally associated with the fall harvesting rites and now popularly believed to have considerable efficacy in turning parboiled turkey into gold. It is not meant to indicate that hinterland audiences are actually battering down the doors to get in, but that they will do so the minute word gets around. The phrase is a magnificent morale-builder and has been known to carry whole trainloads of actors back to Grand Central and right through a two-week run at the Belasco.

Sometimes, of course, tryout audiences are so sparse that this particular fetish cannot reasonably be invoked. In this case it is customary to pound the hotel service table, upsetting the coffee cups stacked high on it, and stoutly insist, "There's an audience for this play!"

This is a fairly safe rubric. For one thing, you are not immediately required to explain that you are thinking of a Maori tribe you once spent a hot summer with, and, for another, you are using a formula which is subject to endless adaptation. Three weeks after the show has closed you can insist "I *still* say there's an audience for that play!" without permanently injuring your standing as seer.

Some out-of-town soothsayers make a profound study of audience reaction. These hawkeyes are likely to come back to the hotel room, flop onto the nearest unmade bed, and announce, "Well, they weren't laughing, but they were enjoying it."

There follows a detailed analysis of how the audience sat absolutely quiet, completely attentive to the comedy before them. The possibility that they were transfixed with horror does not, as a rule, occur to these gentlemen. (I always liked the switch worked out by a friend of mine after he'd come from a particularly gamy farce: "Well, they were laughing, but they weren't enjoying it.")

There are a good many variations on these basic runes. If you will listen carefully, you can hear them drifting in on any still autumn night: "I'll tell you what we've got—strictly a New York show."

This means that Boston has been unkind and that they were mad to think of unveiling it in so unenlightened a burg in the first place.

"I think we can get it past the critics."

This is immediately followed by instructions to the director to play the show as fast as possible, on the theory that what the critics can't see won't hurt them.

Then there are the breathless long-distance telephone calls—Philadelphia, Washington, Hartford, Pittsburgh—to find out how the other fellow's tryout is doing. The witch doctor who has just put through the latest call drops the receiver imposingly, turns to his tensed associates, and, suppressing the wild joy that wells up in him, mutters sympathetically, "Poor guy. Boy, has *he* got a bomb!"

This is the cue for a hilarious round of self-congratulation, not because your rival is in dire trouble but because you follow him into New York, and everybody knows that if you follow a flop you're bound to have a hit.

Of course, there is a somewhat opposed school of necromancy which holds that you are better off following a hit, because a hit softens up the atmosphere and makes everybody more generous. You just pick the superstition which most appeals to you, or, perhaps, the one that works out in your favor.

Black magic in Boston takes still other forms. There is the sudden, intuitive communication which reveals that a show's difficulties will be altogether resolved by replacing the actress who plays the second assistant parlor maid. There is the theory that it is the costumes that are "killing" the show. The producer of a disastrous failure with which I was all too closely connected once brightened the Boston morning with the momentous announcement that what our show needed was a new ground cloth.

There is great confidence in the notion that all will be well if the new juvenile lead can simply be flown in from Hollywood. Hollywood is not the magic formula here; "flown in" is. An actor who took a train would do nothing to lift the spirits of a flagging company; the image of Apollo actually descending from the clouds is everything.

Nor is the cabalistic urge confined to those medicine men who are sweating out failures. A potential hit breeds the same crossed fingers, the same over-the-shoulder glance at Hecate. The man who has a show that is going well in Wilmington is a man who is worried to death—you will find him circulating miserably among his friends begging them to moderate their enthusiasm. He doesn't want his show "overbuilt." The fact that one of the most overbuilt shows in history, an item called *South Pacific*, turned out to be thoroughly up to its overbuild does not deter him: Dick Rodgers may have a more sympathetic poltergeist.

There is the producer who stakes everything on a good out-of-town reputation; and the producer who prefers to have things go badly so that he can come in "with his hat in his hand." There is the producer who believes it best to book a thousand theater parties so that tickets will be hard to get; and the producer who is nervous about booking too many theater parties for fear tickets will be too hard to get.

In short, there are producers and producers—all of them cultists of the evil eye.

As THE NEW SHOWS take a last bracing breath before the madcap plunge into New York, those of us who simply can't wait bury ourselves deep in the Sunday papers, soaking up little preparatory whiffs of what is to come.

"This new play represents a real departure for So-and-so," we read, gobbling eagerly at the hopeful paragraphs some publicity man has prepared. All season long typewriters are busy in Philadelphia, in New Haven, in Boston, sending ahead the kind of word that is meant to pave the way, whet our appetites, and perhaps craftily shape our expectations.

If a play has been found a little flimsy in Philadelphia, the news will come through that it is "for laughing purposes only, not a message in it anywhere." If a play has absolutely confounded the brighter minds of Boston, we will be duly warned that "this is a play the audience must bring something to." If the subject matter of a play is slightly delicate, and no one is certain how it is going to be received, the leading player will send on an interview in which the word "sensitive" occurs with hypnotic regularity.

This sort of preconditioning is obviously sensible, and it has the further merit of offering us all a pleasant pastime with which to while away our Sunday afternoons. Speaking for myself, I find it possible to spend three or four charmingly idle hours puzzling out the answer to the question: What happened to the play in Pittsburgh to produce this particular piece of prose? It's better than helping the children find four hidden faces in a leafy old oak tree, anyway.

There are, however, a couple of preopening gambits that seem to me slightly dangerous, and I'd like to mention them to the press people for whatever the warning may be worth. It is never wise to suggest that the producer has been courageous in doing the play. This tack usually comes from the lips of the leading actress. "I think the producer is so brave," she has murmured between cracked cups of coffee in a Washington dressing room. "Every other manager turned it down. No one would touch it. Not commercial, they said. But our producer isn't simply money-mad. If it never makes a nickel, he'll be glad he did it. He has integrity."

The trouble with this one is that no one wants to ruin a man's integrity. Suppose you went to see it. Suppose you paid money to get in. Suppose the show made a nickel. The man would be corrupted—all his courage gone for nothing. The audience would much rather stay at home where it can continue to admire his gallantry.

I sometimes think it would be better if the interview read as follows:

"The one thing you've got to say about our producer is that he hasn't a shred of taste. Not an ideal anywhere in that third-rate brain. All he cares about is making a fast buck, and, believe me, he's picked the play to do it. Never have I seen such a pot-boiling, audience-baiting, commercial piece of corn. It'll run forever. We'll all hate ourselves, but, what the hell, it's a living."

This play, I feel, now has a chance.

Another approach that must be used with caution is the "Not everyone is going to like our play" approach. "This is not a play for every taste" is the way it goes. "Some of our audiences loathe it; some have come back five, six, seven times and mean to see it again and again." (These are not, as may be thought, investors; they are ushers.)

The sly appeal imbedded in this routine is, of course, the appeal to the Superior Taste. The management suggests that only people of taste will like the play; everybody in the world considers himself a man of taste; therefore, everybody in the world will come to see it. It doesn't work out that way, though. Although you know yourself to be a man of taste, you have a trembling apprehension that your taste may have certain limits and that they may be reached somewhere just short of this particular Walpurgisnacht. You note also that people who like this show tend to go five, six, or seven times and you have no intention of going to it—or to any other show from *Guys and Dolls* on down—five, six, or seven times. A prospect so terrifying must be cut off at the roots. In addition, you have, at one unlucky time or another, been caught in a lobby with the kind of people who do seem to attend certain shows five, six, or seven times and you are not eager to repeat the experience. You scratch the show.

Then there is the announcement that "our play is about loneliness, about the waste of human values, about the emptiness of modern life. Our principal characters are, respectively, seventy-five, seventy-six, and seventy-seven years of age. There is no violence in this play, no conventional drama—how could there be? There is just this sense of loss—of failure. We do not try to solve the problem. There is no quick solution. If we can just get some one person in the audience to point a finger and say 'This is appalling—this must be *stopped*,' we'll be happy."

The temptations aroused here need not be discussed. Suffice it to say that nothing short of casting Mickey Rooney in one of the principal roles, and having Mr. Rooney give a twenty-minute concert on the trap drums immediately following the performance, could save the enterprise. In general, press agents should avoid describing a play in terms calculated to send people directly to Elliott Murphy's Aquashow or, should that entertainment be closed for the winter, to set them to dwelling fondly on its remembered glories and patiently waiting for its early resumption.

Beware, too—O savants of the press corps—that alarming phrase about a play's being of the kind you must "bring something to." As someone has said—my wife, I think it was—whenever I am asked to bring something to a play, I bring a book.

It can't be easy for the publicity man. I see him now, staring at a new show on the Philadelphia boards, and wondering what in heaven's name he is going to say about it. There are times, I believe, when it would be best just to announce the name of the show and the fact that "seats are on sale for the next sixteen weeks." That sounds confident.

TWO

Great Expectations

~ 1 ~

As I sip a late-summer gin-and-tonic and study the announcements saying that the first six shows of the season are now in rehearsal, the next six are getting ready to go, and the six after that are making book on which of the earlier productions will fail quickly and so provide *them* with an available playhouse, I am invariably approached by a man who wants to refresh my gin-and-tonic and ask me a question. "How's the new season going to be?" is the question, and the man who asks it always looks as though he expected an answer.

Personally, I never know how a new season is going to be. Who can say what fiery visions have successfully committed themselves to paper, what lumpish doodlings have mysteriously endeared themselves to producers with money, what odd combinations of the right writer, the right actor, the right director, and the right mean temperature are about to be born? One of the real pleasures of going to the theater is the pleasure of being fooled: you may think you've divined something of the character of an enterprise in advance, but the actuality is always—for good or ill—astonishing.

I guess there's only one thing I'm sure of each year: that the public will support a surprising number of second-rate entertainments before the season is done.

This distresses a great many people. One of the battles I'm everlastingly getting into has to do with the relative taste of those pleasant folk who persistently bundle their ready cash toward the town's box-office windows. Being an innocent sort, with high and impracticable ideals, I keep announcing that the taste of the general public is genuinely good and that the best is honorably supported. "How can you say such a thing?" scream my companions, putting their glasses on sharply, the better to see me. A barrage of horrifying examples is now hurled at me, a veritable drum roll of obviously sentimental or obviously illiterate or obviously carpentered exhibits which have, despite their transparent deficiencies, caught the fancy of the public.

The attitude isn't a new one, of course, nor one articulated solely, and shrilly, by cocktail-party companions. You'll come across it, neat as a pin, in the measured and altogether delightful prose of Harley Granville-Barker. I'd been having a splendid time leafing the old Barker lectures, "On Dramatic Method," finding myself wonderfully stimulated by any number of odd remarks: the author suggests, among other things, that if Othello and Iago are conspicuously oversize and unlifelike creatures, the dramatist in Shakespeare has simply made a world that never existed before and then challenged the poet in Shakespeare to make it exist now. That's good reading, and good practice.

At this point, however, I stumbled over a reference to the audience that had thronged into the Elizabethan playhouse: "its public, like our own—but like every public, I suppose, anywhen and anywhere—had been more remarkable for appetite than taste."

There you have it again. Even Shakespeare's customers, we are told, were lacking in discrimination. They supported Shakespeare, true. But they also cheerfully swallowed down an awful lot of trash.

Holding the beliefs I do, I bridled as I read. A minute later, though, it had occurred to me that in this little offhand thrust there lurked a hint of the whole truth of the matter, maybe even the end of an argument. It seems to me that what we are always objecting to is not the audience's taste but its appetite—an appetite so wholesome and so hearty that it not only gobbles up all the first-rate work that is available to it but, smacking its lips, descends carnivorously on all the second-rate fare, too. And if such a notion is possibly true, can there conceivably be anything wrong with it?

The supply of first-rate work is, at any time, painfully small. It is, I think, always and immediately welcomed by the greedy people who pay for their tickets. (I've never held much stock in those "lost cause" plays that are defended by a handful of partisans; so far as I know not one of them has ever reversed the verdict of its initial audiences and established itself as a masterpiece.)

But with the supply of unmistakable "bests" so sadly limited, what is a man with love in his heart and enthusiasm in his bones to do for the rest of his dinner?

The only thing he can do, I guess, is to take what's left, the smörgåsbord of second-bests, and to take it in as uncritical a manner as possible if he's going to manage to enjoy it.

If you catch a fellow, then, galloping off to an entertainment that offers something less than the required amounts of truth, beauty, and rich compassion, it may not be because he is lacking in taste; he may have exercised his taste and still not satisfied his appetite. He may be acting out of an excess of affection rather than a deficiency in intelligence.

As a matter of fact, we're extremely lucky that he does often behave in this way. If the customer actually could be held to the loftiest standards of "taste," coerced into attending nothing but Gold Seal exhibits and staying piously away from all low-level enchantments, the theater would be bankrupt before you could say Agatha Christie. It's plain enough that appetite does outrun taste. But if it didn't, we'd all be broke.

∽ 2 ∾

I SOMETIMES get to thinking that what the theater needs is more hacks. "Hack" is a pretty unpleasant word nowadays, and it doesn't just mean a playwright who turns out second-rate stuff. It means any writer who writes to order, writes rapidly, or, in a burst of thoughtless vulgarity, writes more than one play every three years.

Somehow or other, the contemporary American dramatist has convinced himself that wooing the muse is a long, private process in which he had better not embroil himself too frequently if he wants to keep his inspiration pure. A season in Italy, perhaps, while he "tunes up." Then a hideaway on the Arizona desert for eighteen months of profound creative anguish. (If it isn't slow going, it isn't respectable.) Finally, production, and back to the beach at Cannes.

There's no doubt at all that getting a production through the Broadway mill is exhausting, but I keep wondering whether our playwright hasn't additionally exhausted himself by his determination to suffer. I wonder whether he hasn't invested altogether too much time, too much foreboding, and too much introspection in a project that is, three times out of five, going to close in three weeks anyway. The object of the prolonged soul-struggle is, of course, quality. But I wonder whether we're really getting all that quality out of it.

What started me off on this somewhat irreverent train of thought was a little note in the Empire Theater's last official program. The management had, in honor of the Empire's sixtieth year and its approaching demolition, reprinted the stage bill of its very first production—a successful but probably undistinguished little item called *The Girl I Left Behind Me*. The piece was by David Belasco and Franklin Fyles; as the program cheerfully pointed out, it had been "written for this company."

Suddenly I was reminded of an almost forgotten world of established acting companies, permanently occupied theaters, and playwrights who did not find it demeaning to help keep a going concern going. The contemporary playmaker who found himself grinding out a vehicle for a star (there are, alas, no more year-round theaters begging for stopgap entertainments) would feel mortally embarrassed by his descent into the artistic underworld and would spend a great deal of time sheepishly explaining to his friends that he had simply had to do it for Tallulah.

While I was still brooding over the matter, I came across—in Ward Morehouse's *Just the Other Day*—the following description of Owen Davis' work methods:

> He was at his desk early every morning and in the course of a day his penciled scrawl would fill many pages of dialogue. He worked swiftly and frequently finished a full-length play in a month or six weeks. His dramatization of F. Scott Fitzgerald's The Great Gatsby was done in about three weeks.
>
> When he brought down his final curtain he didn't feel that he had earned a holiday for himself. . . . He would merely refer to his idea jottings, get out some fresh paper and a collection of sharpened pencils, pull up his chair at his work table, and start all over again, writing, in large and legible letters, ACT ONE on a glistening sheet.

That's hack work. And anyone who wants to can raise a perfectly legitimate question about the enduring value of Mr. Davis' prose. In passing, though, it should be remembered that the gentleman managed to bag a Pulitzer Prize with what was approximately his 250th play.

Accepting all this as hack work, there's one obvious thing to be said for it: it kept quite a few people working for quite a long time. This is a positive virtue—actors remain available, playhouses don't get sold to television, and so on. The theater stays in business against the day when its poets may come along and make it better.

But there's another curious circumstance connected with these 9-to-5-and-no-nonsense work methods. They sound a lot like the work methods which must necessarily have been used by such widely admired manufacturers as Shakespeare and Molière. Both men had theaters to fill. When one vehicle proved unprepossessing at the box office, another had to go in in an unthinkable hurry.

Both wrote directly for known actors and were not above tossing in a couple of extra parts just to keep friends employed. Each produced an almost indecent body of work. (The Greeks were a little lazier, confining themselves to three plays every two years; even at this sluggish rate Sophocles somehow succeeded in signing his name to 120 of them.) All in all, it leaves you with the suspicion that our best men have been found among our most incorrigible hacks.

The answer, I suppose, is something that everybody has known all along: genius is an accident. The playwright who stores up his energies, nurses his psyche and finally sits down to the typewriter with the solemn thought that "This is going to be a first-rate play, no matter how long it takes me to make it one" is just as likely to produce a clinker as Clyde Fitch ever was. (Mr. Fitch once had two plays open against each other on the same night.)

The man who tells himself that he is first going to take a year off and then write a profound play is, I rather imagine, the man in his age group least likely to succeed. In fact, I don't know how, once he has scared himself to death with this announcement, he is able to go on at all.

And, contrariwise, the man who happens to have a little native talent on his side doesn't seem to damage it much by ripping off casual epics as often as his fellow workers in the theater require.

Being prolific isn't in the best of taste these days, and it would be idle to pretend that urgency always, and automatically, produces masterpieces. It doesn't. But neither does the caution we currently admire. If anything, the historical evidence would seem to come down hard in favor of the fellow with the fewest inhibitions and the fastest pen.

ᕙ 3 ᕗ

ONE OF THE NICEST THINGS about the London theater is that you can go to a second-rate play on purpose.

You wouldn't do that in New York. You may, indeed, find yourself staring at second-rate stuff on Broadway with astonishing frequency—but never because you started out with that in mind. If you do wind up at a routine domestic comedy in New York, it is only because someone has assured you that it is really much more than routine domestic comedy—that it is, in fact, first-rate. Or you may conceivably settle for an inferior entertainment out of sheer desperation, because you've got out-of-town friends on your hands and can't get into anything you know to be better. Even when you go out of that fabulous appetite that demands more than quality can ever produce, you must first convince yourself that the chances of a miracle are very, very good. The tacit understanding in the American theater is that every theatergoing adventure is going to be—and had damn well better be—a rare and unforgettable experience. An understandable bitterness is often the result.

The British theater is a great deal more candid, and a great deal more relaxed, about the matter. It offers, with no apologies at all, at least two flatly and imperturbably opposed levels of playgoing. During one recent London summer, for instance, it was possible to satisfy one's presumably higher tastes by traipsing off to the Haymarket, where John Gielgud, Ralph Richardson, Sybil Thorndike, and Irene Worth were giving superb performances in a quasi-Chekhovian cameo called *A Day By the Sea.* Admirers of Edith Evans and Christopher Fry could purr with honest contentment over both the performance and the writing of *The Dark Is Light Enough.* The best is always there for those who insist upon it.

But it is also possible, in London, to turn squarely about and march off to an Agatha Christie thriller that doesn't pretend to be anything more than an Agatha Christie thriller. There were, that particular summer, two Christie whodunits enjoying placid and profitable runs, and neither of them aspired to an intellectual stature greater than that of a 25-cent reprint plucked from the drugstore racks. Neither of them, it might be added, had even that faint gloss of bantering sophistication which lifts an entertainment like *Dial M for Murder* just one notch higher in the social scale and thereby secures it admission to our own more elevated stages.

Going to one of these straight-faced but unmistakably genial entertainments is, in fact, an experience exactly comparable to settling down for the evening with any detective novel you happen to fancy. You know that you are settling down to trash; but it just so happens that you want to give an evening to trash, and you have the evening to give. As theater, it is depressurized—casual, undemanding, irresponsible, amiable.

You drop in, let's say, on one of Miss Christie's murderous bonbons. You notice at once that the hushed and slightly frigid atmosphere that pursues the "best" in theater is missing. The audience hasn't quite pulled itself together after stashing away the dinner dishes and hustling the kids to bed. It certainly hasn't dressed— what's good enough at noon around the house is good enough here. Nor has the tempo of the day undergone any solemn change for the worse: the playgoers are flushed, busy, noisy, pleasantly knockabout.

The women have lugged candy along. The men may smoke. It's about time, by the way, that someone scotched that pretty legend about the prevalence of smoking in London theaters. You are not permitted to smoke in the presence of Sir John Gielgud or Dame Edith Evans; if you want to scatter ashes all over the carpet you have got to do it in theaters where the entertainment itself is more relaxed.

Even the ushers are at their chattiest and most companionable, the starch all gone from their uniforms and from their manners. No one—neither employee nor customer—tries to invest the occasion with any air of false importance, and a cheerful slackness prevails.

There is no orchestra in the pit at this particular enterprise. There is an organ, merrily wheezing out the tunes of the day in the best silent-movie manner. When it is time for the house lights to dim, the organist obligingly plunges into baleful mysterioso thumps and wails, in an even better silent-movie manner. As you take a last quick glance at your program, you come upon a friendly announcement in heavy black type: "There are no Revolver Shots in this play."

If there are no revolver shots, there are splendid absurdities involving quick changes of costume, concealed identities and perhaps a tricky triple solution to the crime. The actors are by no means embarrassed by the relatively primitive work they are called upon to do; they love it, are loved in return, and are never above glancing directly at the audience for approval after a particularly good riposte.

When the evening is over, no one is in a hurry to go home. And no one hates himself for having come: he knew exactly what he was getting into.

London's second-level theater is by no means confined to old-school mystery melodramas. Glancing at the billboards announcing new shows soon to come in from the provinces, you will discover the name of a star, the name of his show, and, then, in almost larger letters than the title, the emphatic warning: "A Family Comedy." The special audience and the aesthetic level that this unknown work is shooting at are clear from the outset. Or you may visit a minor comedy that has been running for two years, only to learn that it has never at any time played to a sophisticated audience; it never asked sophisticates to come.

Musical revues are extremely popular in London, and a good many of these belong in the same unambitious, come-if-you-have-nothing-better-to-do category. Instead of straining mightily to compete with Rodgers and Hammerstein, a company of eight or ten players may toss some simple scenery onto the stage of a tiny theater and settle for the improvisational gaiety of a careless, but also carefree, vaudeville show.

A London revue doesn't have to be better than *The Band Wagon* to survive; it has only to pass the evening in pleasant idleness. The London theater is lucky, I think. By refusing to be on its best behavior all the time, it has left room for the idler, the family outing and the lowbrow. (We have more or less effectively discouraged the lowbrow from bothering with Broadway; no American manager would consider for a moment tagging his incoming play "a family comedy.")

And the virtue of this amiable conspiracy isn't just that it keeps so many actors and writers at work. It has the good grace to invite a much larger segment of the public into the playhouse. It helps form a habit. The man who enjoys Agatha Christie but doesn't care much for Chekhov may, after he has acquired the habit, feel generously inclined to return the basic compliment: he may be willing to leave a little room for Chekhov.

∽ 4 ∾

I DON'T ALWAYS pick up my aesthetic principles from detective stories, but a minor British thriller by Edmund Crispin made me quite a happy man not long ago. Here I was, trying to get interested in a not very interesting plot, when I came across this illuminating little jab at theatrical do-gooders:

> Sheila McGaw, the young woman who produced the plays at the repertory theater in Oxford, traveled third-class. She did this because she thought that art must return to the people before it could again become vital, and she occupied herself with showing a volume of Gordon Craig designs to a farmer who was sitting next to her.

The farmer, of course, thought the lady was out of her mind.

For me, anyway, the episode summarizes one of the profoundest mistakes we make nowadays as we try to rekindle some kind of theatrical enthusiasm in the common herd. It's a matter of psychology, I guess. Every time we brace ourselves for an approach to the mass audience, we think of ourselves as going slumming.

We are always going to "bring" the theater to the masses. Why don't we ever think of bringing the masses to the theater?

This may be a mere matter of terminology, but I doubt it. It seems to me that there's an awful aura of handing-down-the-word about us as we make patronizing overtures to the "ordinary" customer.

Every once in a while I find myself stashing away cold fried chicken and plastic cherry cobbler in the company of a couple of hundred innocent banqueters and a guest lecturer who is going to tell them something about the theater.

What the lecturer invariably tells them is that the theater is a beautiful, beautiful place (this is the same theater we go to every week, mind you), that it is a temple of the arts and a custodian of all that is priceless in our culture, that in some esoteric way it is "worthy" of preservation, and that they had all better send a check somewhere right away if they want to preserve it.

The pitch is riddled with overtones. For one thing, it helps solidify in the public mind the already strong notion that the theater is not so much an entertainment as a charity. "Support" is the word that keeps cropping up, as though the stage were an infirm relative unable under any circumstances to earn its own keep. A form that was meant to be all excitement and exhilaration is soberly presented as an object of pity. (Things may be tough in the theater, all right. But I wonder whether it wouldn't be a good idea to keep this a deep, dark secret—to pretend instead that, if any member of the congregation dared venture his way into a playhouse, gaiety would be his reward.)

This virtuous appeal has the further unfortunate effect of shrouding the theater in a mantle of granite, of turning it into a monument.

The audience is asked to preserve it, not even with such affection as it might bestow on a batch of old love letters, but with that sense of civic responsibility with which it was once asked to preserve Old Ironsides. The stage becomes an institution, roughly comparable to the Smithsonian.

You get the feeling that something once happened that is worth remembering, even to the point of erecting a bronze plaque, but that nothing is happening now. Did this vision ever excite anyone into reaching for his pocketbook, let alone into heading for a box office? My guess is that it will stimulate exactly as much enthusiasm as was aroused by the campaign to preserve Mark Twain's house in New York.

In general, we are terribly busy telling people what they ought to do for the theater. It might be more helpful to start asking people what they think the theater ought to do for them. Instead of saying to the customer "This is what you should like," we might try a tentative and tremulous "What do you like?"

Playwright Terence Rattigan has, I think, a view of the matter that is both friendly and realistic. In the preface to his *Collected Plays* he tells us that he has invented, for his own theatrical guidance, an ever-present Aunt Edna. She is "bound to be someone's aunt, and probably quite a favorite one. She plays bridge rather well, goes to church on Sundays and . . . is a hopeless lowbrow."

As he works, Mr. Rattigan keeps reminding himself that unless the playwright really pleases Aunt Edna, he is lost:

Though by no means a vindictive old lady, nothing, I fear, will prevent her from avenging her unsatisfactory afternoon by broadcasting that evening in the lounge of her hotel in West Kensington: "Oh, it was so dull, my dears, don't think of going to see it. So much talk, so little action, so difficult to see the actors' faces, and even the tea was cold."

She will be listened to. Aunt Edna always is. . . . Aunt Edna is universal, and to those who may feel that all the problems of the modern theater might be solved by her liquidation, let me add that I have no doubt at all that she is also immortal. . . . She is universal and immortal, and she has lived for over 2,000 years. . . . I believe that Aunt Edna sat on those hard stone seats at Athens, clutched her neighbor's arm in her excitement, and whispered: "My dear, do look at that blood on the actor's mask. He's supposed to have blinded himself. How thrilling."

Mr. Rattigan is not wholly intimidated by Aunt Edna. He knows that "she rather enjoys a little teasing and even, at times, some bullying." But he does have an honest respect for her taste and intelligence: "She understands ideas much more readily than is usually supposed" and in 2,000 years "she has never rejected the best." Finally, after some years of working in the theater, the author claims to have discovered that "in pleasing her I was only pleasing myself."

We do spend a lot of our energy these times showing Aunt Edna volumes of Gordon Craig—and sternly stressing her obligation to us. We might do a great deal better by sounding her out.

THREE

Opening Night

1

New York opening nights are, I gather, world-famous for their catastrophic importance. My London friends tell me that a show can dawdle through its first performance there, get very modest notices, and still manage a tidy run—or, conversely, play to bravos, sweep the press, and never earn back the production cost. In Paris, if I am reliably informed, a set of really belligerent reviews can mark the beginning of a controversy which assures the show of running long enough for everyone to see it, if only to let them in on the argument.

If New York audiences do not, as a rule, openly argue with the critics in this way, it isn't because the critics write unanswerable reviews; they don't. It is because the general audience is not very much in love with the theater and must be badgered into attending certain entertainments by a set of notices in which adjectives such as "magnificent," "enthralling," "unforgettable," and "exhilarating" play so large a part as to make the theatergoer's absence seem a social breach.

It is widely believed that the New York reviewer's verdict on a play is nearly final, and the reviewer is therefore most often painted as a slaughterer of innocents, a man whose principal dedication is to the task of keeping the maximum number of people away from the theater and the maximum number of plays from succeeding. The reverse would be closer to the truth. One of the first things a New York newspaper critic learns is that he must all but explode with enthusiasm, must in fact seriously overwrite himself if he is to push people into the theaters at all. The fact that he is willing to do so, willing to perjure himself above and beyond his actual respect for a play, willing to employ all those extravagant, overworked, and downright embarrassing adjectives in the cause of theatrical liveliness is the real measure of his devotion to his trade.

Let me take you down through a single day's advertisements in the New York theatrical columns during a season in the 1950s— and the handy quotes that the critics ladled out. One by one, this particular season's plays were "stunning," "magnificent," "exuberant," "distinguished," "not to be missed," "enormously enjoyable," "the stage at its best," "exhilarating," "as engaging as anything we are likely to see in a long time," "enchanting," "full of wit, talent, and splendor" and "extraordinary." I tell you, old Athens never had a season like this one. (Since the season in question was universally considered one of the worst in the memory of man, I leave to your imagination the quotes that turn up in a good one.) The contemporary New York critic is, quite clearly, willing to do everything short of hawking tickets under the marquee in order to convince people that there may be some valid reason for attending a Broadway theater.

The critic is committed to ecstasy; anything more temperate, or more accurate, is denied him. Let's say the play is modestly attractive, rather engagingly performed, and reasonably—though not extraordinarily—entertaining. The New York reviewer who told the truth, who called it a "nice little play, pleasantly acted," would—if popular legend and passionate press agents are to be believed—be signing its death warrant. Apparently no one would go to see it. Because he has so often been told this, the critic at once dismisses the possibility of writing a calm, reasonable, balanced notice, shrugs off the shreds of integrity he has left, and proceeds to do nip-ups in print over a show that actually has left him only mildly complacent in his seat.

Within the week, as I write, two so-so enterprises have opened in New York. The first is a comedy with quite a few bright lines and a narrative of such magnificent irrelevance that the lines seem to have been imported wholesale from some other play. The second thrives on the energetic, shrewd, but less than inspired work of a single actor. Neither of these ventures is ever going to cause any international stir, or, for that matter, be remembered in New York after a few months. But each is respectable enough, and interesting enough, to be worth the casual attention of the so-called "regular" playgoer. In order to get that "regular" playgoer into motion the critics must wallow in rich and unrestrained prose. The first event was—I quote—"altogether scintillating," "irresistible," "utterly hilarious," and "captivating." The second was "sheer magnificence," possessed of "extraordinary power," and among "the truly great experiences of our time." The critic, rereading his notice at breakfast the next morning, must frequently yearn for a theatrical experience as overwhelming as the one he has just described.

There is, by now, an unwritten law to the effect that no critic may write a so-so notice. He must even be careful about the amount of qualification he inserts into an otherwise ecstatic paean. According to present theatrical superstition, one paragraph of very mild, more or less apologetic, quibbling may do no harm; two paragraphs may blow the whole thing to smithereens. The hawk-eyed playgoer, scanning the notice for some indication that he will be within his rights in staying away, presumably deduces from the qualified paragraphs that *this* is what the show is really like, that the praise which has preceded and followed them is so much cant intended to save the faces of certain reputable personalities associated with the production, that the critic is really a master of the "no opinion" or hedging review, and that there are mysterious forces afoot bent on trapping the unwary into attending an obvious turkey.

Nor is the astute playgoer willing to abide by the favorable verdict of a single critic whom he admires, or whose reputation over the years commands respect. He *seems* to ferret out all the notices, looking for that one bad one that will tell the truth and free him of obligation. Not long ago a new play by a distinguished and usually successful dramatist drew seven out-and-out raves against a minority of two dissenting opinions. The show closed in two weeks. More recently, and much more implausibly, a show opened to eight out of nine glowing reviews. The audience apparently found that ninth one. In any event, the production rapidly withered away. As you can see, the "regular" playgoer is very much on his toes.

The critic must even be wary about the particular *kind* of praise he bestows, about his choice of superlatives. I can remember when a New York reviewer, enthusing about a musical show, made the mistake of calling it "intelligent." Next morning the show's press agent was hot on the wire. "What are you trying to do—kill us?" he wanted to know. "Intelligent," it seems, is not a box-office word, above all for a musical show. There are others like it—"distinguished," "dignified," "searching," "impressive." To the New York audience these are synonyms for "deplorably dull," and they offer handsome excuse for spending the evening in a comfortable bar. The respectable show which is simply "worth a visit"—never say that; it means "don't get caught dead in the place"—must be described as "dazzling," "delectable," or "downright superb."

It is small wonder that when a show comes along that is obviously, unmistakably, hopelessly bad, the average critic turns on it with unholy wrath. For once he may release the other side of his vocabulary; for once he may square it with his conscience, balance things off for the fruity lyricism demanded of him the rest of the time. Confronted with a show that could in no circumstances be salvaged, he explodes in obvious relief. This, of course, immediately gives him the reputation of being a savage and smart-alecky tyrant who is dedicated to destroying the theater and displaying his own verbal virtuosity. Whereupon the legend of the "seven assassins" acquires new heart and fresh health. Oh, it's a vicious Circle, all right.

Or so sayeth a practicing reviewer.

∽ 2 ∾

SINCE THE SUPPOSEDLY all-powerful reviewer must huff and puff mightily if he is to exercise any of his reputed power, and since in a good many cases the hysterical shilling is quite unsuccessful, a candid man might well cock his eye at the legend of critical "weight" and turn skeptical.

But let's give the legend its due—for the moment. Let's suppose that seven daily newspaper reviewers do really control the fortunes of all new plays on the Broadway boards. To the degree that this popular picture is a true one, it is also an extraordinarily peculiar one.

Strictly speaking, the critic has no place at the birth of a play at all. The theatrical experience is a personal one between author and audience, an intuitive meeting of minds which either takes place successfully or fails to do so, and the only legitimate judgment that can be passed upon a work of art is that passed by the audience. The play is written for the audience's pleasure; only the audience can say with any finality whether, or to what degree, it has been pleased.

An author projects his dramatic image from the stage; the audience receives it in the auditorium. Here are the positive and negative poles of an intuitive experience. Either a current of delight is set up between them and the play is an incontrovertible success, or there is a failure of contact and the play is an unsalvageable failure. The relationship of author and audience is intimate, immediate, and absolute. The measure of the author's work is the response the audience finds itself making. From the actuality of this response there is no appeal; no amount of formal rationalization will change what has really happened, no amount of "correct" theorizing will alter the theatrical fact in any fundamental way. The audience has the first, and the last, word. Between stage and spectators exists a closed circuit, a straight line.

In the past there have been many attempts to modify, or even to reverse, the audience's instinctive response, but the audience has never lost a battle. Sir Philip Sidney may have decried the absurdities of the Elizabethan stage, but the audience loved those absurdities, supported them, and preserved for us the most successful form ever to have been invented for the English-speaking theater. Chapelin and Scudery may have found almost nothing right with *The Cid*, and may even have attempted to vote it off the stage. Today we examine the errors of Chapelin and Scudery, not those of Corneille. Molière was told that *The School for Wives* was no play at all; thanks to the insight of the audience, it continues to play today.

Criticism often professes to find great, though hidden, value in plays that have failed in production. Try as it may, it cannot restore those plays to the stage or succeed in making audiences like them. The critic who attempts to reverse the judgment of an audience, to "instruct" it in taste, is the critic who deals in lost causes, the Don Quixote of the arts—a bore and a fool. Criticism also has a habit of finding fault with what has succeeded in performance. There are those who, working as purists and noting serious lapses of clarity and coherence, describe *Hamlet* as a "magnificent failure." The only trouble with this carefully worked-out judgment is that

Hamlet has never failed. Shaw could not abide *The Importance of Being Earnest*. A critic may be brilliant, but his brilliance quickly turns to sophistry the moment he chooses to work apart from, and without complete dependence on, the initial verdict of the audience.

Ideally, then, the critic has no business in a theater until the audience has returned its verdict. His work begins with that verdict, and rests upon it. The experience must *exist* before it can be analyzed. Once author and audience have met, however, there is a genuine function for the critic to perform. He enters the scene—a little later, so that the audience reaction will have had time to come clear —as an observer. The first thing he is called upon to observe is the one root fact of theatrical life: the play is either getting over or it is not getting over. His task—this is the true historical role of criticism—is to explain the fact which confronts him. If the play is moving its audience, he asks *why*, and then carefully answers his own question. If it is not moving its audience, he asks *why not*, and again answers—to the best of his ability—the critical question he has posed.

The true identity of the critic is that of analyst and interpreter. His function is to reduce to rational terms an experience that has taken place in intuitive terms—to state objectively what has happened subjectively. His great contribution is that he is able to work out an almost mathematical equation for values that have hitherto existed spontaneously and imaginatively. He extracts a body of abstract principle from something that has been all flesh and blood. This, by the way, is a tremendous contribution: it helps the author to understand what he has done and what he has not done; it helps a younger author to learn his craft; it confirms the audience in its delight or helps make intelligible its disappointment.

All the literary criticism that we preserve and revere has been of this "interpretative" kind. Looking back over theatrical history, we do find another kind: "judicial," or, in effect, censorial criticism— the attempt to dictate to the audience. But "judicial" criticism has been so often in error, and in the last analysis so impotent, as to cast serious doubt on its validity and usefulness as a method. "Interpretative" criticism, on the other hand, has added steadily to our knowledge and has itself become one of the glories of the language.

The critic in his best—and, I think, his only valid—function serves as an onlooker who explains. If the relationship between author and audience can be taken as a straight line, the critic stands at a point of vantage where he can observe this straight line: the author, the audience, and the current that flows between them. He stands at the apex of a triangle, where he can look down upon its base. His broad and sympathetic point of view embraces the totality of the experience, but it does not intrude upon the experience or attempt to short-cut it in any way. The critic stands detached and alert, ready to note the success of one impulse along the line and the failure of another; later he will help us to understand the magic which has prompted our response, or the ineptitude which has kept us from responding. He is our *raisonneur*.

When, however, we talk about the contemporary New York reviewer as a "dictator," we mean to say that he has plunged down from his perch at the top of the triangle, cut across the direct line between author and audience, and inserted himself at a midway point in the experience. Here he assumes control of the current: when he decides that author and audience should come together, he brings them together; when he decides that contact should not be made, he shuts off the possibility forever. He anticipates and short-cuts the actual response of an audience, usurps its prerogative of personal judgment. He has taken on the judicial-censorial, rather than the interpretative, function, and, to the dismay of everyone, he has apparently made it work.

It is possible to debate certain aspects of this damaging picture. It may be said, for instance, that the first-night audience with which a newspaper critic sees a show constitutes a valid author-audience relationship and that the critic, as he watches the show, is sensitive to the general response that is being made. In this light, he is simply working very rapidly: observing the line of contact and forming judgments about the play in the same instant. Quite apart from the extraordinary intelligence that would be required to accomplish this ambimental feat, very real objections must be raised against any such notion. The first of these is that the opening-night audience in New York is not a genuine audience but an assembly of specialized trade interests. Since the reviewer's next-day notice is immediately effective and helps determine whether or not there will be any paying customers thereafter, it follows that no true audience may ever see the show—not, at least, until after the critic has handed down a favorable verdict. Further, the critic is himself perfectly aware of the specialized and unreliable nature of the first-night audience and is at great pains to disregard it. It is a commonplace of contemporary New York criticism to acknowledge that the first-night audience "blistered its palms applauding" and then to point out that the applause was wholly undeserved. As the situation now stands, the critic's vote is polled without reference to audience behavior and prior to the appearance of any actual audience in the theater. The verdict is reached *in vacuo*. The audience's right of judgment has been thoroughly usurped.

Small wonder that from time to time cries of outrage go up against the critics. Regularly, playwrights turn upon them, actors turn upon them, producers turn upon them. Elmer Rice once retired from the theater rather than subject any more of his work to their absolute judgments. Elia Kazan was party to a paid advertisement that labeled them "the Jukes boys of journalism." The *Critics' Digest* circulates the rumor that Maxwell Anderson has written a letter to Brooks Atkinson of *The New York Times* in which he announces that he will write no more serious plays until Atkinson has left the *Times*. It is interesting to note, by the way, that all of these attacks have come from the creative people of the theater. None has ever originated with that body whose prerogative has actually been usurped—the audience. And this is, I think, an important clue to the situation in which we seem to find ourselves.

Until now I have spoken of the critic as though he were an active factor in this situation. He isn't. He has not actually chosen to surrender his detached and objective position at the apex of the triangle. He has not deliberately fought his way down into the experience itself and forced himself between author and audience. He has not asked for the power of life and death over plays, has not arrogated it unto himself, has not bullied himself into the middle of things.

I doubt that there is a single New York critic who is happy about the power that is attributed to him or who believes that his actual possession of it could ever be a healthy thing for the theater. To the degree that he has such power, it has simply been handed to him, whether he wants it or not.

He couldn't have wrested this power from the hands of the audience if he *had* wanted to. The audience cannot be compelled to buy newspapers; having bought them, it cannot be compelled to turn to the drama pages; having turned to the drama pages, it cannot be compelled to read the critics; reading them, it cannot be compelled to abide by their opinions. If it elects to do all of these things, this has been a free choice, freely made—and probably for a reason.

Nor has the contemporary New York critic's power over the audience come about as a result of his incontrovertible brilliance. It is always conceivable, and it has sometimes been demonstrated in the past, that the stylistic force, the impeccable taste, or the clearly superior knowledge of an individual critic may earn for his work tremendous and terrifying personal influence. I think I shall offend no one by suggesting that our hurried and harried journalists are not of the tribe of Lessing, that they have not come into their present authority by the sheer glory of their work. Some of this work is exceptionally good, considering the circumstances in which it is turned out; but none of it is so irresistibly compelling as to have created, out of its own indisputable quality, the situation we now imagine to exist.

If we honestly believe that newspaper criticism is all-powerful today, then we are forced to a further conclusion: that in the last thirty or forty years the audience has voluntarily surrendered its privilege of judgment. It has, in effect, abdicated. Somewhere along the line the New York audience reached an important decision: it no longer wanted the opportunity to investigate and evaluate the theater personally; it wanted instead to have this work done for it in advance. It deliberately chose to abide by the word of seven journalists, to rely heavily upon the combined opinion of these men.

That this must have been a free choice on the part of the audience is abundantly clear. Thirty or forty years ago journalistic criticism in New York was as severe as it is today, and in general as well written as it is today. It was also considerably less powerful. It is legendary that George M. Cohan almost never got a good notice for one of his musical plays. Cohan himself was regularly attacked as brash, vulgar, and cheap. He was at the same time the most popular audience figure in New York, the man who owned Broadway. It is not necessarily to be supposed that the audience did not read what was written of him. It probably read the criticism of the day, weighed it, then went to the newest Cohan show and made up its mind for itself.

William Gillette forbade the quotation of criticism in his advertisements, no matter how favorable it might be. When his manager did at one time insert a favorable quote, Gillette was outraged. He felt himself demeaned by such tactics. If Gillette felt himself superior to daily criticism, and in no way dependent upon it, it was because he was *not* dependent upon it. His audiences were not really guided by it. They preferred to come and make their own decisions.

This was no doubt a healthy time, theatrically speaking. Criticism was perfectly free to say what it pleased, without feeling that it bore absolute responsibility for the financial state of the theater and all its members. Producers, actors, and authors were free to operate in direct relationship to their audiences, without agonizing side glances at what they took to be the special interests of critics. Audiences went frequently to the theater, under their own power, unpersuaded and uncontrolled, perfectly capable of speaking for themselves.

The factor of outspoken criticism is constant between the two periods. It is not criticism that has changed, or brought about any over-all change. The variable that has brought about such difference as exists is the audience. Forty years ago it could take a critic or leave him; today, we believe, it takes him.

But this drives us into further, insistent questions. Why has the audience changed its mind? Having freely asserted its right in one period, why should it freely surrender that right in another? Is it really possible to shift the blame for the present dilemma from the tyrannical critic to a listless audience?

I think not. The audience is always pleasure-hungry, avid for whatever delights are available. If today it seems to have become sluggish, wary, unassertive, and dependent, we must seek a still deeper cause, a further explanation for this uncharacteristic behavior. We cannot help but turn to the stage itself and ask what has happened on it during the last forty or fifty years to so bore, distress, and alienate an audience that it should become willing to surrender all its rights in connection with the theater and beg for the protective guidance of men who are hired for the purpose.

Reviewers should be made to examine their consciences regularly. But any examination of conscience thorough enough to do the theater some future good will have to begin at the roots: in the plays that have persuaded audiences to give up. Such critical power as exists can come only from a profound distrust of the theater on the part of its customers—from an experience of boredom, a conviction that most new plays will be dull in the same old way, and a demand for protection by a body of advance scouts.

We can't really believe in the power of the critics without also believing in the poverty of the stage.

∽ 3 ∾

Now I AM GOING to let you in on a secret. The stage is, indeed, less popular than it used to be. The body of regular playgoers is much smaller than it used to be. The critics are somewhat more powerful than they used to be. But they are—even in our straitened circumstances—not half so powerful as everyone imagines.

Of course, it's going to take all the zest out of life if I succeed in permanently mending the breach that has long existed between the creative people of the theater and the newspapermen who are hired to criticize them. But I am going to have to try. There is just too much suffering going on.

Miss Faye Emerson, for instance, simply cannot be permitted to endure anything more. It wasn't enough, during one recent season, that Miss Emerson should submit to having her clothes torn off her back, her hair mussed, and her heart broken during the course of a melodrama about brainwashing. She was also forced, once the notices were out, to face the fact that she would have the clothes torn off her back, her hair mussed, and her heart broken for only three consecutive performances. Come Saturday night, she would never again be able to play that stirring eleven-o'clock scene in which she stood with one foot on a rickety drawbridge and the other on terra firma while her captor-lover, sobbing on his knees, slowly raised one trembling arm toward a wall-switch that might or might not raise the drawbridge. The drawbridge, to put you out of your suspense, never went up; but the closing notice did.

Wearing an appropriately tragic veil, Miss Emerson stumbled away into the bright night of a local television studio, there to mourn her loss. The authors, she told us in syllables as brave as they were broken, had worked long, hard, and beautifully. Enormous amounts of money had been spent, some of it by loyal friends who had helped bring the play into town after disastrous reverses on the road. All the work, all the money, all the loyalty, all the beauty had been wantonly wiped out by certain capricious reviewers who had been so delinquent in their clear duty to art that they should now be ashamed to pick up their pay checks on Wednesday. The pain was plain, real, and far-reaching; for all I know, it is still reaching people by kinescope, sending wave after wave of outraged woe into the air we breathe daily.

A week or two thereafter Miss Kim Stanley was back in print. Miss Stanley is in print nearly as often as the reviewers are; she can be distinguished from them, however, by the vigorous quality of her prose. To the luminous and evanescent Miss Stanley, the critics have long been a bunch of "fatheads." Just *how* fatheaded was being freshly demonstrated by their reaction to a psychological fantasy in which the lady in question, after spending an evening chasing her three life-size alter egos through the woods, at last clutched all three of herself to her breast, glared at the morose father whose indifference had destroyed her childhood, and contentedly murmured, "It's all right—he's alone, but we've got each other."

Having immersed herself in psychology during the preparation of this play, Miss Stanley was in an excellent position to analyze the critics' otherwise inexplicable impatience with so noble a work. They obviously had identified themselves with the "father" image in the narrative, had bridled at the suggestion that they were unkind to children, and had revenged themselves by spanking everyone and everything in sight.

Strictly speaking, Miss Stanley was being kind to her tormentors: she was gently and patiently taking them by the hand, explaining what had caused their little outbursts, and helping them toward true self-knowledge. For a moment it seemed as though we were all about to enter a new period of tolerance, understanding, and deep therapy. When, however, the financial handwriting appeared on the backstage wall—this particular entertainment posted its closing notice twice, just to make things sadder—Miss Stanley hied

herself off to a television chamber, let loose with a few heated remarks about all that work and all that money and all that beauty,
and the fatheads were in the fire again.

They are, of course, used to the heat—and it cannot be said that
the fresh scorching accomplished anything practical at all. Brooks
Atkinson's lip did not tremble as he came early to the Winter
Garden. There were no tears to be seen in Richard Watts Jr.'s
eyes as he escorted Miss Nancy Berg into the Broadhurst. John Mc-
Clain did not volunteer public confession at Broadway and Duffy
Square, and it is even reported that John Chapman sneered. Over
the years the reviewers have learned to sit their thrones with the
sensitive, rueful, ironic detachment of philosophers; they know the
ways of this wicked world.

They know, among other things, that no matter how deeply they
are loved, no matter how exquisitely they may be thought to write,
no matter what heartfelt posies and magnums of Mumm's come
officeward at Christmastime, there is always lurking somewhere a
small, nasty voice that will whisper "one of the Jukes boys" in a
large paid advertisement. A slumbering prejudice, more firmly in-
grained than those of race or class, lies eternally coiled to lash out
against them; and they go their ways sweetly resigned to the sting of
the serpent's tooth, stoically conditioned to the loathing of the
loveliest creatures in town, utterly impervious to everybody's
anguish. They can neither be moved by pity nor shaken by spite.

Has someone just lost seventy thousand dollars, or three hundred and seventy thousand dollars, on an enterprise the reviewers
condemned? The newspaper critic's obligation is not to the man
who has invested a thousand dollars in a project he hopes to make
a profit on; it is to the reader who has invested five cents in his
newspaper and is on the verge of investing an additional $7.50 in
a theater seat. The reviewer cannot switch allegiances—cannot
permit himself to dwell forlornly on the money that may be going
down the drain—without becoming a hireling of the producer and
a Judas to his job.

Has a great deal of work gone into the project? An enormous

amount of work must have gone into the building of the Tower of Babel, the organization of Nazi Germany, the writing of Ben Jonson's verse tragedies. The plea that judgments should be arrived at by a careful study of the time sheets and cash disbursements associated with a given production cannot be taken quite seriously: it would mean, I believe, that the Critics Prize for one recent season ought to have gone to a production of the *Ziegfeld Follies* which closed prematurely in Philadelphia. So much for time and money—in the critic's view.

What of beauty? Have masterworks been sacrificed on the altar of the seven deadly egos? Apart from the two morsels mentioned earlier, here were some of the plays of that same season which managed the rather difficult feat of irritating *all* seven reviewers and therefore may be said to have been whacked out of existence by the newspaper onslaught:

One in which a seafarin' fellow came home from "out there where it's clean and free" to discover that his wife was sleeping with her new husband, and thereafter stood under the nuptial window baying like a hound-dog;

one in which an Austrian brothel-keeper stood under three talking wall portraits, announced in accents closer to the Chippewa dialect, "I bake 'um cake like never before," and did bake a beaut with strawberry icing;

one in which a young actor who wished to convince us he was drunk crossed his eyes for three quarters of an hour, though without impairing his ability to blow directly into the socks he wished to put on his feet;

one in which a jealous woman reached into her rival's bodice, ripped out a pair of falsies, and hurled them across the room;

and one in which an officer on a spaceship said to another, soberly, "Lose your amazing tensions, Lieutenant; I too have father-bonds."

Four or five of these expensive treasures (total cost around four hundred thousand, total man-hours incalculable) came in quite early in the season. The critics, sensing a decline in beauty from the year before and detecting a faint aura of "Oh, hell, let's produce *something*" in the crisp fall air, began to batten down their respective hatches. They are well aware that a weak season on Broadway means open season on reviewers; when love and money are lost in bucketfuls, someone—preferably someone who has opened his big mouth—must be made to pay; if reviewers are mere honest reporters in a good season, they are dirty rascals in a bad—they are, in fact, the *cause* of the bad season. Warned in advance, and defensively girded with strong arguments on the matters of time, money, and beauty, they stood their ground.

The critics were not—and are not—going to be shaken by pathos or bested in debate. So far as I know, no show in recent years has salvaged its investment by putting Little Eva on television, by issuing statements that do not so much question as define the ancestry of reviewers, or by taking those candid space ads in which the producers acknowledge the press blast and then tell you how much Jean Arthur, Militza Korjus, and other members of the regular audience loved it. Practically speaking, you can't beat "the boys" by taking a stick to them.

What, then? Will this agony never cease? Must every playwright chew his pencil stubs and his nerves for two or three tooth-breaking years, every performer draw nuance after nuance from the depths of his or her being during months of preparation, every backer reach into his billfold and haul out hard-earned cash reserves, only to see all of this industry, affection, and generosity whisked into nothingness on a single evening, by a few hastily written, obviously capricious words in the press? Can't we lick this thing?

We can. We have. The critics are being beaten all the time—and I don't mean to be so fatuous as to suggest that they are regularly beaten by the simple, canny practice of producing good shows. They are being beaten by good shows, mediocre shows, and pedigreed dogs. How is this mean little deception accomplished? It is first of all accomplished by surrendering one's daydreams and looking very, very hard at the facts of theatrical life:

Item. The critics are, in the majority of cases, impotent. While you stifle your howls of outrage, let me explain. The newspaper notices may be said to be influential, even decisive, when they are unanimous. That is, the appearance of seven thoroughly negative notices in the daily press probably does mean that a show is in danger of its life; the appearance of seven thoroughly favorable notices probably, though not certainly, does mean that lines will form at the box office immediately.

During the season we've been talking about only nine out of the first twenty-nine new productions received unanimous approval or disapproval. Seven of the nine were uniformly blasted and closed quickly. Two were uniformly praised, and ran. But these two were not the only ones to make a run of it. Eleven of the twenty-nine remained on the boards long enough to pay back their production costs and qualify as "hits." What kind of notices did *they* get?

The remaining nine, or a majority of the shows then basking in "hit" status, received what are called "mixed" or "split" notices from those unpredictable reviewers. Well and good, you say: when the balance was in favor, the show stayed; when it was against, the show folded. But you're guessing. It didn't work out that way at all.

Let's take some of the close splits, four reviewers on one side and three on the other. Two domestic farces drew precisely the same verdict: 4-3 *against*. One of them vanished shortly and the other galloped on and on. Or tilt it the other way. A lavish musical and a cheerfully foolish little melodrama both drew 4-3 splits *in favor*. The tilt in favor didn't help in either case; both died.

Glance at some wider differences of opinion. An imported teacake that ought to have appealed to the ladies won a 5-2 favorable nod; so did a revival of *Major Barbara*. The teacake crumbled swiftly, while *Major Barbara* not only lasted the season but then went confidently off to the road. (Bear in mind, if you can keep any part of this arithmetic in your head, that a show with a 5-2 favorable verdict collapsed while a show with a 4-3 negative verdict survived.)

And let me add one mystifying contender to that 5-2 favorable squad. In the same period a serious play about wartime treason opened to five genuinely good notices and two mild quibbles; this average should have—in the mythology of our time—betokened success. A day or two later one of the producers was on the telephone to a friend, whispering in a strangled little voice, "Do you know what we've got? We've got a private hit." No one much was showing up at eight-thirty. After a few weeks of empty houses, the "hit" turned off its lights and took down the favorable quotes out front.

Let's sum up, thus far. Most shows get mixed notices. These shows, however, do not succeed or fail in proportion as the mixture is good or bad. Ergo, in the majority of cases the newspaper notices do not actually determine the fate of somebody's favorite child; some other factor, or combination of factors, steps in to monkey with the teeter-totter.

Item: The average ticket buyer hasn't the faintest notion of what the over-all critical verdict may have been. Who—apart from those good souls closely bound to the production—reads *all* the notices? How many people buy—and read—more than three newspapers? How many more than two? How many out-of-towners, whose support is necessary to any smash hit, have done more than glance at the verdict of a single magazine?

It is a very good thing for a reviewer to go to cocktail parties: good for his arrogant soul, I mean. There he will be exposed to, and chastened by, several conversational openings. The bluntest of them is: "What did you think of such-and-such a play?" Here the convivial fellow is honorably letting you know that he doesn't read you, that he doesn't mean to read you, and that he couldn't possibly follow the meanderings of your prose if he did.

He is swiftly succeeded by the pale but intense lady who gets a death grip on your lapel and furiously asks: "*How* could you have possibly praised the Old Vic production of *Troilus and Cressida?*" It is no good explaining that you didn't; she will simply think you are a coward and are lying to her. And when the conversation gets general enough for sweeping statements to be made, out of the burgeoning smoke will come the hoarse, let's-have-it-now challenge: "You're a critic. Will you *please* tell me why the critics always go for a merely splashy musical like *Fanny* and then turn down a really significant play like *Time Limit?*" (By actual count, the musical called *Fanny* drew four negative notices and ran for two years, while the wartime melodrama known as *Time Limit* drew six favorable notices and shortly failed; I am putting this in here because I never did succeed in making myself heard at that party.)

One of the sad little things a critic soon learns—and very few producers seem ever to learn—is this: people forget. They begin by reading so few reviews that they have only the haziest and most inaccurate impression of what "the critics" said; and they end by forgetting what the critics they did read did say.

I have myself had the fascinating experience of listening to a famous actress denounce a favorite reviewer of mine for what she considered unreasonable reviewing; for three long paragraphs she went on, quoting impeccably with what seemed to be total recall; and every scorned word she quoted was not his but mine. (Did I tell her the truth? I did not; I'm a coward.) I have also on occasion accepted congratulations for notices written in my accustomed space by a young colleague who sometimes relieves me. I accepted them, let me say, with a becoming modesty. The average ticket buyer, in case anyone wants to know, is print-blind and recall-poor. Two months after a show has opened total confusion reigns.

Of course, every potential customer *thinks* he knows what the critics thought of a show. But something is going on here that has nothing to do with reviewing. Since the customer was inadequately informed in the first place and has had a severe lapse of memory since, he is not dealing with criticism at all but with a vague yet tenaciously held impression.

Where did that impression come from? Partly from hearsay— from that most gloriously unreliable of all methods of communication, the grapevine. But mostly, I do believe, it comes from deep inside the customer's private soul. Somewhere far below the levels of newspaper-reading consciousness lies a little Freudian censor that keeps rubbing its antennae together and sending out sharp, insistent messages like "Now *that's* something *I'd* like to see!" or perhaps "Not for this kid!" And these messages tend to *become*, in the customer's mind, what "the critics" said.

Every show that is produced brings with it its own atmosphere of expectation, for good or for ill. It either *sounds* likely, or it doesn't—to the customer. *Can-Can*, with a score by Cole Porter, sounds exceedingly likely; the critics can be graceless, or even downright grumpy, without injuring a month of its two-year run. *Time Limit*, being about brainwashing, doesn't sound likely; the critics can stamp and shout like so many carnival barkers and not help it. The morning after I expressed my own dissatisfaction with a play called *The Fourposter* a friend called me on the phone to say that the review had made up her mind for her; she grasped that *I* didn't like it but it sounded exactly like what she wanted to cuddle up with. People cuddled up with that one for years.

The atmosphere that stirs expectation, that tantalizes the secret hunches all theatergoers have, is composed of many things, some tangible and some not so very. Titles count. (*Sixth Finger in a Five Finger Glove* is not a good title; *The Strong Are Lonely* is not a good title; *Bells Are Ringing* is a good title.) Personalities count. ("I've always liked that nice Walter Pidgeon.") Subject matter counts. (Do I want to see a play tonight about treachery in a prison camp?) Timing counts. (I may want to see a play about treachery in a prison camp next year, or I may have wanted to see one last year, but—tonight?) Circumstances count. (Is it Eugene O'Neill's last play, and what did he say about his family?) Curiosity counts. (What in heaven's name can *The Waltz of the Toreadors* be like, and how much do I want to find out for myself?) The curve of the moon counts.

And reviews count, perhaps more than I've indicated in this good-will message. But they do not, in the majority of cases, count a show in or out. They are influential, to tell the simple truth about it, *only* in relation to the expectation we've been talking about. They constitute one variable element in a great complex of elements.

Suppose the reviews for the tremendously successful *Auntie Mame* had been less good than they were. Would it have mattered much? Very much? The man who had heard about Patrick Dennis' novel and who was enchanted by the thought of seeing Rosalind Russell again had in effect made up his mind. He might, for the moment, have been a bit dashed by reading something lukewarm, or even chilling, in a section of the press; but in a week he'd have forgotten Kerr's hasty comments ("Oh, *he* doesn't like anything!"), he'd have received reassurances from some adventurous friend that "audiences are loving it," and, needing nothing more, he'd have been off to the playhouse to claim his inalienable right to happiness.

Expectation—the way a show looks in the Sunday advertisements, sounds in the gossip columns, or adds up in the "hunch" department of the playgoer's brain—is probably the one truly determining factor in the success or failure of a play. Expectation nudges the playgoer in a given direction, either toward or away from the box office. The critic may confirm this predisposition and so start a stampede, in which case he will seem to have been very powerful indeed. Or he may try to nudge the playgoer in an opposite direction, against his inner conviction. Here he may have some small influence, though the reviewer who once tried to keep people out of a musical gem known as *Mr. Wonderful* or to drive them into a Bernard Shaw play with the unprepossessing title of *Misalliance* knows just how slight it is.

And whenever a genuine elbowing contest develops between criticism and expectation, it is expectation that is going to win. A newspaper critic is powerless to send people thronging to a play they suspect they are going to hate; and he cannot, short of police action, keep them out of an enterprise they are confident they are going to enjoy.

The critic can, then, be beaten—but he must be beaten before the fact, not after it. (Don't take a stick to him the next morning; pull the rug out from under him six months ahead.) To the producers and playwrights, the actors and articulate actresses who would like to get the best of those vultures perched high above Times Square, I'd say: ask yourselves if the title, the content, the company, the timing, the circumstances, the confidential report from astrologer Vincent Lopez all have a lively, provocative ring about them; ask yourselves if your respective mothers would like the show; ask if you'd go to see it were it produced, and acted in, by somebody else. When you mention the project to your friends, do their faces fall? Do they stand expressionless? Or do they seethe with jealousy that you've got your hands on the script or the part? What kind of weather does the play really suggest?

The entrepreneurs who go about their work in this slightly mystical, eminently dishonest way are probably going to leave those poor fellows, the reviewers, sitting lonely by their unwashed office windows, calling out to an unheeding populace that passes them by, and wondering just how long their obviously superfluous jobs are going to last.

But why am I telling you all this?

∽ 4 ∾

THAT DRAMA STUDENT was in here again today, with his stub pencil, his notebook with little rings around the top of it, and his cold, cold, skeptical eye. He asked the usual warm-up questions, diffidently, with a kind of oral shrug, letting me know that *he* knew perfectly well what all the answers would be.

How was the season? What do I think of revivals? Were there any promising new playwrights? What can be done for really talented young people who are forever barred, by secret agreement among people on the inside, from getting a toehold on Broadway? Wouldn't it be a good idea if critics went to rehearsals, or carefully read the manuscript of a new play, in advance?

These, as I say, are feints. The young man, who is preparing an article for his school paper or a report for his class in Drama Criticism 209, is leading me on, letting me expatiate, letting me feel that I have but to speak and the world listens, before he nails me.

Finally he has given me enough rope. Now he fixes me with a stare of astonishing candor, curls his lip slightly and delivers the kicker. "Mr. Kerr, exactly *what* standards do you have for evaluating a play?"

He knows, and he knows that I know, that I have no standards of criticism whatever, that I am simply having a personal ball for myself when I write my review (there's a phrase we could do without —"having a ball"; the whole of next season will be automatically improved if every up-to-the-minute playwright will eliminate it from his manuscript) and that my reaction to the play has been subjective, capricious, uninformed and closely related to the state of my digestive system on that particular evening.

As a matter of fact, this question, which is calculated to make any reviewer fumble, stutter and look shifty-eyed, does not come from the classroom killers alone. It comes in long questionnaires from university professors and on lavender paper from women's clubs. Even the late Barrett Clark, long the editor of the Dramatists' Publishing Company and a man very much in the know, could not resist posing it.

Once, when Mr. Clark found himself disagreeing with the critics on the objective merits of several such minor plays as *The Curious Savage* and *Four Twelves Are 48*, he began to wonder "whether courses might be offered in some university for the benefit of practicing reviewers, where they would be forced to study the theory of criticism and to read and report on, say, 2,000 plays a year." (Right here and now I refuse to read 2,000 plays next year.) "We need," Mr. Clark further reflected, "better educated men and higher standards," thus tentatively committing himself to the skepticism of my beady-eyed young friend.

As reviewers go, I'm relatively lucky. When someone asks me to enunciate all my precise standards of evaluation at the drop of a disbelieving eyebrow, I can always say, "Well, I'm really a novice at this game and I don't expect to have any standards for another forty or fifty years." But what does Brooks Atkinson say? Mr. Atkinson has been on *The New York Times* since 1926 and he has got to have absolute, and absolutely articulated, standards.

Does he say, "Well, I give twenty per cent for integral harmony between theme and climax, twelve per cent for catharsis, eighteen per cent for direct characterization, eighteen per cent for indirect characterization, twenty-two per cent for main plot, sixteen per cent for subplot, eight per cent for exaltation, two per cent for neatness, and the balance to all acting companies having a preponderance of blondes"? Does he carry a scientifically graded tab sheet to the theater with him and score off points in the light of the firmer principles of Aristotle, Castelvetro, Scaliger, Dryden, Lessing, Diderot and William Archer? I have met Mr. Atkinson, and I can assure you that he would rather cover the waterfront (which he does, by the way—he is an authority on tugboats, with very high standards) than engage in this sort of academic crap game.

I can remember that when I was in college we all suffered acutely from technical standarditis. Our special target in those days was George Jean Nathan. (Mr. Nathan was mature when I was a sophomore, and still is.) Mr. Nathan always seemed to be contradicting himself—or us, I forget which—and it gave us great pain. Someone named Constance Frick finally wrote a doctoral dissertation, later published by the Cornell Press, in an effort to discover whether Mr. Nathan was principled or unprincipled.

If I remember correctly, it turned out that Mr. Nathan was unprincipled and also correct about ninety-nine per cent of the time. Taste is in large part a matter of exposure, and since Mr. Nathan has clearly been exposed to more plays than anyone else writing just now, it follows that—even though he does not spend much time in tossing words like "peripeteia," "crisis" and "empathy" around— his judgment is going to be a little sounder than that of the *cum laude* in Dramatic Criticism 209.

It seems to me that this whole matter of taste—and of the absolute standards it is presumed to rest on—is pretty widely misunderstood. There are all kinds of canons of criticism, and a good many of them are thoroughly sound. I'm not one for junking a hard-won dramatic principle just because it is two thousand years old. But this sort of thing is groundwork, the cutting of baby teeth. It is something to be investigated at the student level, something to be soaked up.

Once it has been soaked up, however, it should be expected to disappear into the general taste, the informed substratum of the man; it is not meant to be paraded pontifically, used as an intelligence quotient, or brandished as an esoteric cudgel over the heads of the folks who are just trying to find a good show on 45th Street. Anyone who pretends that he seriously wants this last kind of criticism—stacked with technical jargon, splitting terminological hairs —is a person fully capable of reading the program notes for a string quartet with real relish.

As Mr. Nathan took care to remark, when asked to write his own introduction to the Frick book: "I might confect a foreword gratuitously rich in quotations from Brunetière, Sainte-Beuve, Coleridge, Hazlitt and, satirically, the drama critics of the present-day tonier weeklies and monthlies, thus testifying to my liberal library education and boring the reader, who is seldom deceived by such extrinsic shenanigans, no end."

And Barrett Clark, having posed the problem of standards, special training and genuine erudition, finally got around to answering it with a counter-question: "Who has a deeper knowledge of the history of drama than George Jean Nathan, or John Mason Brown, or George Freedley, or John Gassner? And besides, who in the world would be qualified to conduct such courses? Precisely the men I've been talking about."

Asking a reviewer to tick off his standards in a few polite words is a lot like asking your grandmother for a mathematical description of how she used to make her four-layer caramel cake. And a man who can deliver the goods in a neatly wrapped package is probably a man who has memorized the words but who has absorbed into his blood stream few of the things they stand for. I'd say, beware the glib purist—there has been no osmosis, and he may be a fake. The sound man has a *habit* of principle, but the chances are a thousand to one that he has long since forgotten the phrase and the formula in which the habit was first rehearsed.

⋘ FOUR ⋙

Seats on Sale

⋘ *1* ⋙

I AM fascinated by alibis, especially alibis for not going to the theater. I suppose "alibi" is a curious word to use in this connection, since no one under the sun is obliged to hie himself to the playhouse at regular intervals, irregular intervals, or any intervals whatever.

But a lot of folk seem to sense theatergoing as an obligation and to carry a mild guilt complex around with them. At least they put themselves to considerable pains to explain why they don't go, and the elaborate explanations they whip up often have a fine fishy air of unreality about them.

One of the commonest plaints heard at cocktail parties, literary conventions, and meetings of the mothers of the Peter Pan Day

Nursery School is the wistful thought that everybody would love to go to the theater but that nobody can get tickets. I frequently find myself yapping about the disappearance of theatergoing as a casual habit—the "drop-in" attitude toward playgoing—and I rarely get past the first faltering sentence without having to duck a broadside: "Of course we want to go to the theater! We'd like to go to the theater every week! But you can't possibly get tickets except months in advance, and who wants to plan his whole life around your 'casual habit'?"

There is usually so much vehemence, not to mention shining sincerity, in these protestations that I find myself going back to the show-business weekly, Variety, to take another look. Variety lists both the possible grosses and the actual grosses of every show on Broadway, so that you can tell at a glance approximately how many seats went unsold in any given week.

Take a recent listing. (This was an especially good week at the box office, not a dull one; I'm not trying to stack the cards.) There were twenty-five shows on Broadway, not counting one-man or one-woman operations. Of the twenty-five, exactly seven were selling out.

This means—I don't think the mathematics are too involved for me—that no fewer than eighteen entertainments had tickets available, tickets that were eventually dumped into the wastebasket. Eighteen managements would have been only too happy to pick up a little unplanned "drop-in" trade.

But let's be entirely honest about the matter. Four of the available shows were reasonably close to capacity—within one or two thousand dollars of it, say—and a customer might have been turned away more nights of the week than he would have been welcomed. (He still might have snared a seat for tomorrow night, though, or for next week.)

Let's concentrate on the remaining fourteen—or more than half of the enterprises running. Here there were all sorts of unfilled seats, anywhere from one fourth to better than one half of the auditorium. Anyone who'd had a sudden, lunatic impulse to put on a coat and dart off to a show might have sauntered up to a box office as late as 8:40, been greeted with extraordinary courtesy and perhaps even a pat on the back, and trundled down the center aisle with a bright, fresh stub in his fist. And—to harp on the point—he'd have had half of Broadway to pick from.

For the spur-of-the-moment customer this is a brighter picture than is usually painted. Outline it, though, for the non-theatergoing theater-lover, and you will get a very fast comeback: "Who wants to see the flops?"

Our notion that the shows we cannot see are the only ones worth wanting to see is a deeply cherished but not entirely sound one. It is, I think, a part of the alibi, a psychological device calculated to keep us comfortably absent, and comfortably virtuous, forever. Checking back over that *Variety* listing, I find that there wasn't an absolute dog in the lot. Real dogs die quickly and each of the fourteen available entertainments had some chance of catching on.

There are genuine successes that never do sell out. A Shirley Booth starring vehicle, *The Time of the Cockoo*, was listed—both critically and financially—among the hits of its season; yet it had very few capacity weeks during its eight-month stay. *I Am a Camera* was forced to shut off its top balcony for want of sellout patronage. It was a hit, too. Neither was ever very hard to get into.

Of the various ventures that are not precisely hot tickets at any given moment, some are simply on their way to success and may yet go down in the yearbooks as "memorable." (You can always pride yourself later on belonging to that wise and select group that actually remembers them.) Some others are roaring successes of earlier seasons, now past their first bloom.

Some are geared to special tastes (yours, perhaps). And some are mild and inoffensive evenings that may prove entirely tolerable to anyone looking for a mild and inoffensive evening. (On a drop-in, no-fuss basis, all things are possible.)

In any case, a show that is actually playing has not yet qualified as a flop, and the cry "Who wants to go to the flops?" is at the very least premature. A show isn't a flop until it closes. The only reason a show ever closes is because nobody comes.

Most of all, it would be nice if we could kill off that damaging legend which insists that all Broadway box offices are trimmed with barbed wire. Most Broadway box offices—more than half of them as a rule—throb with delight at the sight of an unexpected stray wandering in with a light in his eyes and a couple of bucks in his hand.

∾ 2 ∾

I HAVE NOW come across—Variety is once more my source—the worst theatrical news of this puzzling decade.

A reviewer likes to be as cheerful as possible as often as possible. It becomes him, considering the despicable nature of the work he is most frequently called upon to do. But this particular bit of information is so alarming in its implications, so unsusceptible of any optimistic interpretation, that we'd better just bow our heads and get on with it.

Variety reports that the seats hardest to sell nowadays are the cheapest seats in the balcony. Even the biggest hits are having trouble with the gallery, and have been having trouble with it for some time.

Mr. Roberts, in its heyday, couldn't sell its $1.20 tickets. Season after season reputed smashes look nervously at their upper reaches. "Whatever the reason," the report goes on to say, "lively second-balcony patronage is now the exception rather than the rule."

This, by the way, knocks into a cocked hat the strongly entrenched theory that what is wrong with the contemporary theater is the high price of seats—the theory that playgoing has priced itself beyond the reach of the average customer. It is precisely the seats that are within the reach of the average customer that aren't being sold.

What all this means, of course, is that no new generation is coming into the theater. Passionate playgoing always begins high up under the roof. The kid who is on an allowance, the student who has had to skip two lunches in order to scrape up the cash, and what *Variety* calls "the hand-holding young couples on lean budgets," all see their first shows from these dizzy, dusty and usually overheated heights.

The admitted fact that the galleries of most theaters aren't spectacularly comfortable has nothing to do with the case. When you first fall in love with the theater (if you do) you don't really mind the long, labyrinthine climb, the patient swapping of binoculars; nor are you bothered by the fact that when you say you have "seen" Katharine Cornell you really mean you have seen a radiant blur that has been identified for you as Katharine Cornell.

My own theatergoing—and that of all my friends—started from a precipitous perspective that provided a magnificent view of the front half of the stage floor, the top side of the performers' toupees (bald actors were unusually dazzling), and the music sheets which flickered into yellowish life whenever the orchestra prepared for a cue.

For a good ten years I never did see an actor make an upstage entrance or exit (characters simply swam in under the proscenium and, later on, inexplicably swam out again), and I must have been a mature twenty-six before I saw what all of a Mielziner set looked like. When I finally got out of the balcony and onto the main floor it seemed strange—and not in every case an improvement.

My own generation has slowly inched its way down to the orchestra. Apparently there's nobody behind us.

Variety has simply brought into the open what has been on the grapevine for quite a while. We were speaking a moment ago of *I Am a Camera*, one of those plays that did nicely with its $4.80 seats and nothing at all with the $1.20 allotment.

What is startling in this particular case is not that a John van Druten play of decided quality should find itself in such a curious fix but that a successful play starring Julie Harris should run into the problem. Miss Harris is a brand-new star, just out of teen-age roles—a rising, glowing symbol of a new generation in the theater.

One might reasonably expect her to pack the galleries, to command that first fanatic loyalty that attaches to the promise of a new career and that takes delight in building up an "I-saw-her-when" tradition. Ethel Barrymore's fans, if you believe their claims, were faithful from *Captain Jinks of the Horse Marines* right down to *The Corn Is Green*.

But Miss Harris' own generation is apparently off in the woods someplace, indifferent to her—and their—claims upon the theater. Only the affluent middle-aged are willing to guarantee her stardom, to urge her on; and they're going to be pretty decrepit by the time Miss Harris, at forty-two, decides she is ready to play Juliet.

The current situation amounts to a violent reversal of what used to be standard theatrical experience. Until eight or ten years ago, producers sold out their balconies months in advance, long before they knew whether they were going to have anyone in the orchestra at all; the loyalty was upstairs, the doubt downstairs. A good many shows were forced to close while gallery trade was still thriving. The impoverished youngsters were still interested, interested even in flops.

To have lost this kind of interest is alarming. The alarm is a little muted at the moment because the topsy-turvy box-office behavior we've been talking about carries an illusory sense of well-being with it: as long as you're selling the expensive seats, you're not much inclined to worry about the inexpensive and less profitable ones.

But the temporary nature of this felicitous condition is obvious: we're now selling $4.80 seats to people who conceived a passion, at $1.20 a palpitation, ten years ago. To whom are we going to sell them in 1963? Total strangers?

The ominous emptiness of those steeply pitched tiers suggests that our current theatrical practice appeals only to a middle-aged taste, that our playwriting and performing methods have little or no interest for anyone under thirty, that we have not yet found a dramatic or theatrical way of reflecting, getting in touch with, or otherwise attracting the next generation.

We have young actors, actresses, directors, and writers. What we don't seem to have along Broadway is young playgoers, and any minute now we'd better busy ourselves trying to find out what the A.W.O.L. crowd might cotton to.

～ 3 ～

In our efforts to locate the A.W.O.L. playgoer, it is possible that we misunderstand what he is looking for. Too often we try to offer him comfort. We do have a habit of thinking of theatergoers as delicate souls, soft of limb and short of wind, who must be led by the hand to the playhouse, slipped into the lobby before they realize quite where they are, and thereafter cushioned and coddled as tenderly as possible.

Broadway managers spend vast portions of their energies, for instance, battling to get their shows into the most convenient theaters. The thought of opening a new venture as far up as 48th Street has been known to give sound men the shakes; people can't walk that far. The notion that a playgoer might be able to find his way west of Eighth or east of Seventh is unthinkable; people get lost.

The general theory, I guess, is that all potential customers are born at Broadway and 42nd, and the shock to their nervous systems is so great that they never again can manage more than two square blocks at a time. They totter forth feebly at 8:15. Unless a theater is so situated that they cannot help stumbling over its curbstone and landing on their faces in the foyer, the jig is up.

Getting them in is only part of it. Once they are there—this is the latest theory, anyway—they must be nestled in the coziest conceivable quarters. Quite a few playhouses have been installing "divan" seats lately—plush and satiny lounges for two, equipped with adjustable arm rests.

And when you hear any talk of the theaters of the future, the talk you hear is about bars. In time, the playgoer is to be soothed in all his senses, if not rendered completely insensible. Easy does it, the maxim goes. Make the theater painless and you will make it profitable.

Maybe. My own guess is that the true playgoer is of slightly hardier stock than this, a reasonably rugged fellow with a streak of pioneering blood in his veins. Suggest to him that there's a good show on 44th Street and he may or may not drop in. Suggest to him that there's a fairly good show hidden in an old loft in Greenwich Village and he will drop his drink, forget about dinner, risk the subways, take his chances of getting lost on a branch of Christopher Street no cab driver has ever heard of, and come up panting at the drama's new hideaway.

Once there, he will scuff down a concrete aisle to lower himself—perhaps with a silent prayer—into a creaking seat which would put any version of the medieval iron maiden to shame. He will find himself seated so close to the thundering floorboards of the stage that any splinters flying off—or any props not held securely by the actors—will land, without warning, in his lap. (During a recent Village season I was on the receiving end of one broken clay pipe, one Capezio dance slipper and one extremely flexible rubber knife.)

Should he develop a thirst, he will have to wrench himself loose from the cast-iron chair arms which have by now locked themselves tightly under his ribs, rise and go across the street for his drink like any other law-abiding, unpampered citizen.

They're short on sybaritic appeals at the Cherry Lane and the Theater de Lys. The Phoenix, normal enough in its interior appointments, is a long way off from the security of 44th Street. And the Circle-in-the-Square, for three years Mecca to the intrepid playgoer, was so risky a labyrinth that the Fire Department called a halt until it could turn itself ino a "cabaret."

Not all of our present-day frontiersmen, I suppose, have the stamina to make it to the Village. Some get as far as the Barbizon-Plaza, and settle. Others have been known to endure the discomforts of the Jan Hus House (a church basement with solid oak pews and a flat floor) and then draw the line.

But they go. And, in an exceptional number of instances, they stay. During the 1950s, as everyone knows, a great many rockets have gone up on the far-flung fringes of the city—*End As a Man, Bullfight, The Girl on the Via Flaminia, The Threepenny Opera, The World of Sholem Aleichem, The Iceman Cometh* and three or four others. Given a sudden sign in the night sky and a whiff of odd excitement, the audience casts off its fancied indolence, its fabled concern for its own deep comfort, and takes to the rockier bypaths.

What lures it out of its accustomed haunts, of course, is the promise of an unfamiliar experience, the exhilarating hope that the theater is doing something *else*. A hint is quite enough. The slightest suspicion that the theater is somewhere shaking off slumber, and stretching its limbs, sends all sorts of normally sensible people scurrying great distances to do desperate battle with wooden benches, winding cellars, and—sometimes—a creaky elevator crawling six flights up. If there's anything mysteriously tempting on the stage itself, the tribulations only add zest.

When we try to explain the absence of balcony customers along Broadway, we tell ourselves that the balconies just aren't comfortable enough. But that doesn't really seem to be the answer, does it?

We make a mistake, I think, in trying to lure the customer back by promising him convenience. What we ought to promise him is an obstacle race, with a whale of a show at the end of it.

∽ 4 ∾

I KEEP REMEMBERING the last ten minutes of an off-Broadway venture called *Bullfight*, and while I am probably tempted to read too much into this singularly effective climax I do think it sheds a little light on the problem of excitement—or lack of excitement—in the contemporary theater.

Bullfight is the first produced play of Leslie Stevens, and Mr. Stevens is one newcomer who means to be a newcomer, not a fourth carbon of his tired elders. While the story of his play is not especially original—two sons of a famous matador destroy themselves by aping their long-dead father—the style in which it is told is thoughtfully rebellious.

Mr. Stevens has preferred not to bore us with the painfully complete and snail-paced detail of the realistic theater. He is after the high spots—the crucial moments of anger and passion and pain—and it is only the high spots he writes out fully.

For the rest he uses pantomime. The necessary transitions from emotion to emotion, the local color, the exposition, the slumbering tensions that prepare a clash to come are all presented as sheer movement—movement that is every bit as evocative and about twice as rapid as dialogue might have been. Whatever is merely informative is quickly and musically described; whatever is genuinely dramatic erupts into language.

Theatrical prophets have, of course, been urging something like this for years. Usually the effort has led to solemnity, ambiguity, and pretentiousness. Mr. Stevens does not wholly escape the customary traps. He is sometimes sucked into marshy rhetoric ("Your father gave you pride and a sword, your mother gave you fear and a flower"), and his concrete images are sometimes compromised by symbolism (a girl slips off her skirt and uses it like a bull cape to tantalize an overwrought male.)

But most of the time the spare use of dialogue and the lavish use of physical activity does its job. A very graphic cockfight, for instance, is conveyed by nothing more than the backs of some agitated spectators. And what really counts is that climax, a battle in the arena proper.

It's a long time since any reasonably practical playwright has dared set his biggest scene in an open, bustling, intensely theatrical place—not since the movies took over, anyway. Because the movies could offer a real bull ring, a real crowd and a whole corral of real bulls, the theater sighed, sank back onto the sofa, and gave over all thought of competing with this kind of excitement.

What the theater forgot was that it could match any other art form, excitement for excitement, in its own way. There is even a sense in which the solitary matador, standing on an apron stage and swirling his cloak away from an invisible bull may be more exciting than Tyrone Power doing the same thing in Technicolor. Because the film is able to show the entire arena, the throng of thousands and the onrushing enemy, it *must* show them. By cutting from hero to crowd to bull, it creates one kind of thrill.

The thrill that is possible to the theater is of a slightly different sort—the thrill of being alone with a man at the center of things, of standing where he stands and feeling only what he feels. When the actor at the Theater de Lys spun violently and crumpled as a non-existent horn ripped into his side, there was an audible gasp from the audience. Belief was complete, and the audience was unusually close to the character whose emotions it shared.

If the motion picture possesses the virtue of literal spectacle, it also falls under obligation to literal spectacle—and the obligation inevitably eats away at whatever is intimate and personal. The theater's obligation is to psychology. But it may, if it is inventive enough, pursue that psychology into any sort of whirlwind, into the fever of large-scale battle. Shakespeare, after all, took us right onto Bosworth Field, right into Lear's thunderstorm.

The principal distinction of *Bullfight*, then, lay in its prodding reminder that plays take place in a theater: on a platform that may jut out over the audience and command its belief by the actor's power of evocation. Even on Broadway, there is a beginning consciousness of this power, a dawning rediscovery of things theatrical.

The fact of the matter is that the theater hasn't been theatrical enough for quite a few years now. "Theatrical" has, in fact, become a dirty word in our time. We've been much too proud of our chaste exclusion of showiness, of emphasis, of direct appeal to the audience. When we have praised actors we've praised them mostly for the restraint they've shown in keeping themselves tidily tucked away behind the fourth wall.

At last there are signs of a crack in that wall, indications that it may go tumbling down into the orchestra pit any minute.

In our realistic theater, the imaginary "fourth wall" has generally been presumed to stand at the proscenium arch, where it constitutes a silent aesthetic barrier between players and public.

Actually, the term was never meant to suggest such a barrier. When Diderot first used the phrase, the theater's "fourth wall" was thought to be at the back of the orchestra seats; actors and paying customers were to be admitted into the same agreeable society.

Somehow or other, though, we managed to push it up onto the stage and make a curtain of it—a transparent curtain, perhaps, but a maddeningly real one nevertheless. We came to understand that the players were sheltered behind it and that we were lucky enough just to be permitted to eavesdrop.

Ours is the only theater in history that has dared isolate actors and audience in this peculiar way. The great theaters of the past—and the not-so-great ones as well—all blasted through the imaginary wall. Sophocles' choruses sang to the assembled holiday mob; Shakespeare's heroes spoke to the people who had coughed up their pennies; the leering villains of the last century leaned over the footlights and acknowledged the fact that there was somebody on the other side of them.

I suppose it must have been the faintly apologetic, and emotionally cheesy, "aside" of the nineteenth century that made us feel that every sort of contact was terribly false and that we had best dispense with the effort altogether. In any case, we did dispense with it, very firmly, and we have subsequently persuaded ourselves that the divorce of artist and auditor was a healthy improvement.

Psychologically, there are a number of things wrong with the stern pretense that no customers are present. In the first place, it isn't polite. In the second, it makes for a decidedly chilly relationship between people who are supposed to be enamored of one another. And I suspect that the practice has played some part in alienating contemporary audiences from the theater. For years and years now our actors have behaved as though no one was listening. After a while, no one was.

During the years of aloofness, only one form has kept up any sort of running relationship with the people who have dropped in for the evening. That form, of course, is musical comedy—a carefree confection in which the heroine, though she is holding hands with the hero and giving him a nod now and then, is really singing to you.

If musical comedy has been the healthiest form of our time, the form most able to bear present-day costs and to grow in aesthetic stature into the bargain, its candid friendliness toward the customer may well have helped it along.

But the so-called "legitimate" theater has tentatively begun to turn around and stare at the ticketholders, too. In *The Teahouse of the August Moon* David Wayne trotted out in front of the bamboo curtain and made you feel as though you were welcome in this once slightly gloomy temple. Playwright John Patrick knew you were there, too: he kept offering you charming little fragments of scenes you wouldn't otherwise have got, linking them together with helpful comment from his talkative master of ceremonies.

In a minor farce called *The Solid Gold Cadillac* the fourth wall took a nice, minor beating. Fred Allen's voice kept needling you via a sound system that wasn't exactly stereophonic but did put the show on an over-the-shoulder basis. The front of the stage kept erupting into motion-picture satires on sugary television commentators, playful exercises bent on pointing up the fact that you were in a playhouse, where all things are possible. The acting style was not altogether intimate, but when Loring Smith launched into his windmill recital of "Spartacus to the Gladiators" there was no mistaking which side of the house he meant to entertain.

The unfamiliar excitement of the two Paul Gregory-Charles Laughton excursions into directness—*Don Juan in Hell* and *John Brown's Body*—lingers on. Both ventures strode to the footlights and stepped over them. The usefulness of this formal freedom did not become fully apparent, however, until the same producer-director combination applied it to what would normally have been a "straight" play. With *The Caine Mutiny Court-Martial* a perfectly realistic courtroom situation was so mounted that the witness stand frankly faced the audience. One by one the principal performers marched to it. One by one they played long scenes dead center, and out front. Instead of being absorbed into a private universe carefully cut off from the customer, they were on spectacular public display. It was no accident that Lloyd Nolan, as the disintegrating Captain Queeg, was now free to give what remains one of the most shattering performances of our time. It is interesting to notice, too, that the motion-picture version of the same story—with wind and wave and the whole horizon at its command—was not able to duplicate the intensity that flowed from an almost bare, drape-surrounded stage.

Razing the fourth wall is not going to solve all of the problems of our theater. But I feel confident it's going to help. A "welcome" mat on the doorstep is always more attractive than a sealed and silent barrier.

∽ FIVE ∾

In the Playhouse

∽ 1 ∾

I DON'T KNOW whether or not we are going to get any new theaters very soon, but now that the licensing regulations have been loosened up to permit the construction of auditoriums in all-purpose buildings, we may indulge in a decent hope. In fact, I was feeling mildly optimistic about the whole business until a letter turned up in the mail suggesting that someone inaugurate a competition in theater design under the new, relaxed rules.

Suddenly I realized what the first flush of enthusiasm would bring us—great to-do about new auditorium shapes, convenient staircases, accessible lounges, multiple exits, and room for that long-lost bar. But nary a word about brightening up the center of all this: the stage.

If we are really going to think about building new theaters, it seems to me that we ought to give at least passing attention to the possibility of some new stages, too. It would be nice, for instance, if one or another chandelier-happy architect could momentarily tear himself away from the problem of what the ceiling is going to look like—one looks at the ceiling only during the performance of excessively bad plays—and give a moment's thought to breaking the hundred-year stranglehold of that three-toed sloth, the box set.

We've grown awfully used to the jam-packed peephole stage that was wished upon us by the nineteenth-century realists, so used to it that we've forgotten how inhibiting it is to actors, playwrights and designers alike.

The picture-frame proscenium arch is such an old and familiar story that we rarely imagine what it might be like to have actors erupt beyond it. The complete canvas walls, the solidly constructed staircases and the ubiquitous doorways have become theatrical second-nature; we don't quite envision the play big enough to rear back, shake off all this constricting paraphernalia, and confidently expand to something more than life-size.

But, however accustomed we may have become to it, we have been putting up with a whittled-down stage. The scene designer has been forbidden to soar. His problem is one of tidy enclosure, and he has been pretty much reduced to an interior decorator.

The actor has been forbidden to raise his voice (it would seem insufferably noisy in that plausible apartment) or to extend his arm in anything resembling an emphatic gesture (he would be in constant danger of sweeping the bric-a-brac off the mantelpiece).

The playwright has found himself building his play to conform to his scenery, instead of building his scenery to conform to his play. It's a rare dramatist nowadays who follows his action where his action leads him. He spends most of his time contriving, curtailing and even distorting his action in order to draw it all into that single expensive, immovable set.

Nor does the audience come out of this cabined, cribbed and confined stage procedure much better. Quite apart from the psychological fence that our proscenium arch sets up—with the actors on one side of a defined line, the audience on the other, and a polite indifference between them—there are quite a few incidental penalties.

Though we have geared everything else in our theater to the scenery, the amount of scenery you are likely to see will depend on where you sit. From the balcony you may very well miss the entire back wall. From extreme right or left of the main floor you may be denied the thrill of contemplating certain of the tapestries, telephone nooks and flower-studded end-tables that have been carefully created for the occasion. The usual solution to this problem is to change the shape of the auditorium; it might be a great deal simpler to change the shape of the stage.

The proscenium arch, of course, was never the invention of a dramatist; it was brought into the theater by the scene designer, for the special purpose of framing a paint job he'd done. When it was first brought into the theater, however, it presented no particular difficulties: the painting was directly inside the proscenium, the actors were out front on a three-sided apron stage. You could see the painting from any part of the house, and the actors were completely free of it.

We have—unfortunately, I think—spent the last hundred years moving actors and scenery upstage, sucking everything in and under. The time has come for a forward push again.

The scenic tail has been wagging the dramatic dog for so long that, even when we do find ourselves on a new kind of acting area, we tend to bring all our old habits of thought along with us.

One of the virtues of theater-in-the-round, for instance, is its supposed freedom from the scenic encumbrance. More and more, though, I notice the wood and canvas piling up on these small, central stages: if not an entire house, then an entire skeleton of a house. There is now talk of building gridirons into some of the more successful arenas, so that still more scenery can be imported, and flown.

We have psychologically accepted the burden of the realistically built-up, and scenically circumscribed, stage. How little it really brings us was demonstrated not long ago at the Martin Beck. For reasons of economy, Arthur Miller's *The Crucible* was played, during its final weeks, with a handful of essential properties—and against no other background than space and light. Boris Aronson's original settings for the play had been excellent; they had also been remarkably uncluttered. But they were not, in all honesty, missed. If anything, the somewhat rhetorical play profited by its release from concrete surroundings, gained in belief through its adventure into the open.

It isn't necessary to turn rabidly antiscenic, though, in wishing for a more flexible stage. You'd have to be ascetic indeed to want to dismiss the color, the sweep, the evocative power and the gaiety that sensitive designing can bring to certain entertainments. Designing itself is happiest when it is freest—in the stylized strokes, the easy fluidity and the wide-open wing space of modern musical comedy.

What anyone might reasonably ask for is a stage so shaped as to emphasize and project the actor, a stage that might help him disentangle himself from the environmental obstacle race he is now running, a stage proportioned in such fashion as to make the subordinate scenic art really subordinate, and a stage on which everything important might actually be visible.

After which we can go to work on that very welcome bar.

❧ 2 ❧

ALTHOUGH IT MAY NOT seem very likely, I have been having a wonderful time with a book called *Sources of Theatrical History*. Professor A. M. Nagler, who directs graduate studies in the field at

Yale, has combed the libraries for eyewitness accounts of earlier theaters and obligingly packed them back-to-back in a single expansive volume.

Thus we get a glimpse of Thespis, who may have been the first actor, nervously explaining to a legislative busybody that acting is really quite a decent profession. We get a flash of Euripides flying into a temper with his chorus boys.

We discover that, long before Stein's or Max Factor had worked out make-up bases appropriate to each and every character type, the Greeks had charted the appearance of their stage women as follows: curled virgin, demimondaine, second demimondaine, talkative, hoary-talkative, concubine, beautiful courtesan, golden harlot, virgin slave, and slut.

We get fine descriptions of what once were orthodox methods of producing classical tragedy: one in which Queen Clytemnestra shared the stage with 600 mules, another in which Oedipus the King played out his tragedy accompanied by a constant bodyguard of twenty-four Turkish archers.

Best of all, though, are the on-the-spot reports of what it was like to go to such theaters: of the sections reserved for decent women and the sections reserved for women with something else on their minds; of the gate-crashing gallants who considered it a mark of dishonor not to be able to outwit mere box-office attendants; of the humane practice of stopping a bad play dead in its tracks—a practice which, if pursued nowadays, would get us all home earlier much of the time.

The audiences of yesteryear come nicely alive on these pages: what they ate, what they threw at the actors, what they threw at one another whenever a riot started are all lovingly listed. For a book which was intended primarily as a research manual, Dr. Nagler's *Sources of Theatrical History* makes attractive light reading.

It also suggests to me that no one has yet done a sufficiently factual job on our own time to make sure that future historians will get us right. To spare them the desperate labor of piecing together odd bits and pieces out of theatrical reviews ("The first-night audience seemed to be having a good time") and to keep them from making mistakes, I submit the following notation:

The twentieth-century American audience was an extraordinarily docile one. It did not choose the plays it went to see, but submitted basely to the guidance of seven or eight journalists, called critics. It did not go to the theater on the spur of the moment, or in a wave of exhilaration, but carefully laid plans for attendance as much as three to nine months in advance, meanwhile adjusting lives, marriages and possibly even childbearing to the impending date.

It did not attempt to enter the playhouse without payment, but lived in a special fear, approaching terror, of the man at the box office. Timid inquiries about seat locations were occasionally heard, and there were spasmodic bursts of letter writing to the Sunday newspapers, but there is no record of heroic self-assertion in the lobby of any theater.

Entering the theater on the night of performance, the furtive playgoer was commanded to keep moving, to buy a souvenir program and to check his hat and coat. Many playgoers did these things.

Most playgoers walked in reverent silence down a heavily carpeted aisle to their seats, looking neither to right nor left; seat locations were fixed, and it was not permissible to wander about the house looking for a friend to sit next to. Hand-waving was substituted.

The playgoer was permitted neither to drink nor smoke. It became customary after a while to indulge in such things rather heavily before the performance so as not to yearn after them too much during the play. Chocolate creams were occasionally eaten, but the slight crackling sound made by the paper in which these were wrapped brought such a sharp turning of heads in the vicinity that the custom was largely abandoned, or indulged most surreptitiously. In general, the audience wished to give the impression of rigorous asceticism and grave indifference to physical pleasures. The atmosphere was religious and devotional, giving rise to the speculation that the twentieth-century drama was closely allied with the church.

Conversation was forbidden after the rise of the curtain, and anything above a light whisper was instantly shushed. Late-comers were not welcomed but reproved in stony silence. The curtain, as a rule, went only halfway up. Some authorities maintain that this was due to the fact that most stage settings of the period represented ordinary living rooms and that such living rooms did not require the full use of the proscenium opening. Others insist that it was a further mark of that caution and restraint which so characterized the period.

The settings were severely formalized, varying almost not at all from play to play or year to year. They consisted of three walls with convenient doorways, together with a sofa at downstage left and a table at downstage right. Occasionally this was varied by placing the sofa at downstage right and the table at downstage left. There is some evidence that the bookshelves that adorned the back walls were also varied in shape and size on rare occasions. It was customary, upon the rise of the curtain, to applaud this setting, whether out of familiarity or out of sympathy with the designer is not known.

No member of the audience was permitted to sit on the stage, although the actors sat a great deal. The actors did not acknowledge the audience's presence at any time, neither looking at it nor speaking to it; the actors spoke only to other actors. They spoke quietly, subdued their gestures, engaged in as little physical motion as possible and went directly home after the performance. It was not customary to cheer them at the stage door.

No criticism of the performance was voiced while the play was in progress, and very little of it during the intermission. It was usual for a member of the audience to reserve opinion until some friend had expressed his, and then agree with it. There was often a momentary burst of unseemly gaiety at the beginning of the first intermission as various members of the audience greeted old friends in the lobby, but this was discreetly balanced by remaining in one's seat during the second intermission in order to avoid meeting the same friends.

Not all members of the audience reached the lobby during an intermission. Many filed in orderly and patient fashion toward an exit only to be turned back for the next act just as they were on the point of lighting cigarettes.

Attendants were also provided to make sure that no cigarettes were lighted until the first wave had hit the streets. This was true in inclement as well as clement weather. Rest rooms were provided for those agile enough to negotiate an almost perpendicular stairwell to the basement. A mild orange juice could be purchased in the foyer.

Those who remained in their seats during intermissions were temperately regaled by the appearance of four or five musicians who played inappropriate selections dimly, for fear of making a vulgar racket. The earlier American theatrical practice of allowing spectators in the balcony to shout down requests for their favorite tunes no longer obtained.

Such members of the audience as might find themselves not enjoying the show were required to remain in their seats until the fall of the last curtain. Occasionally it might be noticed that, at the beginning of the third act, not all of the seats which had hitherto been occupied continued to be so; but those who had departed had made their egress so tastefully, not to say secretively, that it was as though they had never been there. No man ever left the theater without a good excuse, such as that he had lost his glasses or that his mother had died, though not in the theater.

Those who remained were rewarded with a number of curtain calls and continued to applaud politely for as many curtain calls as the actors wished to take.

In general, twentieth-century man considered himself favored to be let into the theater, and fortunate to be let out.

The legitimate theater was not especially well patronized during this period.

๛ 3 ๛

As a rule, I see more men than women sleeping soundly in the theater. I go on opening nights, when it is rather hard to sleep—people keep crawling all over you to their seats at all hours—but, in the few rows that I can take in at a single glance, there is nearly always some gentleman with the contemplative power, the immunity to distraction, and the single-mindedness that are needed to drop off in trying circumstances. Occasionally a woman manages it, but men have the edge.

The ability to sleep during a Broadway performance is usually attributed to cocktails, but this, I think, is a canard. Women have been known to lap up not only their own Martinis but substantial portions of their husbands' and still stay giddily alert through three long acts. The power of the male to remain erect in an evening suit while achieving a state of delightful oblivion is unique. It has been worked out carefully over the years, and represents no easy victory. It has been helped along, of course, by the clamplike rigidity of the seat in which he has been placed, but the triumph is an earned one and we must not take it from him. The male has learned how to deal with a theater which has, for some time now, been principally designed for his wife.

While the old boy dozes off, his wife's eyes dart restlessly over the stage that has been set for her. She checks the fashionable living-room interior for helpful hints in homemaking. She wonders whether tonight's arrangement of bookshelves would do for that reshuffling of her husband's den she has in mind. She checks the draperies critically. She contemplates the placement of the sofa. She makes a note of the tea service. She frowns at the rather nervous dab the ingénue has just made at grouping some flowers in a vase.

She sets her lips grimly as the outspoken comedy maid unsuccessfully tidies an antimacassar.

Of course she studies the gowns—usually by Valentina—and wonders whether brassieres mightn't be better after all. She awaits each entrance of the principal actress breathlessly: to see what she will be wearing. The acts of the play are, for her, divided into the turquoise with the flair (Act One), the scalloped beige (Act Two), and That Peach Monstrosity (Act Three). Each coiffure as it appears is examined, taken down, rinsed, reset, and this time properly modeled to the face it adorns. Later she can tell you everything you want to know, and quite a bit you don't, about color clashes, bone structure, and the inadequate concealment of avoirdupois.

From time to time she attends to the play. These times usually have something to do with love. Though the Greeks got along without love altogether, though the Elizabethans treated it sparingly, and though Molière was satisfied with kidding it, the contemporary playwright knows that somewhere in the course of his action two people must clutch at each other, murmur endearments, come to a misunderstanding, and make it all up by 11:00 P.M. Indeed we have become so accustomed to this procedure that lately the thirty-three basic plots—somebody named Polti once said there were thirty-three—have been reduced to one. Every play is a love story with some other gimmick thrown in. The gimmick may be politics (the woman guides her candidate through the labyrinth of dirty male chicanery), it may be science (she discovers radium while he is making dinner), it may be mayhem (she is locked in a house with a psychotic killer), or it may even be sex (she is attacked by Marlon Brando). But whatever the special coloring given to it by way of variety, somewhere in the play sweetness must raise its head like a flower, look longingly for spiritual companionship, and submit delicately to one kind of embrace or another. Anything else would be sordid. It would also leave women in the audience with very little to do once they have completed their hawklike inspection of the décor and the décolletage.

To be properly historical about this, I would have to go back a couple of hundred years. Time was when plays were acted entirely by men and so, very reasonably, were mostly about men: kings, conquerors, and ravaging brigands. In these plays something happened about every three minutes and no tea was served. Sleep was impossible.

Along about the time of the English Restoration, though, actresses were introduced into the theater—in the interests of morality, as that great humorist Charles II put it—and within a very few years the old tragedy had given way to the "she-tragedy," usually a sad play about Lady Jane Grey or one of her equally abused contemporaries.

With the coming of the eighteenth century, the female of the species had begun to worm her way into all forms of literature— she had been taught to read, that was the fundamental mistake— and Robinson Crusoe was being ruthlessly replaced by Pamela. The standard comic plot for the entire period became that in which a virtuous and fashionable woman succeeded in turning her rake-hell husband into a pious lapdog, and if, by the end of the century, woman had stooped to conquer, she had conquered nonetheless.

In the nineteenth century she took to tidying up the stage. Hitherto drama had been a rather florid and barbaric affair in which the actors—and sometimes even the actresses—raced through abandoned graveyards, secret caves, and monstrous castles, usually at the tops of their voices. These things, it was decided, lacked refinement and reality—reality is the way decent people behave when they are at home with their wives—and they had to go. An actress-manager named Madame Vestris had a lot to do with getting them gone. She was one of the first to lay real carpet on the stage floor, to hang the right sort of pictures on the right sort of stage walls, and to get all the other actors to modulate their voices. She had a husband who worked with her and who is understood to have modulated his voice.

At just about the time that stage design was being turned into a supplement to *Better Homes and Gardens*, the feminist movement came along and, with it, a theatrical spokesman. Ibsen cannot really have known what he was doing when he wrote all those plays about women who were smarter than their men (Nora), stronger than their men (Hilda), more passionate than their men (Hedda), or at least less diseased than their men (Mrs. Alving). But he did it, and he must bear some responsibility for the drama as we find it today.

As we find it, it is domesticated, housebroken. Our plays are plays about intimate family affairs in which, to the clatter of coffee spoons and the swish of housecoats, a noble, upstanding, and long-suffering lady (a) urges her incompetent husband past the point of no return, (b) reclaims him, like the simple country girl she is, from the evils of drink and things like that, (c) supports him tenderly while he rides to destruction on a smile and a shoeshine. Meanwhile she rears his children, cuts flowers, graces his home, and spurns the amatory advances of men who understand her for the superior being she really is. Oh, yes. In my historical rundown I forgot to mention *Candida*.

Over the years men have found little secret escapes from the tyranny which the female of the species has latterly exercised over literary forms. There was, for instance, the detective story, in which some of the older and more exciting values—male heroes of unusual prowess dealing brilliantly with colorful and terrifying circumstances—could be pursued on the sly. And there was the Western movie.

But forces have conspired against even these small satisfactions. Roy Rogers has taken unto himself a wife, who now appears in his pictures. The day of male companionship, when the two cowhands rode over the horizon at film's end, is over, and Gabby Hayes has been reduced to television.

It remained for Dorothy Sayers—a woman—to fix up the detective story by inventing Lord Peter Wimsey and that woman he married. Miss Sayers finally got things around to the point where, in a vine-covered cottage, her victim was killed with a flower pot. I think it was at this point that the male, as a class, realized he was licked.

It is one thing simply to give up reading paperbacks, or going to Saturday-afternoon movies, and quite another to have to continue going to the theater in the company of the woman who picks the plays. To deal with this last humiliation the contemporary male has clearly developed an astonishing muscular control—perhaps he has nursed himself along by dipping into Hindu philosophy—and a beautiful serenity of mind. I watch him as he nods at the Lyceum, and I think I can tell, from a certain expressive play of his otherwise complacent features, from a twist of the lip here and a raised eyebrow there, what he is dreaming of. He is dreaming of William S. Hart or, if he is old enough to remember the theater of *Secret Service* and *Sherlock Holmes*, of William Gillette.

There is this to be said about the whole thing: modern competitive society takes a terrible toll of this man's energies. Sleep is vital, and it is good for him to know where he can get it.

❦ 4 ❦

I WAS TAKEN to my first musical comedy when I was five years old. I ran into my first cancellation due to laryngitis when I was five years and two months old. There I was, in the company of a gracious aunt, all decked out in my matinee best, an exceptionally large package of peppermints tucked hopefully under one arm— and no performance. I've made a fascinated study of theatrical laryngitis ever since.

As I have come to see it, there are four basic reasons why a singing performer is struck down before his time, incapacitated at the very moment when he has succeeded in landing a job. They are, in the order of their clinical importance:

(a) *Good notices.* Nothing is harder on the lining of an actor's throat than the thought that that lining is a silver one. Let a critic make a few pleasant remarks about the quality of a certain larynx, and said larynx at once begins to throb a little. The throb is at first warm, gratified, just a bit proud. A comfortable vibrato can be detected at the second and third performances. Good little larynx, its owner seems to be murmuring, how sturdily it holds this whole production together. And it's a very brave larynx, too—spending itself prodigally night after night in the interests of everyone's happiness.

Of course, no one can tell exactly how brave it is unless it has a few obstacles to overcome: a little scratch in one vocal cord, say, something like that. And, curiously enough, a faint scratchiness does show up one otherwise enchanted evening, just enough to call for a quick throat spray.

Now is the time for nobility. The larynx continues to pour out its song over the insistent scratchiness, over the gallons of throat spray, over the temperature that develops in the second week, over the penicillin that modern science has created especially for the occasion. But the point of no return comes at last: the understudy must go on.

This is maddening to the performer, of course, and he deserves every ounce of sympathy we can spare him, for he must now sit in his hotel room and answer telephone calls from every member of the company plus all three assistant stage managers telling him how magnificent the understudy is, how the understudy is holding the performance together, how there were no refunds demanded at the box office, and how earnestly the management hopes he will take his time about recovering. "Don't come back until you're *really* fit" is what everyone says. Fitness follows in a matter of seconds for many performers. There is always the chance, however, that the understudy himself—under the pressure of so much enthusiasm—will develop laryngitis, and even the score. But to get back to our list:

(b) *Bad notices.* It is easy to see why spiteful comment in the press quickly brings on vocal disability. As everyone knows, the conductor of the orchestra is a malevolent creature, just biding his time and waiting for a reasonable excuse to increase his volume and drown out everything on stage. The critical suggestion that one of the entertainers is not up to par is a very good excuse; by rendering him totally inaudible the conductor will actually be *helping* the show. We are off at a gallop. The unfortunate singer, startled within an inch of his life, now tries to sing even louder than the devil's carnival that is going on beneath him, and is soon home in bed.

(c) *The likelihood of a long run.* The show is open, the broker call is tremendous, out-of-town buyers are reported to be paying up to one hundred dollars a seat for the privilege of coming in forty minutes late, and tickets are on sale for New Year's Eve two years hence. If the producer can look so far forward, why not the actor? He sees himself as he will be on New Year's Eve two years hence— an older man, his hair thinner, his waistline thicker from a thousand after-the-show snacks, his wrist paralyzed from signing all those autograph albums, his voice and nerves and home life shattered. He deserves a rest. He takes one.

(d) *The likelihood of a short run.* I'm sorry, but I can't explain this one. By all the perverse laws of show business, a performer who is on the verge of being jobless should be at the peak of his mental, physical and creative powers. The facts are otherwise, though: there is documentation to show that, when a production is good for about twenty-four performances, a really alert player can miss eight of them. It may have something to do with the death-wish; or then again it may be nothing more than an understandable need to compress the disabilities of a normal engagement into an unreasonably limited playing time. A man has his standards to keep up, after all.

I wouldn't want to give the impression that these occupational hazards are confined to singers. Dancers, for instance, have a laryngitis of their own: it is called, I believe, the strained tendon. What sets dancers apart from their colleagues is the fact that their need for therapy occurs most often during out-of-town warmups: get a dancer in New Haven and you've got a dancer with glass ankles.

It has been suggested to me that if a dancer is resting up in the Taft Hotel during the rewriting and restaging sessions, it is absolutely impossible to alter the choreography he or she has made so unforgettable, and he or she will then be able to take that same favored stance—feet wide apart, hands spread-eagled, shoulders hunched—on opening night in New York. I must say that I don't care much for this explanation. It smacks of libel, and, what's more, it isn't complicated enough.

Playwrights have their own variation of the malady. Many's the man who, immediately after a resounding smash, has found his typewriter buckling, his pencil-hand wavering, his confidence undermined by the regular arrival of weekly royalty checks. The laryngeal playwright, however, may at last take heart. A fellow named George Axelrod has ingeniously solved the problem. In his play *Will Success Spoil Rock Hunter?* the canny and devious Mr. Axelrod has shown us the way to the future by writing a season-long success composed entirely of his symptoms.

This report is, needless to say, incomplete. There are rumors abroad that laryngitis of all kinds may be caused by such unidentified factors as hard work, taxing jobs, exhausting hours, and pathological inflammation of the membranes involved. I'm not prepared to say whether there's anything in the notion or not, but I've got researchers working on it.

SIX

Nightcaps

~ 1 ~

"Some shows are so bad," the lady at the party was saying, "that when you get home afterward, you don't even want a drink."

For some reason or other, this struck me as a profound remark, and I have been chewing on it ever since. Obviously, it's an upside-down statement. It flies in the face of every psychological and philosophical truth we cherish. Bad shows are, by all the rules, supposed to *drive* you to drink, and the ashen customer who stumbles out of a lobby at intermission time and into a little bar across the street, never to be seen on 44th Street again, is one of the hardiest figures in our folklore.

But is he a real figure, or is he one of those gay little legends we invent to make light of our wounds? When a show really gets inside a man's nervous system and shatters it with the far-reaching efficiency of a dum-dum bullet, does he seek solace or does he seek revenge? I suspect it's revenge.

Listen to a fellow struggling onto the sidewalk and into his coat after a bout with a bona-fide turkey. One word out of his wife and she gets her head snapped off. He's never going to buy *her* a drink. What he's going to do is get into a cab, preferably by injuring the couple who have been waiting for one at that spot for twenty minutes, inform the driver of his destination and his absolute indifference to said driver's views on Saudi Arabia, and give him the kind of tip that will cause his own seething venom to stir, like a poison, in one other heart.

If it's a matter of a train ride home, you'll know this man by the heartfelt snap and crackle with which he opens his newspaper, producing a sound you haven't heard since you stopped exploding paper bags in your youth. Should his wife ask for a section of the paper, she will get the financial news and the obituaries, and she will get them in a condition fit for packing crates of dishes on moving day. Meanwhile, one foot dangles ominously in the aisle, ready to bump, and be masochistically bumped by, every passenger who gets on at 125th Street or Garden City.

By the time our ravaged victim is home his first fuming outrage has settled to a fine, steady, low-tension hum, the ironic, abstracted, lovingly nursed resentment of an experienced man who knows that the universe is after him and that its treachery can be met only by a grim-lipped disillusion that mocks at the very thought of hope. He doesn't raid the icebox because he knows perfectly well there's nothing in it that wasn't there last night—and wouldn't you think that somewhere in the world there'd be a woman who'd do some shopping? He doesn't let himself consider a bourbon-and-soda because it would take three of the blasted things to make him feel any better, and besides he doesn't *want* to feel better. What he wants, as he stomps up the stairs to lose the cap on the toothpaste and pull one of the rings off the shower curtain, is to make somebody pay.

If the somebody who pays has to be himself—well, there's a kind of occult justice in that. The score is evened, the spite expelled.

And why should a single bad play bring on this passion for self-immolation, this subsequent rejection of all the finer things of life? People have been known, after all, to slip away from a dullish social event and enjoy a furtive nightcap in the quiet of their own castle. If people weren't perfectly willing to sit through bad movies, there wouldn't be any such thing as double features. A book someone has insisted you read can turn out to be a thoroughgoing frost, and life goes on. Why not after a play?

I'm sure one or another expert will tell us that too much money has been involved: dinner, cabs, orchestra seats, train fares, whatever it costs to put baby-sitters through college. Speaking for myself, I'm not certain that our extraordinarily powerful irritation stems from the fact that everybody loves money and money has been lost; it may be that these folk love the theater and the theater, for the moment, has been lost. Paradoxically, we fly into such intense rages because the theater can be so intensely wonderful. Our fury is in direct proportion to the fun we know is possible.

Most of us have a memory of theater that creates an expectation of theater, a standard that has been set and that we very well mean to see kept. At one time or another we have dropped into a playhouse, been unexpectedly lifted a few feet above the floor, and been left with a three-day glow. If we can't remember too many of the three-day variety, we have a fairish collection of twenty-four-hour glows stashed away.

The theater, perhaps because it is a communal enterprise and so multiplies one customer's joy by every other customer's joy, has a curious carry-over quality, a tendency to extend its heady good will on into the night. We expect its brimming enchantments to have a little staying power, to last until we can get over a table with a few equally fortunate friends and catalogue our joint delights, or until we can make it back to the apartment and raise a toast to our pleasure. And when the Scotch comes clinking out of the liquor cabinet it isn't because we want to dismiss an experience, but because we want to prolong one—to savor it, nurse its echo for a while, greedily and gloriously keep it alive. I think the lady at the party was right, and I intend hereafter to make mental note of whether the project of the evening was a two-drink, three-drink, or no-drink play.

∽ 2 ∽

JUST TO TORTURE MYSELF, I have saved up my memories of a few no-drink plays:

There once was, for instance and for a very short time, an exhibit on Broadway called *A Red Rainbow*. Its title required some explanation. The *Red*, I believe, stood for Communism. The *Rainbow* stood for the light in the heavens on the day Communism took over. The audience stood for more than can possibly be imagined.

The moral of this piece, so far as I was able to grasp it, seemed to be: if you happen to know a subversive personally, shoot him dead. At least that was the novel and presumably sympathetic conclusion toward which author Myron C. Fagin drove his characters.

Toward the end of the evening an outraged American was to be seen waving a gun at a decidedly disloyal newspaper columnist. "There is only one sure law for you," he screamed as he plugged the enemy in a penthouse apartment, "the law of the dead dog. What I do here tonight some brave Frenchman will do in France, some Swede will do in Sweden," and so on. As the curtain fell, a hearty Homicide Inspector was clapping the high-minded gunman on the shoulder and announcing something to the effect that "This man will be tried for the crime of saving America!"

Quite apart from the curious ethics which were hereby urged upon us all, *A Red Rainbow* was a fascinating exercise in juvenilia on several counts. To begin with, the play—and the use of the word "play" in this connection amounts to the most shameless flattery—was extremely complicated.

Its first act was a sort of mystery melodrama (who killed columnist J. Kerrigan Kane?) in which all of the suspects twitched nervously and in which the police force tossed about lingo on the order of "Tell the chief that Roxy dame is ready to squeal." It had a certain amount of humor, too. When that Roxy dame was finally interrogated as to her whereabouts at the time of the shooting, she snapped right back, sassy as all get-out, "Okay, wise guy, I'll tell you what I was doin'. Knittin' a mitten for my kitten." On opening night I noted down much better samples of dialogue, but I hastily destroyed them. My comments appear in a morning paper, and they would never have done for breakfast.

The second act took us back—it took me back, anyway—to the actual murder. This is where the politics came in. Quite a few Washington higher-ups were on hand for a cocktail party given by this despicable columnist, and they were one and all furiously in the know. Among the things they professed to know were: the "true" story behind Pearl Harbor; the fact that Alger Hiss was the "architect of the United Nations"; the fact that top scientists on the Atomic Energy Commission were almost exclusively occupied with passing all available information to Russia. There was the further suggestion that the ultimate Communist coup here would come through the labor unions, and the alarmingly explicit announcement—the actors spoke very rapidly at this point, but I think I got it right—that Harry Hopkins had personally turned the atom bomb over to Russia.

In the third act it developed that our columnist friend—syndicated, of course—not only had a sufficient number of Senators in his employ to stifle an antisubversive bill, but that he was the man who, at the time of the Hitler-Stalin pact, placed key Communists at the top of each of our government agencies. In fact, I still haven't given you the picture. He was also the man who pulled the switches for the Black Tom explosion during World War I. What I want to know is, where was he when McKinley was shot?

It is customary in the face of such debacles to say that the actors were valiant. My own impression is that they were out of their heads.

Of course, even our finest players make mistakes. An evening I shall never forget broke upon us when the good folk at City Center gave Judith Anderson an elaborate opportunity to make the same mistake twice. Miss Anderson, having had no success at all with the Clemence Dane–Richard Addinsell fantasy *Come of Age* some eighteen years earlier, exhumed it ardently at the municipal playhouse one wintry night—and provided us all with an object lesson.

It is a theatrical truth that there never is a failure so witless, so pretentious, so exasperatingly dull that it does not attract a handful of passionate admirers who cheer at its opening, weep at its closing, and stoutly maintain that "there is an audience for this play." The scenery has no sooner gone to the warehouse than this eager little band institutes a whispering campaign to the effect that a beautiful thing has been killed, and a turkey is on its way to being canonized. No doubt this is all normal enough, and provides some innocent consolation for the author.

What is not normal is for anyone to take this minority seriously enough to put the play back on the stage. But that is what City Center did—and not stingily, either. Valentina draped Miss Anderson in some dazzling gowns, Noel Taylor dressed the balance of the company in beautifully muted contrasts, Raymond Sovey whipped up a striking ivory-and-gold formal setting, and Guthrie McClintic was called in to stage the piece with thoroughly professional elegance.

But we were still confronted with that play, and a little horror it was. The authors first introduced us to the seventeen-year-old poet, Thomas Chatterton, at the moment of his suicide in 1770. As we watched, numbly, the lad was summoned from his couch by the offstage voice of Death and told that he had never come of age. He never would come of age, it seemed, until he had "shared his secret" with a woman—at seventeen he had apparently had little opportunity to do this—and he was now transported to the present time and the fashionable apartment of a high-living, hard-drinking woman of the world. By the time he had felt her jealousy, her rage, and her rather frosty compassion, he had presumably grown up a bit and was ready to die, which he did.

Anyone who had heard any of the interim mooning about the work was prepared for the fact that it was written in rhymed couplets. But nothing could really prepare a man for the paralyzing effect of an entire evening spent listening to choppy, cryptic, and endlessly repetitious forays like:

> *That's the worst of it,*
> *The hunger and thirst of it.*

As if the belligerent beat of the rhymes was not bad enough, we were sometimes tantalized with off-rhymes:

> *All this fuss*
> *About a pinch of dust.*

The authors did explain that they had written the play in doggerel as being the most suitable verse form for our time. Our time may not be a happy one, but I am still not convinced that it really deserves an entire play written on the artistic level of the Burma-Shave ads.

And I am absolutely certain it deserves something better than the author of a curious enterprise called Sing Till Tomorrow bestowed upon it. In production, Sing Till Tomorrow had two strikes against it. One was the fact that you couldn't hear half of it. The other was the half you could hear.

Since the producer of this exceptionally chewy caramel assembled a group of players who were so deeply immersed in their work that much of the dialogue came blurting to the surface like air bubbles, it will never be possible to know all that was in the author's heart. I should like to record for posterity, however, the fact that at one point in the evening an actor sank into a chair, stared at his opponent, and clearly said, "You have been a sornu-solopia." I have it here in my notes.

As for the words which, in a quaint and tantalizing way, resembled the language of our fathers, all I can do is scrape off a few samples.

The principal character was a small-town druggist who called everybody "son," a practice which became confusing only when he was addressing his wife. This unhappy druggist was looking for a new kind of life for himself ("Pharmaceuticals are your long suit," everybody kept telling him, but he wouldn't listen), and when he was really unhappy he was perfectly capable of roaring, "I'm baring my chest for the town to see and etching 'anonymous' across it in acid!"

His son wasn't happy, either. "You're rocking my wagon!" he was heard to shout at his father. The father, a quick one to take up an image, bounced right back with "Your wagon is overloaded with ideological manure!"

Everyone in the Jean Lowenthal piece was given to imagery. "We're on a fire escape, me going down behind you," moaned the lad. "You incline to me like a hound," cried the pharmacist. "Right now I'm a little tan, but I still know who I am," muttered somebody or other.

There was, in addition, a girl whose chief problem in life was that she had been required to memorize pastoral poetry at a tender age. ("It was absolute drudgery," she said.)

Drudgery or no, the rhythms had stuck to her. "I have no hesitancy about my declarations," she announced sweetly as she entered the picture. When she was offered a sort of trial home at the drugstore, she murmured, "I take a dim view of your blandishments." Later, when it turned out that she rather liked blandishments after all but could not get the boy of her dreams to co-operate, she took to her heels with a real crusher: "I'll go out under my own propulsion!"

Sing Till Tomorrow was, as you may have gathered, so bad that it utterly defeated a reviewer's sporting instinct to compare it with similar miseries out of the past. All one could do was remember the date—December 28, 1953—and start all over again.

The trouble with starting over again is that you run right into something like *Buttrio Square*. *Buttrio Square* was a musical to which all sorts of things had happened. Half of its financing had disappeared during rehearsal. Directors had been switched in midstream. It had had to postpone. The acting company had been forced to dig into its own pockets in order to get the curtain up. Then the worst happened: the curtain went up.

Knowing all these things, no one could have gone into the playhouse without crossing his fingers and wishing everyone well. During the overture you hoped it would be good. During the first number you hoped it would be good. After that you just hoped it would be over.

For *Buttrio Square* was, after all the heroism that had gone into it, a wistful little orphan of a musical comedy with no music, no comedy, and not even very much scenery. What lodged it in the mind forever after, though, was the curious consistency of its musical numbers.

The show opened on one of those picturesque Italian streets with an exuberant band of peasant boys and girls singing something to the effect that this was census day (in Buttrio Square). We were quickly informed that this little occupied village—the supposed time was 1948—was eager to turn itself into a town but was just one citizen shy of the number needed to qualify.

Soon everyone settled down in the open air—the boys' heads on the girls' laps—to sing that Every Day Is a Holiday (in Buttrio Square). Shortly thereafter we discovered that a local lass named Marisa was secretly married, against Army regulations, to a Captain Steve Dickson, and she mooned right off into a ballad called "I'll Tell the World."

This bit of lyrical inspiration, a small masterpiece of its kind, emphasized that she wanted the gentle breeze to know she was in love and that she'd very much like to tell all the birds about the bliss of a kiss. Next, Steve himself turned up to give Italy the nod in a rousing compliment called "No Place Like This Country (in the spring)." His GI underlings, however, replied with an equally rousing complaint called "Take It Away (and Give Us the U.S.A.)."

It was time for comedy now, an element which was supplied, I regret to say, by a young lady in oversize fatigues who notified us that she had really meant to enter the WAC. Her name, however, had happened to be Terry and she was therefore shipped off to Fort Dix, enlisted as a male, and denied a change of status thereafter. Her song—and of course she sang—was called "Get Me Out" and devoted itself to detailing how her drillmaster used to tell her to "stick out her chest" and so on.

In time, Marisa became pregnant, the impending baby—which, incidentally, would swell the local population to the desired figure —was about to be palmed off on the ancient but robust Mayor of Buttrio Square, and the Mayor, played by a fat man with every jowl rustling, gave vent to a sentimental hymn known as "I'm Gonna Be a Pop." Later on, the lovers quarreled and Steve complained, musically, that "One Is a Lonely Number (unless you can add or multiply)." What he was trying to say, he explained, was that "one plus one is two."

The second act had some further observations to make on the wretchedness of lovers ("I keep telling myself it's foolish, this parody of romance, did it ever have a chance?") and the dust and ashes love is likely to turn to ("There's nothing left but only my thoughts in reverie"). I guess the best that could ever be said for the score is that it wasn't derivative. At least I never heard anything like it before.

Things were pretty deadly (in Buttrio Square).

Things weren't so much deadly as fascinating the night that Jay Robinson opened in his own starring production of *Buy Me Blue Ribbons*. Mr. Robinson was then a young man of twenty-one who had, the season before, been dispossessed of the leading role in a play which he had himself financed. But there had been no bitterness in Mr. Robinson. Instead he had commissioned playwright Sumner

Locke Elliott to write him a comedy about a young man who was similarly thrown out of his own production, and he was now prepared to offer the new vehicle, for his mortification and for ours, on a Broadway stage.

Mr. Robinson was utterly unembarrassed by this display of dramatic incest. He cheerfully put himself on the block, allowed himself to be ridiculed for his own pretensions, even permitted a considerable amount of gagging at his virility. He was, in short, determined to seem knowing about his incapacities at the same time that he was determined to feature those incapacities in a major playhouse. Even at this late date, the mind reels.

The play which Mr. Elliott had supplied wasn't too bad as a stock enterprise. It moved with relatively little awkwardness, it handled its stereotyped show-business characters with an ease born of familiarity, it had a few bright lines. But whatever small praise might have been eked out for the play was shot to pieces the minute Mr. Robinson entered it. The young Mr. Robinson—young in years, young in wisdom, young as young could ever be—had picked up somewhere what used to be called a "stage" accent, a habit of pulling his mouth tightly closed to indicate that he had just got off a good one, and a nice, tricky way of banging on doors as he opened them. He entered with a rush and at once draped himself across a balcony, just as though he were in a play. He struck poses. And even when this kind of activity was meant to be satiric—the character Mr. Robinson played was supposed to attitudinize in just this way—you knew that you were really dealing with the lad himself and that the satire was essentially fake.

It is never any fun to poke fun at so ambitious and industrious a youngster. Then as now, a critic can only bite his tongue and call himself cruel. But what is to be done when a player asks for it— on the double? Is he to be let off? With the theater already in such serious straits? When I tell you that the character concluded by surrendering his dreams of overnight stardom and deciding to learn his trade from the bottom up—a conclusion which, if read in rehearsal, could only have resulted in Mr. Robinson's abandoning *this* role as well—the compounded, spine-chilling confusion of the evening must surely be evident.

Mr. Robinson was game, all right. But what is gameness in a man who is suffering from delusions of adequacy?

Oh, I have my memories, I do indeed. There is a hard and fast rule among first-night reviewers that, as they gather on the sidewalk during intermissions, they will speak of their wives, their children, their dinners, their political preferences—of anything, in short, but the play at hand. I have almost never heard this rule infringed— never, as a matter of fact, unless the enterprise was so obviously moribund that half the audience had already taken to the streets, the press agent was obviously trying to conceal himself behind a pillar, the trucking company was waiting impatiently at the stage door to get at the scenery, and the pretense of not noticing would have amounted to being present at the drowning of Pharaoh's army in the Red Sea and politely ignoring the mishap.

One of the few occasions when a reviewer committed himself before press time turned up at the premiere of a gem known as *Hook 'n' Ladder*, a farce in which half the adult males of the company seemed to be running around in Boy Scout uniforms, in which the principal comedienne made a bed by crawling all over it, and in which a hearty drunk kept pressing on his friends a concoction of his own called Old Factory Whistle ("one blast and you're through for the day"). At the second intermission a reviewer whose work I have always admired emerged from the gloom, let his face light up in an inexplicably cheery smile, and murmured, "Well, it's not uneven."

And it wasn't. It had begun with a wow of a laugh-getter in which a gentleman with a pack of ice on his head winced painfully at the slightly squeaky shoes of a low-comedy servant named Ulysses. And it ended, or should have, with a phone call for a fellow who was at the moment unconscious. The character taking the call explained, "He's in but he's out."

It was, in short, the sort of play that gives failures a bad name.

ᴖ 3 ᴗ

BUT EVEN REVIEWERS have their three-, four-, and five-drink evenings—if you don't mind my pursuing this image to its grave.

I'd no sooner got home from a City Center revival of *Carmen Jones*, for instance, than I found myself idly suggesting that I really ought to take our ten-year-old son around to see it while it was still on view. After all, we owed him a little something—musical education and all that.

My wife, who has a bad habit of interpreting everything I say on three levels just as though I were a symbolic play, glanced at me—on three levels—and remarked that an evening concerned almost exclusively with sensual passion and culminating in a love-murder might not wholly absorb the attention of a young man currently involved in the exploits of Rogers' Rangers. Her clear impression was that I was either out of my head or—well, now that I think it over, I guess there wasn't any *other* implication.

As so often happens around our house, I was now forced to examine my motives, knowing them to be devious to begin with. Obviously, I wasn't trying to advance the musical and theatrical education of my son at all. I was simply trying to sneak back to *Carmen Jones* for my own shoddy pleasure and using that poor kid as an excuse. A reviewer needs an excuse to go rushing back to an entertainment he's just seen, of course: anything else would make him seem a vulgar enthusiast, a parvenu, a fellow who couldn't quite manage the detachment, the faint and faintly elegant trace of cynicism, the intellectual austerity required by his craft. One must respect one's line of work.

Clearly, I would have to scratch around among my acquaintances for a sorry soul who had never seen *Carmen Jones* if I was to justify that return trip. (My wife couldn't go back because she begins to sob publicly early in the first act and keeps it up right through Joe's final throbbing "Carmen, my Carmen" over the dead girl's body, and it's hard on her.)

And I was forced to ask myself: what is this hold *Carmen Jones* has over me? By all—or at least some—of the rules, Oscar Hammerstein's recasting of the standard opera into American Negro terms against a wartime background ought to be little more than a stunt. When you stop to remind yourself that Escamillo has been translated into "Husky Miller" and that Don José (Joe) really does sing "You look just like my maw" to his wistful little Cindy Lou, visions of a profound cultural mishap are bound to rise before you.

But they never rise in the theater. If *Carmen Jones* is a stunt, it is the most moving, most genuinely affecting stunt yet perpetrated on a happy public. As Oscar Hammerstein sets a male chorus of MPs to singing "That Honey Girl of Mine" outside a parachute factory, as he provides Carmen with a vocabulary as insinuating as her other charms, as he traces the infatuation of Joe through the tormented declaration of "Dis Flower" to the blind and helpless fury of his threatened vengeance late in the second act, all sense of parallelism, of reconstruction, vanishes. The pleasure of the evening is never the pleasure of making comparisons between the old work and the new; this isn't a game, a swapping of personalities, a card-house built of conceits.

The pleasure is precisely that of a new work, of an exciting story told because the author couldn't resist telling it, and of an exceedingly vivid group of characters who demand that their independence be respected and their emotional needs heard. To watch Muriel Smith, who has played the title role in every production I've seen, entrance her young lover even while she is being hauled off to jail, to hear her sassy voice snap off insulting lines at a magpie clip, to be drawn casually but completely into the irresistible rhythms of "Dat's Love" is to forget not only the familiar libretto but the very fact that the *femme fatale* is in herself a conventional figure, a collection of stock gestures; the flashing image that Miss Smith creates is a particular image, a dazzling discovery, something we've never quite seen before. Mr. Hammerstein has found for this lady—and for all the Joes and Cindy Lous who have come and gone—a new environment that is alive; for the tempestuous people who inhabit it he has found a voice.

I figure I'm going to keep on hearing it until the ten-year-old is old enough to hear it with me, after which he can start a parade of his own.

Dat's love, I guess.

Reviewers can be bowled over. I know that my instinct, as I ground some dirty copy paper into a typewriter the night *My Fair Lady* opened, was to suggest to the readers of the *New York Herald Tribune* that they not bother finishing the piece. Better to use their valuable time sitting right down and writing for tickets. First things first.

What was so enchanting about that fabled first night was watching a new musical grow, like Eliza Doolittle, before your eyes. Eliza, you'll remember, starts out as a tatterdemalion flower girl, hawking her wares on the grubby streets of London. *My Fair Lady* didn't start out like a bona-fide princess, either.

The curtain went up on a blithe little October-night idyll, with Eliza being given a friendly ride in a garbage can while a number of her friends, with brooms over their shoulders, skipped out a few Hanya Holm steps. Pleasant enough. Eliza was picked up by her phonetics professor, Henry Higgins, for a quick schooling in the language, and the sly quips Shaw wrote for his *Pygmalion* pair began to ripple along as before. Still pleasant, if fairly familiar. Old Alfred Doolittle, Eliza's red-nosed dad, wove his way onstage to do "With a Little Bit of Luck" with his patchwork cronies. Most engaging. It was already a good show, if not a great one.

Then two electrifying things happened. Rex Harrison, as the dedicated Higgins, bounced up off a chair to hunch his shoulders, elevate his eyebrows, wag his finger mightily, and passionately spell

out a song called—with great inaccuracy—"I'm an Ordinary Man."
Mr. Harrison's slouch was a rhythmic slouch. His voice was a show-
man's voice—twangy, biting, confident beyond questioning. His
leaps over the fashionable furniture were the leaps of a true enthusiast. But most of all Mr. Harrison was still an actor, believing
every cranky, snappish, exhilarating syllable of the Alan Jay Lerner
lyric he was rattling off, and a fourteen-carat character simply
crashed its way onto the stage.

It was five minutes later, and Eliza was furious with the man who
had called her "a bilious pigeon" while lashing her into a lady.
Alone on the stage, Julie Andrews' enormous eyes flashed, her jaw
turned to cement, and the glorious venom in her heart ripped
across the footlights in a howl labeled "Just You Wait." Miss Andrews had caught you, too, now—she was funny, she was pathetic,
she was savagely true. Eliza wasn't just a doll; she was a demon
with a soul you could understand.

And now that these two utterly credible and magnificently attractive people had asserted themselves—in each case through one
of Frederick Loewe's exuberant songs—they were ready for the
kill. It came about halfway through the first act. Miss Andrews had
slowly—and perfectly—enunciated a series of vowel sounds. You
listened, astonished—astonished because you believed in her so
completely that you didn't really suppose she was going to make it.
Suddenly her delight became yours. And when Mr. Harrison, together with an equally astonished Robert Coote, bounced jubilantly
to the center of the stage and began to kick out a tango rhythm
to the sounds she had just made ("The Rain in Spain Stays Mainly
in the Plain") there was no controlling the joy in the theater. Indeed, very little of the number was heard that night; the audience
cut loose right along with the characters.

After that you couldn't have stopped *My Fair Lady* if you'd
invited the authors of *Buttrio Square*, *Hit the Trail*, and *Carnival in
Flanders* to work over the second act. Oliver Smith's double turn-
tables spun round and round to show off ever more dazzling pa-
vilions, ballrooms, and gaslit living rooms. Cecil Beaton's black,

white and gray costumes for the Ascot races—not to mention the gray-and-orchid he had whipped up for Cathleen Nesbitt—took what breath was left from an already helpless audience. Moss Hart's staging sped by beautifully, Hanya Holm's second-act frenzy at dawn in Covent Garden exploded maniacally, Stanley Holloway and John Michael King hurled song after song from the Loewe-Lerner treasure chest into the auditorium. Pace, taste, and a triumphant good humor rolled on into the night.

The mood at the American premiere of Jean Anouilh's *The Waltz of the Toreadors* was somewhat different.

I think it was F. Scott Fitzgerald who once said that he had come to the time of life when it was always three o'clock in the morning. *The Waltz of the Toreadors* turned out to be the kind of *play* where it was always three o'clock in the morning.

And the odd thing about it was that this time of fatigue and despair and dread of another dawn became, inexplicably, an endlessly fascinating and uproariously funny time.

This was partly due to the fact that General Ralph Richardson, with his mustachios bristling and his voice booming roundhouse commands, was valiantly leading the cavalry charge against the fate that bedevils all romantic men. Mr. Richardson, looking like a cross between a lascivious goat and an exasperated Uncle Wiggily, was cast as an elderly satyr with the soul of a small boy. This boy still had dreams, rather ambitious sex dreams, as it happened. And he had hope, hope that one of these dreadful dawns everything in the world—beginning with women and ending with all felicity—was going to light up warmly, take him in its arms, and make him feel comfortable, satisfied, and thoroughly at home.

Jean Anouilh is not, of course, the dramatist to give him his dreams. M. Anouilh has seen the worm in the apple, the light that fails in the eternal distance. He knows that no matter how fine a breast-stroke a man manages as he swims steadily toward the buoy in the middle of the ocean, he's not going to make it. The daydream, the childish promise of absurd joy, isn't true. A fellow's going to twitch, blink, damn his wife and ugly daughters, and throw up his hands in horror before it's over.

Richardson was just the man to seize every ornery nuance of this hopeless sex-duel in his sheepdog jaws and shake it for the fun, the fury and the pathetic howl of outrage that was in it. It didn't much matter whether he was licking an envelope with the enthusiasm of a cat licking her young, telling boastful and disreputable stories about desirable little girls of twelve, roaring at the "misbegotten frumps" who were his children, or seething at his "great goop" of a soul—the grotesque balance of savagely ironic humor and wistful defeat was everlastingly, superbly sustained. This was the grotesque goat-man of Aristophanes, tempered with a bit of Shaw and a bit of Dagwood Bumstead, and it was—as a performance—magnificent.

But there was more to this curious, caustic, yet immensely entertaining evening than a single performance. Director Harold Clurman had found a way of conveying both the pessimism and the macabre merriment of Anouilh to American audiences. It may not have been the only way, and it may not have been the "right" way; but it worked. He had blown up the nagging fools and preposterous romantics of the piece into attractive Hogarthian monsters, equipped them with voices that seemed to be calling trains, and set them to marching in circus-parade blare about the sword-draped Ben Edwards setting.

Everyone was in on the secret. Mildred Natwick, as a wife who has faked invalidism to keep her husband in her grip, rose in her bed, clutched a sheet about her, hurled scathing epithets at the disappointed "centaur" who had married her—and brought down the house with each seething onslaught. Meriel Forbes sniffed daintily at a pearl-handled revolver that might yet mean suicide—and the sniff was enchanting. John Abbott discussed the marvelous linguistic progress that professional medicine has made with sly urbanity. And John Stewart bemoaned a young man's loneliness with a rigid 1910 decorum that perfectly suited the lithographic lines of the inventive staging.

The Waltz of the Toreadors is a mocking play that demands a taste for sweetened hemlock. It is sometimes blunt, sometimes bitter, sometimes cynical, and nearly always outrageous in its content and its method. But the rapier-thrust strikes oddly true: out of the calculated comic savagery comes an image of battling men and women that is, in its wild and willful proportions, blisteringly accurate.

The temper of Anouilh is not an easy thing to sell to American audiences; indeed *The Waltz of the Toreadors* is the first of his half-rueful, half-rollicking studies to succeed on Broadway. An initial resistance to the unknown must be overcome. There is also, on occasion, an initial resistance to the known.

When *The Diary of Anne Frank* was first published in book form, it was widely admired and, I am given to understand, widely read. Yet I kept running into people who knew its contents "from the reviews," who professed sincere delight that so touching a document should have been salvaged from the horrors of Belsen, and who had, somehow or other, just missed picking up the book at the lending library.

Once Kermit Bloomgarden's miraculously warm production of the Frances Goodrich–Albert Hackett play based on the diary had opened in New York, admiration was again at fever pitch. And right in the middle of all the admiration was another little pocket of unconscious reluctance: I gathered from a few of my friends, not long after the exciting first night, that they were enormously cheered to hear of its success and that they did mean to get around to seeing it—sooner or later.

This vaguely suspended enthusiasm was easy enough to understand. *The Diary of Anne Frank* was the sort of material that conjured up a prior image. Everyone was in favor of a sensitive evocation of what Jewish families went through under Hitler—we all deserved to be reminded—and everyone was sure he knew what the evocation would be like. It would be grim, hopeless, heartbreaking:

a record of extraordinary nobility in the face of persecution, and a searing experience to sit through. One imagined a dark play peopled by the wistful shadows of the condemned.

The Diary of Anne Frank was a radiant play shot through with the exuberant humor, the confident vitality, and even the day-to-day cantankerousness of people who were going to live forever.

There wasn't a consciously noble gesture in it. Joseph Schildkraut, as Anne's father and the man responsible for the safety of the eight souls hiding out in an Amsterdam garret, did indeed find himself laying down stern regulations about the use of water and the sharing of food. It was also his sharp command that shocked the household into a paralyzed hush whenever the sound of danger sifted up from below.

But neither the authors nor Mr. Schildkraut had seen this man as excessively heroic. He was a reasonably good businessman thrown into a situation that needed to be managed intelligently; he was a devoted and generous family man who was much too practical to waste time and emotional energy choking up over the pathos of his lot; he was at his most characteristic when he was making a quick, sensible peace between a jumpy couple who could not help scratching at each other or when he was philosophically admitting to his eager younger daughter that she had now caught up with him in algebra. Self-pity found no foothold in this tense, miniature world.

Nor did the Hacketts pretend for a moment that eight refugees could share a room for nearly two years and remain pitiable plaster saints. The snap of nerves and the crackle of personalities were all about us. The parents of the boy Anne Frank was to learn to love clawed at each other and at their last few possessions—a fur coat, a handful of cigarettes—with a foolish and furious avidity that was as human as it was absurd. A touchy dentist with an allergy to fur-bearing animals and to people as well eventually maneuvered himself into a position where every door in a tiny room was slapped shut in his face.

Gusti Huber, as Anne's patient mother, finally turned on one of the community who had been caught stealing food with a wrath that all but blew the walls apart. And we saw that temperaments may be sharpened under stress but that they do not really change. Whatever the circumstances, the human heart swells in anger, flinches in resentment, fights for its right to be heard.

And it lifts into happiness, too. Soaring through the center of the play with the careless gaiety of a bird that simply cannot be caged was Anne Frank herself, a figure of blithe, bumptious, breathless abandon in the hands of young Susan Strasberg. Not a trace of sentimentality weakened the portrait.

In the earlier scenes, when Anne Frank is fourteen, Miss Strasberg bashed at her roommates with the bold, impudent, headstrong and coltlike confidence of a spirit that was going to conquer the world. The conquest was going to come through mockery—Miss Strasberg was delectable beyond belief as she solemnly strutted around the room after a pompous and fuming neighbor—and through sheer animal energy. As the actress tripped up the boy she "wished were a girl," turned up in a pair of oversize trousers for a sassy impersonation, or pounded her hands against her forehead in adolescent outrage, she was any child testing the universe to see how much it would give. Anne was not going to her death; she was going to leave a dent on life, and let death take whatever was left.

In the second half of the play Miss Strasberg carefully carved out the graceful, sober, quietly determined lines of this girl's too early maturity. She put up her hair—to go calling on a boy who lives just across the room—with an abstracted wisdom. When she had received her first kiss, she moved gently but knowingly through the crowded upstairs room sharing her simple happiness with everyone in it.

When she left the play—the Gestapo was waiting below—she smiled at her family, and you believed that she could smile. The time they had had together was a nice one.

The play that Garson Kanin so lovingly staged was more than a nice one. It was also something more than an "impressive" one. It left a shimmering image behind it because, in a way, it gave no thought at all to tomorrows, cared not a whit for the obvious tears to be wrung from the plight of its characters. It only wanted to tell you what Anne's todays were like—and, as it happened, they were wonderful.

The theater is infinitely flexible, forever putting one or another foot forward to score an unexpected victory. The sudden emergence of Shaw's supposedly unplayable "Don Juan in Hell" scene from *Man and Superman*, with Charles Boyer, Charles Laughton, Cedric Hardwicke, and Agnes Moorehead barnstorming the country in the principal roles, constituted a clear victory for the spoken word, spoken well.

Without benefit of scenery or dramatic costume, the four performers placed themselves at microphones and proceeded to read the daylights out of a long, discursive, but—as it turned out—magnificently actable treatise. The contemporary theater generally smothers us all in an abundance of scenery and swathes of costuming, hoping that the doodads will conceal a stupefying dramatic vacancy. The Drama Quartette, as these explorers called themselves, turned the tables, threw out everything that was expensive and unnecessary, and filled the vacuum with fire, intelligence, and emotional power.

Don Juan in Hell is not a play, or even a part of a play. It is a debate, and that is how the foursome presented it.

But they knew it wasn't a stodgy or formal or rhetorical debate. They came at it with passion, with slyness, with tremendous enjoyment. Nor did they altogether abandon mime. They were on their feet impatiently fiddling with eyeglasses to make a point, giving themselves over to a remarkably uninhibited use of theatrical gesture. And, although they were separated by stools and microphones, they achieved a greater feeling of playing together than do most acting companies bound together by walls, ceilings, and the eternal exchanging of cigarettes.

The first act was Mr. Laughton's, the second Mr. Boyer's. Laughton opened the evening with a modest and ingratiating setting of the stage. But the shyness, the coy mannerisms, did not fool anyone: Mr. Laughton is a killer. He was out for blood, and within a very few minutes he was drawing it. He wagged his head, chucked his chin into his collar, went in for the twinkle and the double-twinkle, and then—just as you were fearing that some damage might be done by way of cuteness—he let rip with Shaw's blasting of man as a creature essentially in love with death in a manner that tore him to tatters, but not the sense of the speech. This might be ham, but it was delicious.

Boyer's work in the first act was relatively disappointing. Forced to cope not only with an accent but with the fact that the lighter and more impudent of Shaw's lines are decidedly English in feeling, he found the rhythm of the language working against him. But in the later portions of the piece, where Shaw is at his most serious and persuasive, the opportunities for straightforward and dynamic reading swiftly became greater, and Boyer rose to a level of emotional performance that hasn't been matched on the New York stage in decades. There was a moment when he seized his microphone and thrust it forward in a spasm of urgency that was at least twice as exciting as the top thrill in an ordinary melodrama. And when he came to Shaw's climactic speech describing the inhabitants of Hell—a listing of categories, a procession of balanced phrases which in the hands of a casual performer might well have proved intolerable—Mr. Boyer drained it of every nuance not by picking at it quietly but by hammering out its contrasts at the pitch of his powers. He did not dissect the speech; he waved it like a flag over the auditorium. Mr. Boyer is no romantic leading man, whatever the movies have done to him; he is a serious actor of extraordinary ability.

Mr. Boyer was a surprise. In *Peter Pan*, Mary Martin wasn't. I always knew she could fly.

She'd always bounced along as though the earth were made of inner-spring mattresses, and that piping, rollicking voice of hers could have carried anyone aloft, wires or no wires, any old time.

Be that as it may, from the moment that Miss Martin zoomed in out of the night through gigantic nursery windows—barely bothering to stop at the footlights—until the moment when she bested the scurrilous Captain Hook in a sword fight by scooping right over his scoundrelly head, Miss Martin and her musical-comedy version of the Barrie fantasy were sky-high with joy.

The flying, lest we get past it, was nothing short of miraculous. For the first time in my own theatergoing experience, it had been designed rather than limited to a couple of quick exits—in effect, it had been choreographed by director Jerome Robbins. Result: it wasn't so much a nervous stunt as a rapturous lyrical experience, and you couldn't help but be popeyed with happy disbelief at the first-act curtain: Peter brushing away the heavens at hurricane force while Wendy and family bobbled gently behind him, with moon and stars slipping swiftly away beneath their dangling feet. It was the way *Peter Pan* should always have been managed, and never had been.

And the flying, after all, was only the half of it. Miss Martin was charming as she abstractedly rocked a rocking-horse in the Darling nursery, buoyant as she skipped about a forest with a paint can full of green paint, rowdy and raucous as she led the stubborn Lost Boys in a rebellious chant called "I Won't Grow Up." With her shock of cropped blond hair, a dagger at her belt, and her man-in-the-moon smile cracking her face in half, she was domestic nectar, no chaser required.

It was clear at the time that the pieced-together score wasn't everything that Barrie's indestructible moonshine deserved: there were tinny and conventional strains seeping up from the orchestra, there was a truly massive amount of mere utility music, and you did sometimes suspect that the producers were robbing Peter to pay Pan.

But there was always that brightly crayoned, picture-book wonderland to go back to. In fact, one of the things I liked best about this particular *Peter Pan* was the fact that everyone—and above all the special-effects man—took his wonder-working seriously. Most productions have cheated a bit, passing over the nonsensical magic hastily and concealing whatever couldn't quite be managed. Not this time. Tinker Bell not only took refuge in a jug, she rolled it around on the mantelpiece. Peter's recaptured shadow danced with him, a giant on the wall. Trees unfolded in full view, arrows sped accurately through the bright-green forest, a door that had just been painted on a house opened immediately, and Cyril Ritchard's sublime Captain Hook boasted a good arm that could stretch itself, snakily, for miles.

Peter Pan opened the theater's childlike bag of tricks and tossed them at our heads in a high, happy, bubbling good humor.

∿ SEVEN ∿

Playwrights

∿ 1 ∿

You could have knocked me over with a coffee ring when I picked up the papers one lazy Sunday to discover that, on the occasion of Bernard Shaw's centenary, a band of British critics had decided to chop the bearded old spruce down to kindling-size.

Not that this sort of re-evaluation isn't perfectly proper. A playwright can set quite a bonfire in his own time; the serious critic's business is to note the size of the blaze in varying perspectives and to try to estimate how much light it is going to give over constantly increasing distances. Shaw may, in the future, flare or fade; a man can't be blamed for making a responsible guess about which it's to be. What stunned me was the particular calendar of charges.

Here they were: Bernard Shaw never drew a fully dimensional

character; Bernard Shaw was not a poet; Bernard Shaw was not really a realist; Bernard Shaw's essential concern was with thought, but his thought was inconsistent and sometimes incoherent.

Do those complaints sound vaguely familiar? They do to me. As I read on, I had the dizzying sensation that time had up-ended, that I was back in college, and that Shaw was going through his middle-American—or let's-make-this-man-plausible—period all over again.

We were an earnest lot in those days. Shaw was a serious social philosopher, and we put on horn-rimmed glasses when we read him. He was also a dramatist like other dramatists—perhaps rather like a dramatist named Ibsen, only with more humor—and when we produced him we gave him the old Stanislavski.

Voices were lowered reasonably; inflections were casual, as comfortably commonplace as we could make them; long speeches were read intensely, with wise little smiles thrown in now and then but with a conscious halo slowly forming behind our reverent heads.

Of course, there were problems. In this somewhat religious universe, Shaw's characters *didn't* seem to have much body to them. To help Shaw out, we added all sorts of tiny humanizing details, observant bits of business designed to flesh out the figures and make them respectably ordinary. And there was an intellectual problem: *Saint Joan* would have been such a nice, clear play if Shaw hadn't perversely made an interesting case for the Inquisitor; *Major Barbara* might have been an extraordinarily useful tract if Shaw hadn't insisted on seeing some sort of virtue in munitions-making. We did what we could: stressed the thoughts we believed in, threw away the difficult ones, trimmed the wagging beard to a gentlemanly shape.

In the end, it was no go. The more we strained for "honesty," the thinner our playwright seemed. The more we strained for a logical "line," the less convincing our evening turned out to be. Shaw had often announced himself a social realist and a major prophet; we had treated him as though he were these things, and what did we have? An exasperatingly ill-formed charade in which the message was curiously garbled and even the fun was nervous. The generation I went to school with finally threw up its hands: it had worked very hard to rescue Shaw from his defects, it had failed, and it could only conclude that the impractical Irishman was just not a very good playwright. Maybe *Candida* was okay, but *Man and Superman* was unthinkable.

I can only speak for myself, but my own dazzled awakening came one spring night when I walked into a nonprofessional production of *Heartbreak House* directed by a man who had discussed playing-style with Shaw. Odd things were happening. The characters had no flesh at all: only minds. They did nothing you or I would ever do in a living room, not even in a living room that looked like a ship: they wheeled about, advanced gloriously to the curtain line, and bounced every happy shade of meaning off the back wall of the playhouse. And they were not worried or sober or poetic or earnest, even though the supposed world behind them was due to be blown up at any moment: they were exhilarated, deliriously happy to be able to *talk* about death, destruction, or whatever.

Nor were they really talking toward a conclusion, forging out a philosophy of salvation: they were thinking, all right, but they were thinking for the sheer joy of thinking, thinking about everything at once and about anything at all, taking immense pleasure in exhausting one line of thought because they would then be able to think something *else*. I need hardly add that they were having fun; and so was I.

With a blissfully foolish expression on my face, I suddenly realized that every familiar criticism made of Shaw was absolutely just—and that not a single such criticism mattered a hoot. Whatever his extracurricular pronouncements, Shaw had never been an Ibsen realist, a Chekhov naturalist, or a manufacturer of salable ideas. His vision was stylized, his language a splendid artifice, his characterization a process of painting and then cutting loose a hundred balloons.

But much more importantly, he had turned an enormous somersault, abandoning the work of the mind for the play of the mind—

the free play, the unfettered bounding around corners, the stretching and tussling and spectacular weight-lifting that any young man
goes in for the moment he discovers he has muscles he can flex.
(When Shaw wanted his mind to work for him, he wrote a Preface
or a pamphlet; he wasn't able to subdue it when there was a wonderful arena for it to romp around in.)

In the 1950s Broadway has succeeded in recapturing what seems
to have been Shaw's intended style: productions by Cyril Ritchard,
Charles Laughton, and Maurice Evans have opened the high-comic
doors again with grace, gusto, and undisguised glee. Shaw is not yet
wholly safe: Laurence Olivier's Caesar was a studied "character"
job; when some inexplicably green actors offered *The Doctor's
Dilemma* at the Phoenix Theater they managed to supply it with
every gloomy and introspective gesture of twenty years before.

But it should be clear by this time that, out of whatever tempera-
mental affinity for the intellectual playground, Shaw did at last
land in a literary tradition rather different from the one we'd so
long imagined: he wound up skipping school in the company of
Congreve, Sheridan, and Oscar Wilde. Or I'd say—at the very least
—that when we try to measure Shaw against the future, we'd be
better off using the yardstick developed by these effervescent gentlemen than holding him to the specifications of a soberer clan.

2

IN THE NEW YORK PRODUCTION of *Long Day's Journey into Night*
Florence Eldridge played a shattered mother—her white hair floating mistily about the damaged prettiness of her face—who convinced herself, with the help of morphine, that others
were the true cause of all her pain. She stretched
her in the blurred light of a foggy seaside after   ble and

"They can't touch me now—I see them, but they're far away! The pain is gone."

This, I think, is what Eugene O'Neill was doing when he put to paper the searing and sorry record of the wreck of his family. He had held up his mother, his father, and his brother at the arm's length of the stage, looked at everything that was ugly and misshapen and destroyed in them, and now the pain was gone.

It *was* gone, too. Though the four-hour, endlessly savage examination of conscience on the stage of the Helen Hayes was deliberately, masochistically harrowing in the ferocity of its revelation, the agony that O'Neill felt whenever he contemplated his own beginnings was not passed on to his audience. It was in some curious and even exalting manner exorcised, washed away, leaving in its place an undefined dignity, an agreed-upon-peace, a powerful sense of completion.

Long Day's Journey into Night is not a play. It is a lacerating round-robin of recrimination, self-dramatization, lies that deceive no one, confessions that never expiate the crime. Around the whisky bottles and the tattered leather chairs and the dangling light cords that infest the decaying summer home of the Tyrones (read O'Neills), a family of ghosts sit in a perpetual game of four-handed solitaire, stir to their feet in a *danse macabre* that outlines the geography of Hell, place themselves finally on an operating table that allows for no anesthetic. When the light fails, they are still—but not saved.

How did O'Neill keep self-pity and vulgarity and cheap bravado out of this prolonged, unasked-for, improbable inferno? In part, by the grim determination that made him a major dramatist: the insistence that the roaring fire he could build by grinding his own two hands together was the fire of truth. You can disbelieve, but you cannot deny him his heat, his absolute passion.

In the production, director José Quintero saw to it that every one of his actors shared O'Neill's violent vision. Fredric March cracked the whip of the flint monarch that O'Neill remembered as his harsh majestic authority from the outset. Laughing a bit too much and a bit too hollowly, working off his nerves with a restless cigar, snapping at every insult like a guilty bulldog, he foreshadowed the whole sodden fantasia of the midnight that was to come. When he reached that last grim debacle, and stumbled to his feet in a slavering but heart-breaking tribute to his lost glory, he made it plain once more that he is the best realistic actor we possess.

Hot on his heels was Jason Robards, Jr., as the dissolute elder brother who may have led the consumptive Edmund (read Eugene) into every sort of vice in order to help square away his own failure. Mr. Robards lurched into the final scene with his hands, his mouth, and his mind wildly out of control, wrenched himself in two as he poured out every tasteless truth that was in him, and subsided at last into the boozy sleep of the damned. The passage was magnificent.

Florence Eldridge made the downward course of an incapable mother utterly intelligible. She did not have the deep, resonant notes that were needed to sustain her woman through the blinding, tragic memories of the center of the piece; she could not quite fight fury with fury. Yet there was a hidden delicacy that was often touching in the shallow gaieties and transparent pretenses of a convent girl who could not survive the world.

Bradford Dillman handled the exceedingly difficult and soul-searching soliloquies of his young would-be poet with swift, sensitive skill, and the David Hays setting was a perfect echo—curving and empty—of the universe these characters wandered.

When the season that brought the play to us was over, it was almost unnecessary for the New York Critics Circle to meet. That *Long Day's Journey into Night* was going to take the annual prize for the best American play—with an act or so to spare—was obvious; when the Circle did meet there was only one holdout among the twenty-one members voting.

To what degree was this vote a sentimental one? Was the conscience of New York determined simply to make it up to the shade of O'Neill for the long neglect of his work after his death? were we all moved more by the fact that the "play" was a terri terribly personal family record—a kind of *requiescat* and *mea culpa* rolled into one—than by its independent power as a work for the stage?

Not at all, I think. More than any other native drama of the season this posthumous thunderbolt spoke with its own rolling, crashing, domineering authority. Whatever it was, it was completely itself, a self-starting dynamo, a display of power that came down like a hammer stroke on the skulls of its—sometimes skeptical—listeners. A portion of the audience did come out of simple curiosity; it remained because O'Neill, in furious command, would not let it loose.

But even when this has been said, a thousand questions stand unanswered. If O'Neill had risen like a mighty specter to reassert himself, to say that the long neglect was unjustified because the hypnotic force of his vision was in some way valid and real, what of all the criticism, the apparently definitive dismissal, of the years between? If it is true that his language was both bald and turgid, and that his most ambitious structures were sometimes sophomoric in design, what *did* O'Neill have that made him a titan still in the late 1950s?

It seems to me that the only way anyone can dig at an answer is to begin by acknowledging that most of the criticism was well taken. O'Neill meant to become a poet and never became one; the worst of his plays are those in which he tried hardest, *Lazarus Laughed* among them. The words lack melody; the rhythms rise by main force, and end in shouting; on paper, O'Neill is simply not literature. The *finis* to all this was really written by the man himself in the late, autobiographical play: when his father helpfully says that he has the makings of a poet, he sneers, "The makings of a poet. No, I'm afraid I'm like the guy who is always pan-handling for a smoke. He hasn't even got the makings. He's got only the habit. . . . I just stammered. That's the best I'll ever do."

Most of what has been said about the hewed-out-of-stone rigidity of O'Neill's characters is probably true, too. It's clear enough, watching *The Iceman Cometh* on the stage again, that these are marble men: blocked out, tooled with infinite care, firm and strong in their external accuracy, and wholly without the suppleness, the surprise and the free play of flesh. The gasp of astonishment that Tennessee Williams can draw from us in a fluid, unprepared gesture that is as uncontrollable as quicksilver yet incontrovertibly true is never a part of the O'Neill armory. O'Neill did not so much paint his characters on water as spell them out on clay.

Profundity of design? O'Neill's shapes were often massive, but the mass is always horizontal: we are taken down a coastline built, quite consciously, of symmetrical boulders, never permitted the natural rise of a pyramid to a point at which it cannot help touching the sky. A Greek myth could be spread out over New England; but this was imported architecture, with too many echoing, empty halls. Freud could be carried into the theater; but he was carried wholesale and dumped. Symbols, when they were used, tended to be too simple: we could see only the mask in front of the face, not the face through the mask. When O'Neill turned from realistic reporting to earnest philosophy he was apt to produce something as bad as *Dynamo* or *Days without End*.

Suppose all these things are accepted as true. What's left? What is left, I think, is a strange irony, an irony almost as biting as any O'Neill might have hurled at his characters. It is possible that the secret of O'Neill's strength and durability is an overwhelming sense of melodramatic scene inherited from a father, and a theater, he despised.

The late Robert Benchley suggested this a long time ago. At one opening night, he reported, he found himself imagining that among those present, off in the wings somewhere, was the ghost of old James O'Neill, looking on in excited satisfaction and shouting, "Give it to 'em, boy!"

O'Neill, as a youngster, was bent on ridiculing and, if possible, destroying the heroic, rococo extravagances of his actor-father and the plays (*The Count of Monte Cristo* notably) in which he appeared. The theater would, with him, become more realistic, more honest, more responsible than it had been in such cardboard kingdoms. And it did: he made his threat good. But deep within the new dispensation, carved out of his own passion, lay a bequest: an irresistible urge to openness, to the roar of outrage, to the head-on clash of souls locked in mortal combat. (The combat took place on a New England farm or in a Village saloon, not in a dungeon; but its sound, direct and shattering, swelled up nonetheless.)

However or wherever the drama was to be arrived at, through endless realistic detail or naturalistically rambling structure, it must at last be arrived at: the moment—the scene—must crack open into lacerating confrontation, into the spectacle of mothers and sons and dreamers and deadbeats clawing mercilessly at one another's throats. *Long Day's Journey into Night* may repeat itself for four hours; but two or three times in the course of those four hours it is going to split apart like a boiler blowing up, with a rush of scalding steam and an impact that jars the foundations of the theater. Where most of his fellow realists turned to implication and even evasion, O'Neill continued to insist on statement: on the plainest, fiercest, most harrowing exchange of statement that any two people could possibly inflict upon each other. (The marble figures are, in a way, good for this; they may not have subtlety, but they have crushing weight.) Whatever the absurdities of James O'Neill's theater, we are told that James O'Neill himself had fire; whatever new channels Eugene O'Neill may have directed the theater into, he brought the fire along.

What did O'Neill do? He gave it to 'em, boy.

⌁ 3 ⌁

THE FAILURES of Tennessee Williams are worth talking about. Mr. Williams, it seems to me, is the finest playwright now working in the American theater; every failure he has represents a real loss not only to himself but to all the rest of us. When so substantial and exhilarating a talent appears, the hope must be for the largest possible body of durable work.

Almost alone among his contemporaries, and without wholly shaking off the realistic tradition that is ours, Williams sees and writes as an artist and a poet. He makes plays out of images, catching a turn of life while it is still fluid, still immediate, before it has been sterilized by reflection. Arthur Miller may sometimes build a better play, but he builds it out of bricks; Williams is all flesh and blood. He writes with his eyes and his ears where other men are content to pick their brains—poetry with them is an overlay of thought, not a direct experience—and his best plays emerge in the theater full-bodied, undissected, so kinetic you can touch them.

The curious thing about Williams' lapses is that they seem to represent a conscious straining away from the virtues that are most naturally his, a rebellion against self that takes the form of wanting to shatter—or escape from—the mirror he has taken such pains to perfect. Life is his for the patient echoing; he occasionally seems to want, wantonly, to silence the echo.

The least of his vices, but one that has been with him from the beginning, is his inability—or refusal—to conclude anything, to find endings for his narratives that will embrace, take account of, and face up to the materials out of which he has begun them. *The Glass Menagerie* simply stops; the play has been so accurate and so touching that we do not really mind. *A Streetcar Named Desire* escapes into the heroine's insanity; the play remains thrilling, but this is to wash out the struggle rather than resolve it. *The Rose Tattoo*—here the matter becomes serious—winds up by junking a character complexity that has fascinated us all evening in favor of a simple sexual gesture, a gesture that is totally inadequate to the needs of the play.

The Rose Tattoo has two exhilarating acts. The first is concerned with the emotional paralysis that overtakes a volatile Sicilian woman living in the Gulf country near Mobile when the husband in whom she takes fierce pride is killed. The second is concerned with her reluctant reawakening at the hands of a man who, compared to her own idea of her first husband, is little more than a clown. While these events are taking place the theater swims in vitality and rich good humor.

In the third act, as Williams casts about for a resolution, both the action and the characterization begin to fray. The heroine has been presented to us as a quicksilver compound of physical passion, intense idealism, and hysterical religiosity. That a single sexual act should reduce these qualities to a happy harmony is implausible; it tends to suggest that there was no real conflict in the first place. At this point we begin to feel that we know the woman better than Williams does—sexual gratification would hold her down for about an hour—and the bland surrender with which Williams waves away her personal torment destroys, rather than absorbs, the complexity that has made her interesting.

It further brings into focus a certain sentimentality about sex that runs through Williams' earlier work, a kind of humorless dedication which leads his characters into locutions like "getting them colored lights going" and earnest apostrophes to "the glory" of it. Where Williams is earthily realistic about everything else, he is somewhat romantic about sex, and his wide-eyed wonder at it all goads him into occasional disproportions bordering on parody—as in a third-act scene during which an avid ingénue tries to break down an agonized but rigidly responsible young sailor. There is some assumption behind these plays that the psychological aberrations of the universe can be quickly settled on one big bed; it is one of the few failures of honest observation in Williams' work.

Both *The Glass Menagerie* and *A Streetcar Named Desire* are vigorous enough in other ways—in many other ways—to make us accept their escape-hatch endings. But the collapse of character in *The Rose Tattoo*, the hasty flight toward an unrealistic panacea, is a more disturbing matter: what was formerly a small structural blight now eats dangerously into the heart of the play, diminishing its human validity. Because the play as a whole fails in this final swift substitution of sentimentality for complexity, we are forced to write off some glorious portraiture.

A similar flight from the concrete to the symbolic, from the hard-rock particular to the hazily general, also began to be troublesome in *The Rose Tattoo*. There had been, it is true, an incidental toying with symbols in *The Glass Menagerie*. Crippled Laura's menagerie of figurines is in itself a symbol; but a shelf of small crystal animals is also possible, probable in the circumstances, and concrete. Less concrete in its use was the photograph of a father who had earlier run out on this unhappy household. In the stage directions for the play Mr. Williams had asked that the absent father's portrait be lighted up arbitrarily—that is to say, without realistic motivation— at certain key points in the dramatic action. In production, this slight gesture toward the abstract was somewhat played down. Its presence, however, suggested a dramatist who rather liked to intrude on the life he had so painstakingly caught, a dramatist whose hand—poking into the world he had created and pointing a finger at certain of its objects—might one day prove as meddlesome as his eye was meticulous.

In *The Rose Tattoo* the hand became much more obtrusive: it went in for tattooing. To serve as a crucial moment in the play's emotional development we were given the sudden, symbolic appearance on the hero's chest of a meaningful "rose." At this vital point the characters were inexplicably robbed of the power to act for themselves; they stood passive and inert while the playwright scrawled significant designs upon them. What is wrong here is that a growing relationship is not permitted to fulfill itself out of the characters' temperaments, though those temperaments are—as we have seen—wonderfully capable. At the very moment of crisis, of the final "coming together" of two thoroughly alive people, something cuts across life and, in effect, denies it. That something is the playwright, impatient now with life, appearing in person.

With his next theater piece, *Camino Real*, the playwright was alone on the stage, playing with puppets. Here life was rejected on two counts: in the content of the play, which seemed to hold that the world is a desert of vice deserving only of abandonment; and in the method of the play, which discarded the three-dimensional universe altogether and replaced it with symbolic placards that could be juggled into various kaleidoscopic patterns at will.

In reading over *Camino Real*, it is possible to discover what Mr. Williams is after, in method at least. He has—quite often—been called a poet; in the sense that a poet works primarily with images rather than with syllogistically reasoned ideas, he has quite often been one.

He has also, along the way, noticed that a good poetic image has very little of logic in it. Words that have no literal relationship to one another are thrown into unlikely juxtaposition, rubbed back to back in odd and apparently irrational fashion. When T. S. Eliot writes that "the evening is spread out against the sky like a patient etherized upon a table," there is no common-sense connection between a sky and a man who is about to be operated upon. When Stephen Crane writes that a mother's "heart hung humble as a button on the bright splendid shroud of her son," there is no realistic relationship between the idea of a heart and the idea of a button. A heart doesn't look like a button, act like a button, or ever—in the ordinary course of affairs—seem like a button. Yet, out of this highly implausible combination a third thing magically emerges: a clear feeling about a mother's emotion.

Mr. Williams, it seems to me, is here plainly after this third thing: the fleeting, stunning intake of breath that sometimes comes from such nonliteral, nonrealistic mismatches. To get it he has constructed a play of calculated *non sequiturs*.

In a courtyard that looks vaguely Mexican but is never identified, a man who is never identified stumbles down a flight of stone steps. An ominous policeman, uniformed but otherwise unidentified, steps out of the shadows and shoots him. The man is suspended for a moment—long enough to talk about a pony he once owned—before he falls. Falling, he is collected by two trash men who cart him off in a two-wheeled container.

Kilroy enters, looking for a "normal American." The first "normal American" he greets turns out to be a French homosexual. The second turns out to be Casanova. Casanova, now a mangy "old hawk," is having a twilight affair with the consumptive Camille. But Camille deceives him with a younger man and, as streams of confetti rain down from the heavens, Casanova is crowned "king of the cuckolds."

Figures in death masks lurk on the stairways. A surly, gravel-voiced man growls popular song titles from a balcony window. Camille attempts to board an outgoing plane, the "Fugitivo," but has lost her passport. Kilroy, an ex-fighter with a heart as big as the head of a baby, barters his Golden Gloves for a chance to lift the veil from the face of a gypsy's daughter. Kilroy's heart is removed by white-jacketed surgeons and turned in at the nearest pawnshop. Byron limps forward to anguish over the ashes of Shelley. Don Quixote comes in for a drink of water. A narrator wanders about asking "Where are we, what does it all mean, what is real?"

These are some of the strangers—the realistically unrelated figures —who brush shoulders in the play in the hope of setting off sparks, of evoking unexpected but nevertheless revealing relationships. Once in a while—as when Kilroy comforts Casanova with a Tin Pan Alley tune, or when the same Kilroy swings his fists wildly against nothing at all—there is a faint whisper of interior vitality, of ironic meaningfulness.

But ninety-nine per cent of the time that sought-after third thing—that fresh, clear picture, that stabbingly felt emotion— never emerges. The odd contrasts are made; but they seem merely odd. The consciously unlike elements refuse to mate; no new reality is born of their union.

Why? I think there are, roughly, three reasons for so thundering a mishap. One is that the business of constructing an intelligible narrative for the stage is not at all like the business of constructing a single image to be placed in a lyric poem. The theater does use poetry; but it climbs to poetry through the development of a coherent narrative and three-dimensional characters; language comes last and reveals these earlier concrete values. The effort to put the methods of language into the topmost position and to treat story and characters as fragmentary tools which can be bandied about in the interests of such methodology—the effort to treat root and branch as though they were the result, rather than the cause, of the flower—is probably a theatrical dead end.

Another reason, no doubt, lies in the author's own imaginative equipment. In the sense in which the term is understood nowadays, Mr. Williams may be called a dramatic poet. But that is, again, not the same thing as being a lyric poet. So long as Williams is working outward from a lifelike stage situation, he hits upon wonderful streaks of earthy imagery; there are dozens of lines in *The Glass Menagerie* and *Summer and Smoke* and *A Streetcar Named Desire* that have the stamp of poetry upon them.

But when, as in *Camino Real*, he turns to the poetic for its own sake, he produces a sort of song-writer's jargon ("There's a cold wind blowing out of the mountains and over the desert and into my heart") and the mildly embarrassed humor of a sophomore who knows he is too ambitious for his own good ("I don't see nothin' but nothin'—and then some more nothin'," a construction which is echoed more seriously in the "nobody ever gets to know nobody" of the later *Orpheus Descending*).

Lastly, and most importantly, Mr. Williams has reversed the poet's intention. The poet is primarily in search of reality; if he permits himself a certain license along the way, an intuitive reaching out for normally unlikely combinations, it is in order to speed up and intensify the search. Momentary unreason ends in a more vivid actuality. Mr. Williams has made the unreason an end in itself, has exalted method above substance, has permitted method— rather than the face of life itself—to determine the shape and degree of everything else in the work. In *Camino Real* there is a strong hint not simply of disgust with reality but of disbelief in it; the mathematics of image-making become more important than the matter out of which images are made. We are on the threshold of a world that distrusts the world and places its faith in some place or thing beyond the mountains: in craft detached from the coarseness of life, in man detached from men.

The drift toward Olympian detachment is given sharp crystallization two plays later, in the thorough and considered revision of the earlier *Battle of Angels* now called *Orpheus Descending*. Here a virtuous young guitar player who has descended into the hell of a small Southern town looks about him in horror. He sees corruption everywhere: in the storekeeper who is a prisoner of her bigot husband; in a once idealistic child who has bitterly sold her soul to the jukeboxes; in the frustrated and hysterical wives of the men of the community; and in the men themselves, swift to dispense "justice" with switchblade knives.

He extends a gentle, gingerly hand to several of the local Eurydices, feeling as he does so that he is touching "corruption," that he is apt to be drawn into the inferno himself. And he is drawn into it. His reluctant surrender to the forlorn and passionate storekeeper involves him hopelessly in the crude and possessive maneuverings of "animals sniffin' around each other" (sex is losing its position as panacea, becoming part of the tainted world). His gesture of kindness to an elderly religious fanatic brings down on him the wrath of a lynch-minded mob. In the end, like the Orpheus of legend, he is torn to pieces by a pack of dogs (Men).

Mr. Williams' theatrical sense is such that his juxtaposition of innocence and depravity sometimes takes on the sharp terror of a blood-drained face staring helplessly up at an uncontrollable fire, a fire that is burning down everything in sight. When the storekeeper stands in ashen disbelief while her husband taunts her with the information that he has helped kill her father, the sting of gratuitous cruelty is keen as a whiplash. When the boy twists his face into simultaneous desire and loathing for the sexual snare that is being drawn about him, the sense of disastrous involvement is painfully clear. When, at last, a trigger-happy sadist puts a bullet through the pregnant heroine's back, the shock is powerful indeed.

Yet behind this succession of shattering crises there lurks an echo of emptiness that will not be quieted. Whatever seems fiercely true in the heat of the immediate moment reverberates hollowly in the larger pattern of the play as a whole, as though an exciting sound had been produced that had no real source in nature. An increasing insistence on pattern—on an arbitrary arrangement of the shape of the world—is evident. A philosophical commitment, begun in *Camino Real*, seems to be hardening.

The hero of *Camino Real* was a wide-eyed innocent with a "heart as big as the head of a baby"; this innocent was subjected to every temptation and torment a nightmare universe could devise; he ended by leaving the universe, in the company of Don Quixote.

The hero of the play that followed, *Cat on a Hot Tin Roof*, was a married innocent, symbolically crippled; he was subjected to the demands of a wife that he enter a venal bed and the demands of a family that he join it in a life of "mendacity"; if his struggle—on Broadway—ended in compromise, it was not because Williams had written the play that way.

The hero of *Orpheus Descending* is a maker of music who has been in the world, been corrupted by it, and risen above his corruption by refusing all entanglements; the moment he has any fresh traffic with flesh and blood he is freshly tainted, ripe for outright destruction.

The special crystallization of Mr. Williams' attitude toward these obviously parallel figures comes when, midway in the third play, our music-maker pauses to define himself.

There is, he tells us, a species of bird that has no legs, no means of touching the earth; it spends all of its time in the air, sleeping— when it sleeps—on the wind; it has a protective coloration that makes it resemble the pure blue sky and keeps it safe from hawks; it can never be corrupted because it never lights anywhere until it is dead. "God has made one perfect creature," this Orpheus concludes. While it is always dangerous to read an author's symbols too literally, it is difficult to escape the inference now: that this young man, like those other young men in *Cat on a Hot Tin Roof* and *Camino Real*, is potentially just such a perfect creature, kept from his destiny by the ineradicable vice of all who walk the earth.

The steady movement of Mr. Williams' later vision seems to me, then, to be toward the unqualified rejection of that perverse complexity—that mercurial combination of good and evil—that we call human. Whatever is explicitly human, whatever actually puts foot to the earth, is unequivocally bad: greedy, treacherous, gross and unsalvageable. The only escape is total escape: the shedding of legs, of the delusion of love, of all companionship except that of Don Quixote. The world is divided into the wholly pure and the wholly impure (or, as *Orpheus Descending* has it, into "the buyers and those who are bought") and is then declared unfit for the wholly pure.

On the one hand we are confronted by angels, virgins, birds; on the other by beasts alone. The middle ground—the ground we walk and stub our toes on—disappears.

For a time there were no endings; for a time there was sex; now there is strategic withdrawal, the substitution of imaginary blacks and whites for plausible grays, of fantasy for flesh.

The brilliance of Williams' best work lies precisely in its admission of complexity—in Blanche du Bois tying a noose around her own white throat, in Alma Winemuller defeating her purposes with every pitiful word she utters—and in the humble acceptance of complexity as the root condition of all our lives. The danger in the growing angel-devil commitment is that we may continue to admire Mr. Williams' passion but fail to recognize his people.

4

IT IS POSSIBLE to respect the "natural" poetic imagery of a man like Tennessee Williams and still yearn for the day when this shall grow, stage by stage through action and character, into language that is admittedly, and powerfully, verse.

Christopher Fry has, in a sense, overleaped our time. He has come out for verse *now*; it has got him into trouble, but it has also made our eyes pop and our ears perk up.

The most striking thing Mr. Fry has accomplished is to have discovered a twentieth-century verse form for comedy—of all things. Matters had got to the point where it was almost impossible to convince anyone that comedy *could* be written in verse, so strong is the stranglehold of prose upon our age. Lip service was still paid to the notion of verse tragedy, because both verse *and* tragedy seemed equally remote to us; but prose comedy had been galloping along at a successful rate and there seemed no reason to wish for anything better. Mr. Fry has given us something better—has found both an imagery and a rhythm for comedy which increases the intellectual and emotional range of things to be laughed at—and his work comes as a genuine surprise.

Broadway had to wait for Mr. Fry's second American showing to take his work to heart. The first Fry venture to appear here, *A Phoenix Too Frequent*, was apparently so ruinously directed and acted as to conceal completely the quality of the play. On the printed page *A Phoenix Too Frequent* seems to me the most perfect thing of its kind since *The Importance of Being Earnest* and, within its limited intention and shorter length, superior to *The Lady's Not for Burning*. It has a sharply defined narrative that is developed with alacrity and precision. By comparison, *The Lady's Not for Burning* seems talky and meandering. But the play has its own virtues and they represent an experimental advance for Fry. He has tried for more complexity and got a richer texture out of it. He has tried for a slightly more rounded characterization and picked up a bit of human warmth. Where the earlier play was a perfect joke, intellectual to the core, the new one is an imperfect but possibly more appealing attempt to capture nature on its own vexing, complicated, and fulsome terms. It keeps shifting gears, and pulling back into first rather too often, but when it gets where it is going you feel you have been with the people all the way. *A Phoenix Too Frequent* is an exercise in detachment; *The Lady's*

Not for Burning is an experiment in participation. Fry asks you to accompany the characters rather than observe them.

There is a perpetual danger of Fry's becoming too fulsome. In one of his plays he has a character settle back and sigh happily, "It's nice that anyone can say anything at all."

And it is nice, now that verse has made it possible. But drama is still limited by the singleness of its action and the things said must have some relation to this singleness. Occasionally Mr. Fry forgets this and indulges himself in the pure delight of all that can be said. I am so grateful for the method of saying it that I am willing to indulge him his indulgence, but the audience isn't likely to, and he will do well to brake his verbal exuberance every now and then.

The effect of talkiness was accented by John Gielgud's performance in the production of *The Lady's Not for Burning* that was imported from England. Where the rest of the company, under Mr. Gielgud's own direction, read contemporary verse as though it were contemporary verse, Gielgud himself was frequently guilty of chanting. The immediate result was that Fry's verse was compared to Shakespeare's in some quarters, whereas the author's chief distinction is that he has found a new form instead of echoing an old one. If Fry is like anything, he is like Shaw in verse.

In a later and less successful play *Venus Observed*, the stuffy Dominic is informing his sister Perpetua that their charming father is a crook and likely to go to jail. Dominic expects his sister to be shocked, but she is a pleasant realist:

> PERPETUA: . . . . *I was able to believe you at once.*
> *Poppadillo has the most beguiling*
> *Jackdaw look about him. But you think*
> *He wouldn't be happy in prison?*
> DOMINIC: *He wouldn't, but what*
> *Difference does that make? Would you be able*
> *To look anyone in the face, with a father jailed?*
> PERPETUA: *Oh, yes, if he were comfortable.*

That is like a dozen passages in Shaw, and Fry has much of the impudent love of paradox, the passion for plain sense, and the hopeful irony of his prose forbear. He has neither the romanticism of Shakespearean high comedy nor the lowness of Shakespearean bumpkin comedy. Even when, in *The Lady's Not for Burning*, he introduces two brothers who seem on the bumpkin side, they turn out to have the intellectual facility and emotional disillusionment of a couple of Shavian Caesars.

That third play, *Venus Observed*, did shake a number of Fry fans in various ways. By the time it appeared in America, in a rather sluggish production staged by Sir Laurence Olivier, two schools of thought about Fry had formed: one which held that the fanciful young comic poet had brought about a joyous rediscovery of the English language, and another which stubbornly held that his verbal dexterity was mere vaudeville, and difficult vaudeville at that.

I remain a Fry man myself, but I must confess that *Venus Observed* gave aid and comfort to the enemy. In the process of dazzling his contemporaries with the rare and rich antics through which obedient words can be put, Mr. Fry had apparently bedazzled, and perhaps even blinded, himself. The language was once more sent sailing through hoops; but it finally tumbled in a little clutter about the feet of some paper-thin people whose behavior was sometimes amusing, sometimes ingratiating, but almost always uncomfortably contrived.

No one should ask that a verse comedy, least of all the kind of fanciful conceit that Mr. Fry so pleasantly invents, be entirely levelheaded about its people. And we should have been willing, momentarily at least, to accept as heroine a young lady who had spent a few years in America destroying such public objects as offended her aesthetic sense. We were, in fact, mildly entertained by the notion that she had spent some time in jail, making restitution. We may have been a little bewildered that she should suddenly draw a gun in a living room and shoot an apple out of a young man's hand, but we expected that Fry would sooner or later have some delectable point to make of the episode. And it was pleasant enough to watch the Duke of Altair, an aging rake who believed himself to have renounced all further conquests, fall in love with her.

But, having accepted all of the author's introductory whimsy, and having finally arrived at the moment of intimacy between Duke and girl, we were dismayed to discover that Mr. Fry had conceived no real relationship for them. No emotion fluttered upward to disturb the glossy verbal surface. Instead, the girl stood prettily in the center of the room and delivered a sparkling apostrophe to the glories of syntax. The speech ran on for forty-one lines, and while it was delivered (by Lilli Palmer) with some gaiety and some invention, it gave the whole show away. Mr. Fry had assembled his unlikely figures only to parse them.

At about the time that *Venus Observed* was being poorly received in this country, Mr. Fry was jotting down some thoughts of his own—for a small book called *An Experience of Critics*—on the creative processes, the behavior and misbehavior of words, and, of course, the critics who had been commenting on his work.

Most playwrights who turn on their tormentors do so in the heat of passion. Smarting under the immediate sting of a set of bad notices, they tend to cast both caution and coherence to the winds, erupting into a breathless invective that is quite as unpersuasive as the play which has preceded it.

Mr. Fry was cannier. He permitted his critics to go on to new targets, fully frocked; he caused his own rancor, if he ever had any, to relax into the graceful coil of the sleeping serpent; he seemed to have taken his hemlock in small daily doses so as to build up a splendid tolerance for the stuff. Then, in his quiet and almost jolly way, he let us have it.

An Experience of Critics may have been only a temporary victory for Mr. Fry, but it was a juicy one. For one thing, Mr. Fry writes better than the people who write about his writing. And for another, he had thought long enough, calmly enough and trenchantly enough to have found some true and telling things to say.

On the critical treatment of still budding talent: "The newly sprouting acorn is dug up several times a week and solemnly told that whatever it may think to the contrary, it is not an oak tree."

On one of the occupational hazards of criticism, noted when Mr. Fry himself attempted to review a play: "I could scarcely hear a word of the play for the noise of my own mind wondering how I should write about it."

On the inadvisability of having infallible criticism: "No man in his senses expects a critic always to be right—indeed, it would be very disconcerting if he were: we should have to believe him."

On the howls that go up when critical thumbs go down: "An artist's sensitiveness to criticism is, at least in part, an effort to keep unimpaired the zest, or confidence, or arrogance, which he needs to make creation possible."

On the vision of versifier Fry at work, as conjured up by the newspaper notices: "I see a man reeling intoxicated with words; they flow in a golden—or perhaps pinchbeck—stream from his mouth; they start out at his ears; they burst like rockets and jumping crackers and Catherine-wheels round his head . . . his typewriter continues to chatter long after it has been put back in the case. Words will grow out of him, like finger-nails, for some time after his death."

The poet's morose account of how he turns from this sort of journalistic analysis of his work to the work itself, sitting like an ancient Indian for silent hour after silent hour until at last he is able to type out an inspired "How," is not only deliciously funny reading; it is also a sharp comment on the easy nonsense which critics often substitute for an accurate reading of a complex creative problem.

Meanwhile, our author was at work on the problem. Shortly thereafter he came up with a fourth major play, the "winter comedy" called *The Dark Is Light Enough,* in which one character turned to another at a fairly heated point in the verbal clamor and cried, "But that's only a word!"

"Still," replied someone who was obviously a friend of the playwright's, "a word stays in the mind—and has its children, too."

And at long last—and in spite of certain very real difficulties in the play—it did seem as though Mr. Fry's words were ready to give up philandering, settle down, and perhaps produce grandchildren. Until now, except for the hint of amiably rooted character in *The Lady's Not for Burning*, the unexpected poet had been having fun with the language—testing it, tormenting it, making it laugh in a manner to which it had been unaccustomed, and sometimes skyrocketing it right over the garden wall. If it had often been exhilarating, it had sometimes been irrepressible to the point of irresponsibility.

In *The Dark Is Light Enough*—my enthusiasm for this play is based on the British rather than the softer and sleepier American production—language was ready to come home and stay with people, even belong to them. As an Austrian countess of the 1860s chose to risk her life and endanger her loved ones in order to perform an entirely quixotic act of mercy, she spoke now with a quiet self-confidence ("I am always perfectly guilty of what I do"), now with tartness ("People are always ready to die for what death will take away from them"), now with humor ("Are you military by nature or misfortune?"). And each of the lines belonged not to a free flight of Mr. Fry's more errant invention but to the woman who was thinking it.

Elsewhere in this melodramatic poem in praise of human generosity there were further evidences of the author's beginning tryst with reality, his beginning fondness for dimension in addition to dexterity. Much of the second act was concerned with an elusive, tantalizing yet thoroughly alive relationship between a good-for-nothing deserter and a woman—the Countess' daughter—who had loved him, lost him, and was now risking the destruction of her second marriage by giving him the time of day and the kindness of her heart. As these two moved clumsily, then impulsively, toward each other, we were never quite certain what this lingering affection meant, or where it was going to lead. But it existed. For the moment something very concrete, thoroughly clothed in flesh, was seen to be working out its peculiar destiny before us—and the moment meant that Mr. Fry had begun to see his characters in terms of their secrets rather than their syntax.

Thus, toward the end of the evening, when one of the puzzled people whose lives had been turned topsy-turvy by a meaningless war paused to remark that he knew a certain truth "in the still of my mind," it was possible to believe that these figures did have still reservoirs, places of rest, behind their bright and eager phrasemaking.

Mr. Fry was slowly and patiently putting flesh on those dancing bones.

5

FROM TIME TO TIME Christopher Fry has interrupted his parade of joyful verse comedies to perform acts of good will. He has written various shorter plays—*Boy with a Cart, Thor with Angels, A Sleep of Prisoners* among them—for church performance, donating the proceeds to his favorite worthy causes. His benevolent habit sheds some incidental light on the problem of religious drama, or, more specifically, drama as ritual.

A Sleep of Prisoners is, in this country, the best known of these plays. In an effort to examine the moral causes for the despair of the modern world the author assembles four men in a prison camp, puts them to sleep and then has them dream out their perplexities in a series of Biblical vignettes. They relate themselves, historically, to Cain and Abel, King David and Absalom, Abraham and Isaac, Meshach and Abednego. They come through the fiery furnace of the last episode to a renewed affirmation of faith.

The British are, on the whole, more tempted to experiment with this sort of devotional drama than we are. The relative success of T. S. Eliot's *Murder in the Cathedral* at Canterbury provided the stimulus for a new attempt to combine theatrical and spiritual values in the manner of the medieval morality play, and several distinguished writers, Dorothy Sayers among them, have followed Mr. Eliot's lead.

There is undoubtedly a certain personal satisfaction for the artist in turning away from the glittering worldliness of commercial success and dedicating himself, however temporarily, to so dignified and imposing a form. I suspect that some of the men and women who do this do it out of gratitude; they have succeeded so well in the world of profane letters that they feel some return of their talents to be in order. In any event, their sincerity and dedication cannot be questioned.

What can be questioned is the wisdom of this renewed attempt at mating ritual with theater. Whenever we become excited about the possibilities of this kind of thing, we tend to speak enthusiastically of the medieval drama; we imagine ourselves going back to a glorious time when church and theater were ecstatically one. We overlook, in our excess of zeal, one blunt fact: that medieval drama, for all its several hundred years of bustling activity, never did amount to anything. It remained an amateur enterprise to the end of its days, primitive and sprawling. If it did have moments of warmth, charm, and even exaltation, these were isolated and fragmentary, and today we must wade through reams and reams of solemn rhyming to find them. The form never did grow up.

There were good reasons for such permanent immaturity, and they are the same reasons which keep A Sleep of Prisoners from achieving valid dramatic life.

Narrative is subordinated to moral or philosophical point; in Mr. Fry's play the action, instead of climbing to a resounding climax, begins over again no fewer than four times so that we may examine its spiritual implications from various points of view.

Characterization is made abstract, so that it shall have obvious symbolic value; the principal figures in A Sleep of Prisoners no sooner begin to interest us as people than they are turned into quite different people, which is no people at all.

And because the story and characters are purposely not lifelike, the language tends to become fuzzy and inspirational as well. Mr. Fry's play ends in a burst of hopeful rhetoric meant to give mankind some confidence in itself and some hope for the future, but it is couched in words that must be picked over in the library before they can be made to yield much profit.

The ritualistic or philosophical drama is, furthermore, a great temptation toward poetic self-indulgence. Almost any writer has a number of exhortations he would like to get off his chest but for which there is no room in the stricter form of his regular work. In a play which does not have to compete for an audience in the market place, and which commands the respect of its audience if only because of the place in which it is played, the writer is free to let the benevolent side of himself relax into too many and too misty phrases.

The Irish playwright Synge once remarked that "the infancy and decay of the drama tend to be didactic," but that great and gay comedies "can no more go out of fashion than the blackberries on the hedges." Christopher Fry is a man for picking blackberries, and he will probably do more for mankind by filling his basket than by donning the cassock and surplice.

This is not to say that the religious intelligence may not, and most profitably, bring its insights into the world of playmaking. The reasonably human scene—with its sin and its defiance and its sorrow—is generally seen and revealed at its greatest depth by men with God on their minds, somewhere. (I am thinking of Sophocles, Racine, and, to a lesser extent, Shakespeare.) It is a matter of displaying what is human under a certain illuminating shaft of light; the trick is to continue displaying what is human.

Graham Greene should be able to manage it. His novels have often seen the one world in terms of the other with shattering success. Why was his first play, *The Living Room*, something less than his novels?

In *The Living Room* a crippled priest sits in a musty parlor arguing long and hard with a defiant psychologist. The psychologist, a middle-aged man with a neurotic wife, has taken the priest's young and inexperienced niece as his mistress.

He is confident of his right to happiness, contemptuous of his wife and of that strict moral code that would put a label of "guilt" on his conduct.

"When I got home last night," the psychologist remarks bitterly, "my wife was in bed with the door locked. Like a jury after the evidence has been heard. This morning she gave me her verdict of guilty."

"Was it a just one?" asks the priest.

"Do you believe in justice? Of course, I forgot. You believe in a just God. The all-wise Judge."

"That kind of justice has nothing to do with a judge. It's a mathematical term. We talk of a just line, don't we? God's exact, that's all. He's not a judge. An absolute knowledge of every factor —the conscious and the unconscious—yes, even heredity, all your Freudian urges. That's why He's merciful."

Around these two precise concepts—the concept of God as exact, and of God as dispensing His mercy in perfect proportion—novelist Greene builds his play. But they do not simply constitute its subject matter, its themes for debate. They also dictate its spare structure, its stern tone, its almost frigid refusal to become emotionally involved.

Mr. Greene, too, is exact. He measures his priest, finds him earnest, understanding, and futile. He measures the lover, shows him as candid, straightforward, and wretchedly self-deceived. He turns to the girl and sees that she is a loving innocent in her sin, but that she is perfectly capable of compounding the sin by giving way to despair and—the final rejection of God's grace—suicide. ("He knows his own selfishness," the priest tells his niece, "and you know your own guilt.") No character in the play is presented in a less than exact light; one of the girl's aunts is genuinely pious and genuinely dishonest; the psychologist's wife is frigid, whining, but deserving of her husband's love.

The author does not cheat; the scales give nothing but honest weight. Yet the play is arid and unmoving. Why? Because, I think, in being so exact Mr. Greene is himself playing God. That is, he is playing God so far as he is able. He is staring dispassionately, with unswayed objectivity, at the terrible tangle that mankind makes of its good intentions, its generous loves, its secret treacheries. He is willing to acknowledge the human impasse at which many lives arrive. And he wishes to suggest that out of this aching unintelligibility God will—in the end—make sense. But as a dramatist he can only show us the impasse, the ache, the unintelligibility. He cannot complete the picture, carry us over into that supernatural understanding that will make everything tolerable, everything just. He is, if the phrase may be allowed, writing God's play without God's talent.

The difficulties of Mr. Greene's sober, literate, psychologically honest play increase as we approach the second of the author's preoccupations—his urgent desire to dramatize, at the climax of the piece, the inexhaustible mercy of God. (Given exactness in the first place, he must go on to mercy in the second.)

This is a theme that has absorbed Graham Greene throughout his literary career. In his violent and engrossing novel of 1938, *Brighton Rock*, an almost satanic young gangster went unregenerate to sudden death. Yet through the novel ran a nagging refrain, "Between the stirrup and the ground . . ." a suggestion that in the split second before death a man might ask God's forgiveness, and be forgiven. The motif is greatly elaborated in a later novel, *The Heart of the Matter*, where the principal sinner is heard murmuring an Act of Contrition at the same moment that he is putting a bullet through his brain.

In *The Living Room* distraught Rose Pemberton—finding no consolation in her religion and no hope of happiness in her future with a married man—crams a handful of sleeping pills into her mouth even as she is mouthing the words of a prayer. Her first prayer is a formal one, a mere gesture; then—and this is the play's most effective insight—she lapses into a prayer of her childhood, a prayer that is meaningless in the situation but transparently sincere. Rose, too, may be saved, may have earned mercy.

But once more the action cannot be completed. The last word about Rose must be written somewhere else, invisibly. A curtain falls on the death of a miserable girl, and as it falls it shuts off our last hope of illumination about the fate of a soul; it also shuts off the one satisfaction we might have taken from an evening of harrowing observation. In effect, Mr. Greene has written a play about mercy that is merciless.

Supernaturally speaking, he cannot show us enough. In choosing to speak supernaturally—to stand quite outside and apart from his impaled characters—he has actually robbed them of that running spirituality which is every mortal's birthright, side by side with his concupiscence. The figures are not so much seen in double dimension as they are denied a dimension which must come later. It has the unexpected effect of making them seem less, rather than more, human.

A possible solution to this two-world problem, however, begins to suggest itself in Mr. Greene's second try at the theater, *The Potting Shed*. And the clue to this play's compulsive fascination, its much greater sense of reality and its sheer theatrical suspensefulness, may lie in a line or two spoken late in the evening.

The revealing remarks come from the divorced wife of a man whose eyes and heart have been hopelessly empty from the time of a mysterious illness in his youth. While she lived with him, and before she lost him not to another woman but to a common and characterless "bed-sitting room in Nottingham," this puzzled wife had felt that she was "in love with nothing." Now, suddenly, he has returned to life, and is quietly asking her to love him once more. But the explicit circumstances of his return to life are frighteningly supernatural; he has come back all tangled up with a miracle.

The sheer size of the event is too much for this candid, decent, honestly affectionate woman. She can go right on loving the man, but she cannot love him as the bearer of a miracle. Her own emotions are much too simple; the object of her love has become much too big. It is impossible for her to live on intimate terms with anything so wildly important; it would even, as she says with a wan smile, act as an "anti-aphrodisiac."

Here the writing has precisely the bewildered but outspoken humanity that is needed if ordinary mortals are to be caught up in the unfathomable wave of the supernatural and still seem to be themselves.

In his second play Mr. Greene remains determined to do what it is almost impossible for the theater ever to do: to explain, complete, and resolve the fleshly terrors and earthbound drives of his characters in terms of a Divine pattern that is essentially invisible, essentially incapable of translation into the concrete world of walls, fireplaces, and proffered cigarettes. Though we can see the trembling hand of the man who is on the verge of suicide, we cannot see the Hand that keeps him from it by opening his eyes to a savage and shattering truth. Yet Greene continues to insist that we acknowledge both forces as real, that we watch them—somehow—engage in actual combat.

He is, furthermore, still unwilling to make this a polite and shadowy battle of mild intimations; he wants it fought as a searing clash of ultimates. There is a general impression abroad that Mr. Greene's religious vision is a macabre and self-flagellating one, that he is eternally looking up into lowering skies and muttering "Somebody up there hates me." Not so. The theme that most haunts him, as we have said, is "the appalling strangeness of the mercy of God." But if he is to show mercy at its incredible maximum—if he is to show the enormous forgiveness that is man's for the asking—he must also show the enormous, indeed the maximum, need for it. He must take his actual men and women to rope's end, where violent despair or equally violent rescue awaits them. Let's grant him the logic of this.

The logic leads him to the key images of *The Potting Shed*: a hero who is ceaselessly pulling at a dog's leash as though he would like to wrap it around his throat; a drunken priest who reels about his rectory searching for his secret supply of forgetfulness and who stops drinking exactly at midnight so that he may rise in the morning to say a Mass in which he doesn't believe; an iron-willed mother who is ready to send her son to any Hell he chooses so long as the lie that was his father's life can be preserved; a serious and deeply understanding psychiatrist who has lost—to death—only one patient, his own son.

Wherever we turn, the stakes are as high as they can be, as high as they were in *The Living Room*. The God who has gambled on these creatures is now defiantly challenged to intervene. He does intervene as He never did in the earlier play: Lazarus rises to walk in the twentieth century. The scale of intellectual, psychological, and spiritual activity is vast indeed.

It is, as Mr. Greene's heroine has humbly but forthrightly pointed out, so wildly big as to be repelling, emotionally defeating. How are we going to catch hold of it, cope with it, feel for it—in the theater as in life?

This time the author has coped by simply telling the limited, human truth about it: our lives may not be happy but they are orderly, and every flash of the supernatural that filters through to them is a baffling, unsettling, exacerbating intrusion.

When the mother of the piece surveys her rigidly kept domain to remark that she doesn't like the new fashion in flower arrangements or "the new fashion of Christianity," either, she speaks in the clear, clean, familiar accents of the rational world bequeathed us by the nineteenth century.

When the despairing priest glances cynically at a monstrous lithograph of the Sacred Heart and mockingly deposits an unwanted bottle of wine just beneath it, he is looking at the standard commodities of piety with the jaundiced eye of the unbeliever who also possesses a measure of taste.

When the enigmatic central figure of the play twists the corners of his mouth downward, lets his hands fall limp, and records the details of his own conversion rather helplessly ("I don't love God, I don't want God, but He's there . . ."), we find the spare words moving because they are the fewest, least rhetorical, most direct words possible in the human circumstances.

A play like *A Sleep of Prisoners* neglects man for message, reality for ritual. *The Living Room* looks at its people from a supernatural point of view that is not dramatized; helpless figures are cast adrift, cut off by a curtain from what may or may not be Mercy. *The Potting Shed* permits the supernatural to enter the room and to contend with the natural, but not at the expense of its nature; the people recoil and rebel, or engage and submit, in a manner that is essentially recognizable. In plumping for God, Mr. Greene has given not the devil but man his due.

EIGHT

Playwriting

∽ *1* ∾

IT IS EASY, and in a way it is generous, to soften the blow of a quick failure by saying that the author of the piece shows promise. But loving kindness on the part of a reviewer may do the playwright more damage than a good sound thump on the head.

When a young writer is really off the track, when he is studiously striving to do all the wrong things, it is no great service to him to urge that he continue in the same vein. What will really help him—though it will make him good and miserable at the time—is the kind of shock that may lead him to question his methods of work, his models if he uses any, and his notion of what constitutes stage life.

Each season we have a certain number of respectable disasters—

that's a curious phrase, but I think it's the right one—written by men who show such technical familiarity with the theater that they would seem, at first blush, to be on their way to eventual success. Because they have grasped the surface niceties of dramatic form, because they have learned how, when and where to make the routine gestures, they suggest that it is a mere matter of time before one of their manufactures begins to breathe.

But this is like creating an endless number of robots in the hope that one day one of them will wink at you. Technical competence can be very deceptive. It is perfectly possible to learn how to shape a play without ever learning how to write one.

These neatly built automatons are almost always properly plotted, textbook style. There is normally a clear central tension, and a complexity to cross it. The necessary characters get on and off the stage appropriately, scenes of quiet are followed by scenes of vigorous activity, the curtains come down on calculated crises. Indeed, they possess everything but a single moment that is honestly touching, honestly moving, honestly alive.

Why? Because their authors have learned to write with their heads instead of with their eyes, their ears, and their noses. They have read too many plays. They are too well trained. They know too much. Instead of rooting up the back alleys of their own experience, ears cocked and eyes open, they have made of playwriting an imitative mental exercise. They have learned the polite forms, and they are bores.

Probably the only playwright who ever learned his trade by shutting himself up in a library for a long weekend was Oscar Wilde, and he was writing a highly specialized kind of artifice. What we may need at the moment are more slovenly playwrights—playwrights who are not so much concerned with the judiciousness of their structure as they are with sudden and stabbing flashes of simple observation. Tennessee Williams sometimes writes a slovenly play, but its untidiness is often the result of too much life. Mr. Williams—especially in his earlier plays—is so full of the actual taste of things that he seems unable to digest them all. For the machine-made playwright everything is pre-digested, and it has no savor.

What is truly tragic about so many of our novices is that they are not really hacks and do not mean to be hacks. A hack writer is a shrewd writer—shrewd about his audiences—and he will shave his structure for the sake of an effect every time. But many of the young men who are turning out lifeless plays are not the least bit concerned with trickery. They are one and all earnest, eager, and high-minded. They are trying to do what seems to them to be the right thing, because they have been taught it or because someone else has done it before them.

What they need to learn is how to be themselves, and how to respond personally, immediately and without too much formal concern to the actual sound and the actual touch of life about them. They need to be much less cerebral and much more kinetic. They need to concentrate on the dramatic moment, not on the over-all mold. They need to soak up, and then give off, the vibrations of an event as it sings in time, and forget all about the chess moves.

It is perfectly true that the greatest play will have both the tang of life and a tautness of form. But the life comes first. A Tennessee Williams can always hope to improve himself as he slowly gains mastery over his appetite. But the man who makes only a well-made play can never improve himself; he can only churn it out over and over again, like a stencil on a mimeograph, endlessly correct and endlessly dead.

The multigraph boys have got a lot to unlearn. They have got to ditch their passion for construction—for the moment, anyway—and acquire a passion for the homely, awkward and shattering small truth. They have got to start with small potatoes that really taste like potatoes, and do the French-frying later. When one of them turns out a play, however crude in form, which contains moments—which contains even one moment—of breath-taking accuracy, of unexpected and even embarrassing honesty, then he will be genuinely promising.

❧ 2 ❧

THE MOST CHEERING REMARK I have heard in a long time turned up in a *Vogue* interview with Jane Bowles. Miss Bowles is the author of a tantalizingly imperfect play, *In the Summer House.* She had, according to the grapevine, spent some nine years shaping and re-shaping the play; she had been through the Broadway production mill for the first time; her play, possessed of a number of unusual virtues, had failed.

A good many playwrights in similar circumstances have emitted yowls of pain, sworn off the theater and at all its practitioners, con-demned the audience for its patent stupidity and retired into the sulking chamber reserved for also-rans.

Not Miss Bowles. After nine years of labor learning to master this peculiar craft, she feels she still has something to learn. "There is no point in writing a play for your five hundred goony friends," said Miss Bowles. "You have to reach more people."

These last few words should be footprinted across Shubert Alley. Or better still, they should be engraved on the lintels of all those Village hovels and uptown brownstones where genuine talent re-sides.

Their importance is not for the hacks of the world; the hacks have always known that the audience must be dealt with, and they have always been careful to deal with it on a somewhat conspira-torial level. Besides, hacks don't have five hundred goony friends. They have five hundred hep friends, each more certain than the author what the audience will lap up.

The very special importance of Miss Bowles's words is for the band of writers Miss Bowles represents—the genuinely sensitive, the undeniably literate. Let's call it, without prejudice, the intellectual upper-crust.

There are a fair number of upper-crust talents bursting to make use of, and make friends with, the theater. The theater can use the integrity, the conscientious style, the feeling for poetry that these people possess. (*In the Summer House* was conspicuously wealthy in these particular virtues.)

The difficulty is that when Literature with a capital L comes to the theater these days it comes from another environment. Our prosy and practical stage—with its blunt, bare syntax and its hammer-and-saw construction methods—doesn't produce too much of its own.

In the course of a Broadway season we are likely to hear anything from "Take your paws off me, you big gorilla" in a patently ill-written play to "In your case, work was in competition with the home" in a relatively well-written one. The man or woman who can write the equivalent of Miss Bowles's first long character monologue in *Summer House* is a welcome visitor.

But that man or woman is likely to come from a literary coterie accustomed to more fragile media than the theater. He or she is bound to have five hundred goony friends. For "goony" read: delicately expressive, emotionally reserved, tightly astringent, or fond of the fleeting nuance.

In other media these preferences are workable. An obscure gesture may make a haunting short story. An unfinished sentence may throw off enough overtones to sustain a twelve-line poem. A cloud hanging low over summer sands may do very nicely for an evocative mood piece (reading time: five minutes).

But the theater is—for good or ill—more robust than all this, more extrovert. A good many literary lights, deeply involved in a first flirtation with the practical theater, have been appalled at what seemed to them excessively bald demands: occasional plain statement, clear progression, frequent emotional openness.

It is at this point, I think, that environmental pressures do their damage. The playwright sits poised over his typewriter; he knows quite precisely what his principal character's next emotion is to be. "The theater," he tells himself, "demands that I spread this emotion across the entire stage, that I let it come out. I can do it elusively, I can let it scurry like a lapwing against the ground, I can let it be inferred during sudden silence. Nevertheless, I mustn't. I must speak up." This much is certain.

"But—" and the playwright pauses. We are at the crossroads now. "But what in heaven's name will my friends think?" The artist's friends are accustomed to inference, to restraint, to the remote echoing of something never, never stated. Isn't it a bit vulgar to say what you mean? Isn't it crude to show what might be deftly concealed and, later, subtly deduced? In making any sort of concession, am I lowering my standards and corrupting my style?

The fear of becoming a hack has, I think, kept many a talented man or woman from becoming a useful playwright. The theater is— if there is no other word for it—cruder than some other arts need be; it is cruder in the sense that it is more direct, more concrete, more expansive, more explosive.

But it may be all of these things at several levels. The hack may say what he means and say it flatly. The talented man may say what he means and say it richly. But the talented man who insists upon his right not to say it at all, to hug his meaning like a secret close to his breast, to serve his goony friends rather than his gaping audience, is better off out of the theater.

All hail to Jane Bowles for her happy pronouncement.

∽ 3 ∾

DON'T ASK ME what I was doing watching an ice show at the Roxy, but I was, and the experience had the usual perverse effect of bringing out the sleeping philosopher in me. I kept watching the skaters make glorious arcs across the entire Roxy apron, felicitously avoiding a sudden descent on the first violinist directly below. I kept thinking of the scale and the sweep that had been added to the human body by the simple expedient of strapping a couple of blades to the actor's ankles. And I also kept thinking how much less interesting, and how much less satisfying, all this was than watching the human body do the same thing, or half the same thing, unaided.

Which brought up the age-old, and still unfinished, battle between the performer and the various machines that have been devised to help him out. Fertile minds have always been busy making the player look larger, sound louder, move faster, and bat longer and lacier eyelashes, and every gift of the mechanical gods has proved as slippery and as treacherous as that floor of ice at the Roxy. (One of the chorines, quite a pretty girl, did come smack down on it before the arabesques were done, and I wanted to applaud her for restoring the species to its proper and happy imperfection.)

The danger—of ice skates that allow a dancer to scoot into infinity, of Inigo Jones's seventeenth-century skywires that hoisted entire acting companies into the invisible heavens, of agile cameras that permit Tab Hunter or whoever to take off for outer space— is not that the performer will be unable to adapt himself to such mechanical marvels but that he will adapt himself too well.

Everything—acting, dancing, eyelash-batting—is made much too easy; first thing you know the entertainer is letting the machine do all the work. Since the machine is impersonal, the work becomes impersonal; the awkward and fumbling and splendidly unconquerable misfit that we recognize as man disappears; and we are all in for a cold winter.

The movies have had a life-and-death struggle with their magical "advantages" from the beginning; if they've lost some ground in the past few years it may be because the machine has, for the moment, the upper hand. Sometimes a man comes along who dominates the whole perilous tangle of angled cameras, unlimited cutting, and the artificial coloring that has been added. When Joshua Logan makes an eight-minute cinematic whingding out of a hayseed picnic you are immediately aware that a firm and imaginative mind has put every cable, crane, and scissors to the service of the rhythm and the meaning of the story. Too often it's the other way 'round: the actor's voice is pitched not at an emotion but at a microphone; the actor's arm is lifted in a gesture not because the gesture is expressive but because it will show up nicely in the back-lighting. The result is likely to be as metallic and hollow as it is technically miraculous.

What has this Sunday sermon to do with the theater? One of the verbal debates I'm always losing is the one about poetry in the theater—and by poetry I mean what used to be meant, formal verse that will take the language of the theater as high as the playwright's blood pressure will go.

Verse, as an idea, is hard to sell nowadays. People who have offered you a drink will snatch the drink right back out of your hand if you so much as mention it. And they have an out, a very reasonable one. Why, they say, need it be verse? Haven't we, within the confines of our own realistic prose, actually achieved a "poetry of the theater" that is every bit as valid as the old poetry of language?

The image conjured up by the phrase "poetry of the theater" is clear enough: a mellow and sensuous wisteria mood, a play of light across the veranda, a conversational rhythm that has its drowsy and its more strongly accented beats, a painter's grouping of sensitive people, an over-all orchestration that has the discipline and variety of a decent piece of music. And I do think there's this to be said for our present practices: the structure of our plays—as distinguished from their language—is becoming rhythmically bolder and pictorially freer all the time.

Still I'm not happy. I have a sneaking feeling that what is called our "poetry of the theater" is largely a poetry of the switchboard. Season after season we are mightily impressed by a number of things: by shimmering cycloramas against which silhouetted players look "poetic" indeed; by liquidly shifting pools of light in which high-priced employees are handsomely bathed; by muted colors and by dazzling colors that rise and fall with the grace of a six-o'clock September sun. We may well be impressed by such embellishments: they're good to look at, and—dramatically speaking—they're meant to help. They *do* help.

But is someone leaning on them too heavily, letting them do too much of the work? When the text is finally divorced from its theatrical cushion, has it very much splendor left? Are we in some danger of getting our art out of amperage rather than out of that surest of theatrical staples, genuine verbal ardor?

Well, I shouldn't have gone to the Roxy.

~ 4 ~

ONE OF THE REAL THORNS in the flesh of the contemporary theater is the fact that what seem to be its very best plays date so rapidly. It's a familiar experience to find ourselves waxing lyrical over the merits of a work, bestowing a prize or prizes upon it, and then—after a lapse of no more than five or ten years—discovering that its artistic glories have been reduced to fine ash. Repertory companies that attempt to include the twentieth century in their hopeful schedules are eternally learning that *Journey's End* and *The Silver Cord* don't play quite so crisply as they once did, and television—currently ransacking the theatrical warehouse—often finds itself stunned by the stodginess of a 1938 box-office smash.

When we try to explain this unhappy circumstance to ourselves, we usually fall back on the notion that history has moved rather too rapidly in recent times. We imagine that the scurry of events and the changes in the national temper are what leave once all-too-topical plays behind, and we resign ourselves to the thought that any work that truly reflects the age around it must perforce pass with that age.

I doubt that the galloping calendar is quite so responsible as all this for our theatrical breakage. There are, of course, merely journalistic plays that vanish with the daily headlines. On the other hand, there are plays that do echo the preoccupations of the seasons in which they were written, that are stuck with references to dead men and dead issues, and that manage to survive as fresh, pertinent and lively theater pieces, in revival, all the same.

After a sixteen-year hiatus, for instance, we were granted a second look at William Saroyan's *The Time of Your Life*. As it happens, this award winner of 1939 not only makes reference to a contemporary phenomenon known as Adolf Hitler but diffuses throughout the evening that vague apprehension and desperate optimism that most of us felt at the time. These haunting echoes, and half-forgotten moods, did not in the least destroy the play, though. If dusty skeletons were heard rattling in the dramatic closet, the work itself had not become a skeleton; it could be listened to with as much pleasure as ever, perhaps a little bit more.

At about the same time Bernard Shaw's very much older *The Doctor's Dilemma* was trotted out for reinspection. Mr. Shaw was not a man to stand apart from the immediate issues of the moment, and certain immediate issues of 1906—of very little interest or validity fifty years later—were unmistakably present in this all-out whack at the medical profession. Tuberculosis was regarded as a matter of almost certain death; and every step of the narrative depended on the assumption. The pseudo-scientific jargon in which Mr. Shaw's bombastic quacks reveled, and by means of which they were satirized, was a jargon that had been wholly superseded; an enormous amount of the evening's comedy came from a florid old fellow's ranting on and on about the need for "stimulating the phagocytes," a process we hadn't heard much about for half a century. But we laughed, anyway. Science may have rendered some of Shaw's terminology obsolete, but neither time nor science had been able to trim the bristle out of the old boy's beard.

As a matter of fact, it is never anachronisms that distress us in the theater. If someone mentions Adolf Hitler, we simply say "Oh, yes, this is taking place in 1939" and adjust ourselves comfortably to what is, after all, an intelligible period. If someone rattles on about "stimulating the phagocytes" we make a quick translation into miracle drugs, antihistamines, or, let's say, "one of the milder antibiotics" and are delighted to discover that the joke holds perfectly good. A play isn't dated by its use of contemporary materials any more than Richard's howl for a horse on the battlefield is made implausible by the invention of the jeep.

What really yellows and stales a contemporary play is, I think, its use of language. We've been inhabiting a realistic, deliberately prosy theater for quite a long time now, and our ambition has been not only to make our subject matter contemporary but to make our idiomatic constructions thoroughly contemporary, too. We've taken considerable pride in our ability to tape-record the accent and the vocabulary of actual speech, to put the words down precisely as they might be spoken by a fellow living at a given address on a given street in a given month of a given year. This is, I am sure, a trap.

Nothing changes so rapidly, or so completely, as the truly common speech of a passing age (the only really unintelligible passages in Shakespeare are prose passages). Whatever is smart, knowing, or idiosyncratically accurate about the conversation of the moment is bound to be rhythmically dead—its special intimations and connotations all emptied out—when the moment is past. The play that leans on these is leaning on air.

If both Saroyan and Shaw manage to survive lapses of time that have sent many another playwright to the theatrical graveyard, it is because neither one of them ever wrote anything that could conceivably be mistaken for realistic conversation. It isn't that these dissimilar men were insensitive to the verbal nuances, or the atmospheric oddities, of the times in which they wrote; it's just that they refused to settle for a stenographic report and insisted on producing illuminated manuscripts. What was only a hazy, half-assimilated reference in the random speech of daily life has been raised to the level of meaningful, and close to poetic, statement.

The authentic speech of a time is rarely very articulate. It is sometimes a stammer, and it is always a form of shorthand. To write a play in shorthand is to run the risk of needing a decoding expert to unravel its meaning once the shorthand system has changed. In turning out *The Doctor's Dilemma* and *The Time of Your Life,* Shaw and Saroyan wrote longhand. Both, in their intensely personal ways, made their characters articulate. And that, I imagine, is why we can still hear them.

∽ 5 ∾

THE TIMING of satire is a ticklish business. We have a notion that, since society is nearly always making a fool of itself in one way or another, the satirist may speak up at almost any time and be heard. We think of him as someone who points out to his startled and suddenly convulsed customers a number of things they hadn't noticed before, and we often credit him with singlehandedly correcting the absurdities he lampoons. Actually, none of this is so.

There is a pinpoint in time when a given subject is ripe for slaughter. It occurs at that moment when everybody—the whole general public—has been fed to the teeth with a given national foible, but when it has not yet found precise vocal expression for its outrage. The audience has, in effect, subconsciously reached the boiling point. The satirist comes along and takes the lid off.

But he is always in danger of being severely burned. Let him strike a moment too soon—before the audience is really ready to share his malice—and his satire will be resented, driven off the boards. Let him strike a moment too late and he will be laboring the obvious, or flaying the already forgotten. He gets a split second in which to pin the tail on the donkey and when he misses the moment he is left looking either subversive or old-hat.

I suppose the most famous theatrical instance of making a joke before anybody was ready to hear it occurred when Beaumont, with or without Fletcher, mistakenly turned out an irreverent little lark called *The Knight of the Burning Pestle*; the time was the early seventeenth century, when middle-class tradesmen first began elbowing their way into the theater. The irritated playwrights promptly set about producing what was intended as a corrective satire—a broad and funny burlesque of middle-class bumptiousness that kidded the aprons off a gauche and meddlesome merchantry. The audience would have none of it, and the play quickly failed.

Some twenty years later it was revived. By this time the same tradesmen had become powers in the community. Their social standing was secure, they had nothing to fear from imprudent actors, they were themselves aware of how pushy and pretentious they had been in their long climb upward, and they were prepared to laugh—a little bit—at themselves. The play was a rollicking success and remained popular for a long time after. Beaumont had been trapped in that tricky time-factor which plays hob with the best satire, which turns it into one of the most delicate and uncertain of all theatrical attitudes, and which once led the astute George S. Kaufman to define satire as "that which closes on Saturday night."

Mr. Kaufman has himself run afoul of the same unpredictable sandglass. *Of Thee I Sing*, one of the most inventive and popular of all American musical satires, was produced twice: once at the beginning of the Thirties, again at the beginning of the Fifties.

When Mr. Kaufman and his collaborator Morrie Ryskind first tossed their lethal barbs at us, in 1931, the time and the topic were perfectly matched.

We had just been disillusioned about the dynamic Twenties, those dazzling years in which supersalesmanship was the solution to every national problem and in which there were at least two bathing beauties to every garage. We had caught on to the glamorous nonsense of having good-fellow Presidents, cheerfully useless Vice-Presidents and slap-happy political campaigns.

As yet no bank had closed. The stock-market crash was still a sort of joke on people who had had too much money anyway. The depression hadn't reached out to touch, and to sober up, every

living soul among us. There was a wonderful twilight period in
1931 when we could look with humor on the great, foolish day we'd
had without worrying too much about how dark the night was going
to get.

Kaufman, Ryskind, and composer George Gershwin mirrored
our mood delectably: here was a gay, lighthearted ribbing of Presi-
dential campaigns that were little more than popularity contests,
of candidates who picked their wives for the quality of their corn
muffins, of legislators who napped blissfully through any and all
legislation.

Two years later none of these things was any longer a laughing
matter, and when the same gifted trio tried a sequel called *Let 'Em
Eat Cake* their work was quickly dismissed as both impertinent and
unfunny.

And twenty years later the atmosphere had changed again, but in
a different way. The dismay of the mid-Thirties, the morbid concern
for our future which made laughing at *Let 'Em Eat Cake* impossible, had happily vanished.

But the satire itself was now unrecognizable. The felicitous moment had truly passed. Though Washington had gone on to new
idiocies, they were new ones; we could peer only dimly at the peculiar and barely remembered targets that had proved so timely a
few years back.

Perhaps nowhere was this more apparent than in *Of Thee I Sing's*
most famous and most fabulous creation: Vice-President Alexander
Throttlebottom. The forlorn little man who was so thoroughly
anonymous that he had to join a sightseeing tour to get into the
White House was surely one of the richest comic inspirations ever
to come out of American musical comedy.

But even though this splendid blob of Jell-O remained mildly
amusing in an extravagant way, the part had lost its juiciest point.
Somehow or other we had heard of Wallace and Truman and
Barkley in the interim. We may not have thought much of some
of our Vice-Presidents; but we had learned to think about them.

And now that they were not so anonymous any more, poor Throttlebottom tended to become a figure of pure fantasy—pleasant, but in no sense pungent. Along with beauty contests at Atlantic City and the notion that a French accent is automatically naughty, Alexander Throttlebottom had wandered off into history—a memorable reminder of a strange and gaudy era, no longer a pertinent political cartoon.

It was later than the satirists thought.

～❧ 6 ❧～

Whenever a theatrical season takes a fair share of its strength from adaptations of novels, and above all whenever one of these dramatizations manages to snag for itself a "best play" award, an old and troublesome question looms large: what price originality?

Mustn't a "best play" be only a play, and mustn't the theater take a very jealous pride in the legitimacy of its offspring?

Invariably, the tendency to borrow from other literary media is looked on as a sign of creative slackness; our drama as a whole is thought to be limp simply because it leans so heavily on prior work.

But, strictly speaking, our own theatrical age isn't much different from any other theatrical age in this respect. Playwrights have always rifled the lending libraries, and critics have always lamented the practice. The nineteenth century devoted almost half its time to stealing from Dickens and Scott. At one point the English theater had become so indebted to translations from the French that when author Tom Robertson called his new play *Ours*, the typesetter automatically set the advertising copy as *L'Ours*. Or so the legend goes.

But the nineteenth century was, creatively, a weakish time, too, and most good people have always thought that the hacks of the period might well have bettered themselves by putting themselves to fresher and more personal invention. The hole in this argument is, of course, the peculiar and puzzling fact that nearly every first-rate work ever written for the theater took its original inspiration from somewhere else.

Sophocles rewrote the stories of Aeschylus, and Aeschylus had, in the first place, been rewriting a standard mythology. Molière cribbed from Plautus, Racine from Euripides. If Shakespeare was the dramatist's dramatist, he was also the kleptomaniac's klepto-maniac, gathering an armful of other men's books before putting himself to the task of turning out a new piece for his actors. Nobody seemed to mind in those days, and if a Pulitzer Prize committee had been in existence it probably wouldn't have ruled out *The Merchant of Venice* just because five or six Italian novels had gone into its making.

Nowadays we mind, or say we do. We like to insist that every dramatist start from scratch and that each of his scratchings be his alone. There is possibly some virtue in the demand—it may keep lazy dramatists from doing merely tired, or merely imitative, work. But there are certain other ways, it seems to me, in which our insistence on total originality may be unrealistic and perhaps even harmful.

For one thing, the constant yelp for wholesale invention tends to put an enormous price on novelty. The basic dramatic themes don't actually change much more than human nature does; and they've all been pretty thoroughly explored.

The nervous playwright, fearful lest he be caught ringing a small change on a standard subject, anxiously seeks out a subject that no one has touched before. Under this pressure he may wind up with something that is only journalistic, only of interest because it is hot from the presses. Or he may wind up with something that is intensely special, intensely private, even intensely introverted.

Told that he must be original, he often becomes painstakingly odd, and a lot of our cul-de-sac drama may derive from a too deliberate search for the unfamiliar. Playwrights, poised over the type-writer, keep asking themselves, "What hasn't been done before?" when they might, with just as much and maybe more profit, ask, "What has been done before that I can do better?"

In any case, the important question is never where the material has come from but whether or not anything specifically theatrical has been done with it. (If something truly theatrical *has* been done with it, then the single important creative contribution that the dramatist can make has actually been made.)

A few seasons ago, for instance, we were offered a "dramatization" of *The Pickwick Papers* which was in no sense a dramatization. It was a leafing and snipping and pasting together of a voluminous novel. Such merits as it possessed were entirely Dickens', and such charms as it had for an audience were the charms of remembering what the original had been like. No new value—no theatrical fusion or theatrical force—had been added. The literate adapter had re-spected his materials but he had not given them vital translation into a new medium. *Auntie Mame* comes to mind as an even more conscienceless scissoring job.

On the other hand, adventures like *The Teahouse of the August Moon* and *The Caine Mutiny Court-Martial* seem to me to belong to quite another breed. Here the materials have been imaginatively reworked, and reworked especially for the stage. The folk-tale style of *The Teahouse of the August Moon*, for instance, was playwright John Patrick's inspiration—an inspiration which introduced a charming, pin-wheel coloration that did not exist in the novel from which it was made. Mr. Patrick had not simply culled ready-made dialogue and situations; he had fashioned something with a face of its own.

Similarly, Herman Wouk's feeling for the stage led him into much more than a condensation of his story of a naval mutiny. He uncovered a dramatic shape for the story that was wholly different—in outline, in contrasts, in shading, in presentation—from his first successful assault on his materials. I think it might even be argued that both these pieces were improvements on the source novels.

But that is not the point. The point is that they can be distinguished, creatively, from the works on which they are based—that the very special vigor of the stage, made up of a verbal intensity and a visual supercharge, has been handsomely taken into account.

Adaptations don't necessarily lead the theater to the level of Sophocles. But they don't necessarily drain it of its characteristic blood, either. They can have, and sometimes do have, a blood stream of their own.

༄ 7 ༄

TELEVISION seems to be the only new competing medium of our time that hasn't scared the theater half out of its wits. The arrival of movies found the theater moaning; radio frightened it, too. But nearly everyone you talk to nowadays chirps merrily on about the boon that TV is going to prove to its oldest brother.

It's a matter of writers mostly. (That, and the fact that the taste for "live" stuff in the living room may create a further taste for "live" stuff in public places.) Where Hollywood once drained the legitimate theater of its writing talent, the newest medium promises to become a handsome source of supply. Because the demand for material is so tremendous, youngsters are being encouraged and developed at an unprecedented rate. In the course of their development they are being trained in a style that is somewhat closer, visually and psychologically, to the traditional stage than to the very busy screen. Their work tends to keep them in New York, and the closer a man is to the theater the likelier he is to stumble into it.

Furthermore, to show that this line of reasoning isn't just so much theory, the statisticians can point to some six or seven promising people who have already "passed over." In recent years Broad-

way has opened its backstage doors to a hopeful handful of scripts
that either originated in the local studios or came from the typewriters of men who spend most of their working hours there. The
daily drama columns steadily indicate that more are on the way.
The trend seems real, all right, and a certain amount of optimism
is clearly in order.

There is, to be sure, a beginning hitch. Of the first ambitious
band to try working both sides of the street, only N. Richard Nash
and Paddy Chayefsky have had anything resembling success (*The
Rainmaker* and *Middle of the Night*). Horton Foote has stirred
up enough managerial interest to get three of his plays on the
boards (*The Chase, A Trip to Bountiful,* and *The Traveling Lady*)
but not enough critical or audience interest to keep them there.
Some lesser lights have seen their names go up on billboards and
come down again so rapidly that these might just as well have been
screen credits slipping by. If most of the work has been respectable,
very little of it has been right.

What's the trouble? Paddy Chayefsky, in his extremely interesting collection of hour-long scripts (*Television Plays*), gives us a
strong, left-handed hint. Mr. Chayefsky is actually plugging away
for the merits of what he believes—tentatively, at least—to be the
proper pattern for small-screen drama.

"In the last year or so," he points out, "television writers have
learned that they can write intimate dramas—'intimate' meaning
minutely detailed studies of small moments of life." Because of the
limitations of time, and the size of the activity that can be decently
embraced by a close-up camera, the stories that serve best are those
that "deal with the world of the mundane, the ordinary, the untheatrical." Television "can only handle simple lines of movement,"
and those simple lines are leading to "one small synthesized moment of crisis."

It is this last observation, I think, that gives us the most helpful
clue to our present difficulties. (I haven't much doubt, by the way,
that Mr. Chayefsky's prescriptions are thoroughly sound ones for

his native medium.) A television play is normally at its most active, the camera at its most mobile, during the early stages of the game. As the story moves forward, it tends to narrow in focus. The first thing you know you're dealing only with a face or two, and you're watching closely for the bat of an eyelash, the twist of a lip, the significant quiver that suggests an otherwise unelaborated change of heart. When the moment of crisis does come, it's not much more than a shadow across a man's face. From a theatrical point of view, the best television plays seem to shrink to a climax.

The theater, of course, works the other way around. An audience doesn't resist a lazy opening: that familiar maid ambling slowly to that familiar telephone won't be dialed out. But Act Two had better be a little bigger than Act One: in emotional range, in the complexity of crossed lives, even in sheer noise. And in Act Three the simple answering of a telephone (with a slow dropping of the receiver and an illuminated staring into space) won't do at all; if you're going to use a telephone, you'd better hit somebody with it. The stage is normally at its most expansive, its most full-bodied, in the last twenty minutes, and anyone whose responses are theatrically trained is apt to feel decidedly cheated by the closing moments of a regulation television play.

In other words, the man who writes for television is building to a grace note at the same time that the traditional dramatist is trying to strike a chord. The two forms tend to move in precisely contrary directions, the one dropping to a sigh while the other is taking its biggest breath, the one diminishing to a pinpointed epilogue while the other is winding up for an all-out Act Three. (If I had to boil this down to a phrase, I guess I'd just say that television writers don't write third acts.)

The playwright who wants to live in both worlds, then, is obviously going to have to equip himself with reversible gears. It should be possible. The biggest mistakes to date haven't come from the grinding clatter of gears being stripped but from the failure to try for any real change of course; too many TV men have simply placed their habitual, quietly "untheatrical" formula on the stage. So long as the distinction between styles is clear, an able craftsman ought to be able to manage both—as the late Robert E. Sherwood managed stage and screen alternately over a long, conspicuously successful career.

∽ NINE ∾

Trends?

∽ 1 ∾

EVERY ONCE IN A WHILE I get a letter from some patient theater-goer wondering why the theater—including the comic theater—devotes itself so passionately to the seamier side of things; why can't there be a little more sweetness and light? My own wonder about the way things are going is why playwrights can't let the seamier side of things be nice and seamy and leave sweetness and light out of it. Not that I have anything against sweetness and light. It's just that I like virtue to keep its place.

As a matter of fact, there may even be a playwriting principle—of immense potential benefit to seamy playwrights—lurking around here somewhere. I'm reminded of what happened to Sidney Kingsley when, a couple of years ago, he wrote a boisterous, bedroomy but not altogether convincing farce called *Lunatics and Lovers.*

Mr. Kingsley had trapped a whole cageful of mink-draped mice and on-the-make males for our scientific observation. These folk were hustlers, the lot of them. Quite apart from their plans for the evening hours, their daytime activities included perfume smuggling, income-tax evasion, and straightforward blackmail. All of these industrious sports were meant to be talented in their various lines of work.

But Mr. Kingsley was afraid we wouldn't like them. He was, perhaps, afraid that the people who write letters to newspaper reviewers would start writing letters to *him,* complaining that the riff-raff who romped around his garish hotel room were essentially a greedy, cold, selfish, disreputable bunch. He therefore set about equipping each of his wayward children with a built-in heart as soft as a mattress and as pure as a triple-sealed Band-Aid.

A little lady we had mistaken for a harlot turned out to be a real dragon of a chaperon, primly prepared to intercept any pass that might have been hovering in the air. An abandoned matron who, we were given to understand, had ditched fireside and family for a rousing fling promptly turned out to be a great one for the pocket handkerchief, dabbing at her eyes and thinking wistfully of those dull, sensible evenings at home. By the time the last act had rolled around, there wasn't a bum on the premises who hadn't come out in favor of marriage and motherhood, and why they weren't all hawking inspirational literature in the lobby after the performance I don't know.

This method seems to me to be wrong in principle, no matter whose play it is softening up. My admiration and affection for a no-good doesn't increase in proportion as he learns to echo sentiments I first heard at my mother's knee. Somehow I don't quite see this character at my mother's knee. I don't even see him at his own mother's knee, unless it is in the act of picking up cigarette butts. If I think of him in relation to his mother at all, it is only to imagine that the old girl probably taught him everything he knows and that her reward consisted in being pushed off a third-floor landing when junior could no longer stand her incessant yammering. In short, I think of him as a no-good you can respect.

When I do find myself working up some affection for a scoundrel, it is not because he is a good man but because he is a good scoundrel. That is to say, he excels at his chosen trade, is magnificently true to his vocation. Whatever the chicanery he is up to, he is adroit at it, inventive at it, unbeatable at it.

I admire a crook because he is a superb crook, not because he has a few commonplace domestic yearnings. What makes any scalawag interesting is his ingenuity, his skill, his imagination, his effrontery, his resourcefulness. To undercut this sort of professional élan by supplying a racy figure with the sentiments of a slob does not endear the fellow to me. It just embarrasses him in my presence and me in his. And it makes it terribly, sorrowfully clear that he is, after all, no better than the rest of us.

A playwright will do well to honor his character's shortcomings. That, at least, is the way all the best comedies have been written, from Aristophanes right down to *The Front Page*. Nor is Sidney Kingsley alone in feeling that a heart-of-gold approach is the safest route to the underworld. The whole contemporary theater likes to adulterate its tougher visions with little rays of sunshine. You could see these peeping through Rodgers and Hammerstein's *Pipe Dream* (the nice kids in a brothel baking birthday cakes) and through Truman Capote's *House of Flowers*. In this last item, which purported to tell the story of a battle of rival bordellos, some of the sweetest people this side of paradise smiled, sang, and deported themselves with the delicacy of a finishing-school faculty getting ready for Founders' Week. True, there was a suggestion, toward the end of the first act, that one of the madams was going to truss a man up in a barrel and heave him into the sea. But I didn't believe it for a minute. Not from that nice Pearl Bailey.

When a comic playwright wants to make us like a lout, a liar, a drunkard or a knave he had best make him the most incorruptible lout, the most incorrigible liar, the most capacious drunkard, or the most errant knave since Falstaff was a very bad boy.

～ 2 ～

I WASN'T REALLY bent on research. I just happened to overhear a couple of trusting five-year-olds watching television one quiet night.

"Which guy is the bad guy?"

"Wait. See who has a mustache."

The conversation not only brought me back to the simple, clean-cut, perfectly intelligible world in which I myself grew up, it made me think. What kind of preparation is this for the *real* theater these kids are going to inherit? As they grow to manhood, and find themselves free to wander the length and breadth of 45th Street, what is going to happen to their touching conviction that villainy is identifiable?

You can't really tell a bad guy from a romantic lead any more. There *was* one thoroughgoing rat roaming our local stages a couple of seasons ago—he was in a play called *The Desperate Hours*—but to look at him you'd have thought he was fresh from Princeton, or at least CCNY. Certainly he sported no helpful mustache. He hadn't a paunch, and his eyebrows weren't shaggy. He did have a rather slovenly, slack-jawed speech pattern, but that has become so commonplace nowadays as to constitute the social norm. (Perhaps precise speech will sometime become the new mark of villainy, suggesting an almost psychopathic arrogance.) The gunman in *The Desperate Hours* was a young, good-looking fellow with a crew cut, and if he hadn't kept threatening to kill people there'd have been no spotting him for the cad he was.

Well, there might have been one way. He had had, as he told us quite a few times in the play, a dominating, tyrannical father. This is a real clue to the new dramaturgy; whenever a character starts to talk about his father, you can look for trouble. In the old days a figure who tended to ramble on about his aged parent was at once taken to be sympathetic, a friendly sort of codger filled with filial piety. Now that we have looked into the psychology of the matter, discovered what harm fathers do in this world, and realized that practically any criminal you tangle with is blazing away not at you but at the father-image he sees in you, the tables are turned, the sympathies reversed. The boy who had a father is the boy you had better keep a sharp eye on. Don't look for mustaches; look for dad. I am a little reluctant to explain this handy principle to my children, but I know it's going to be a help to them.

What they would make of a contemporary work like *The Bad Seed* I don't know. There have, of course, been villainesses in literature before, but they have normally worn a great deal of mascara and displayed a telltale slink. Or flashed exceptionally long fingernails. Even when the villainess was only nine or ten years old, as must have happened somewhere earlier in the long history of the arts, she usually gave herself away in one or another conveniently repulsive trait: she was fat, or she was rich and snooty. And when her opposite in the play, a dainty little cherub in pigtails and crinoline, tripped winningly onstage, you knew where you were at. By these standards *The Bad Seed* is simply confusing, if not seriously disorienting; the dimpled little cherub is the girl the authorities are after.

Of course, it isn't entirely her fault, pretty creature that she is; she had a mentally diseased grandmother. As I see it, there wouldn't be a menace left in the theater if we didn't have the older generation to lean on.

In *Bus Stop* there are no villains. Everybody is lovable, and such trouble as arises comes from the fact that no one lovable person quite realizes how lovable the other lovable person is. The principal bounder in *Tea and Sympathy* is a hearty, clean-shaven, curly-headed schoolmaster who likes to take the younger lads on hikes. And Clifford Odets' *The Flowering Peach* would surely have unsettled anybody. As the play turned out, the cause of all the unhappiness was old, wise, funny Noah—Noah, the Lord's boy. After this one, you couldn't trust anybody.

There came a point, during a recent season on which I kept tabs, when there were just two mustache plays left on Broadway—and one of them didn't count. The one that didn't count was *The Dark Is Light Enough*. In Christopher Fry's verse melodrama a certain Colonel Janik strode fiercely into the drawing room. His upper lip was decorated, his hooked nose and sunken cheeks were impressively threatening, and he at once behaved abominably to some sweet, soft-spoken people. Confidence returned to you as you watched him: here, you told your believing heart, was a man who would wind up properly, with a slug in his back.

But no. The whole thing was a trap. Christopher Fry belongs body and soul to the new school of don't-shoot-him-he-may-be-the-hero dramatics (the variation on this is don't-let-yourself-like-him-he-may-be-a-lout), and he had no intention of sacrificing this man. He wanted us, as the tumult was dying down, to shed a tear or two for him, to understand that his snarl was a necessary snarl, and to applaud his last-minute rescue from the folk who were trying to get their hands on him. In my time, I'd as soon have saved William V. Mong, or Mitchell Lewis, from the mob.

That left *Anastasia*. Here we were back to fundamentals. The snake who stirred up trouble in this one had a mustache. He wore boots. He swirled a cape about him when he entered and when he departed. He breathed hot upon the heroine's neck. He signaled a henchman to clap a hand over her mouth and hustle her into the cellar. He laughed maliciously. He was, or had been, a demon with a horsewhip. He drooled at the thought of stolen money. He clenched his teeth. And—this is the surprising part—he was steadfast. When the whole thing was over, he turned out to have been the villain. *Anastasia* fooled you, all the way.

It also put you back in touch with an orderly universe, a universe in which you could count your friends, cut your enemies, and communicate with your clearheaded children.

∿ 3 ∿

EVERYBODY WANTS TO KNOW what's wrong with the modern theater. Personally, I think it's eating itself to death. By actual count I saw forty-seven meals served onstage during a single Broadway season, and that did not include the occasional preparation of canapés to accompany those vigorously mixed very dry Martinis.

Aristotle once said that a play was an imitation of an action, and the time has clearly come in the theater when the principal actions imitated are those of mastication and digestion. A playwright would no longer be able to get his people onstage at all if he couldn't assemble them for gustatory purposes, and the stage director who did not have the business of laying a table to occupy his characters while they chattered out the exposition would soon be at a loss for imaginative stage movement.

Somehow or other, dramatic stage movement in our time has boiled down to: Act I, setting the table for breakfast; Act II, setting the table for lunch; Act III, setting the table for dinner. This is sometimes, and strikingly, varied by having the actors clear the table, and in an exceptionally exciting play—like *A Streetcar Named Desire*—it may take the exhilarating form of having the actors hurl the dishes to the floor instead of drying them nicely. But the playwright—whether he be given to comedy, tragedy, farce or melodrama—who neglects to feed his company during the course of the evening is a foolhardy fellow who doesn't mind violating one of the most revered theatrical conventions of his day.

The precise thrill that contemporary playgoers are supposed to get from the vigorous clash of Community Plate is not clear to me.

An older audience insisted on broadswords at the least, and a playwright like Shakespeare, aside from letting a man toy with a leek now and then and going in for a fair amount of quaffing, wasted precious little time on tableware. The characters in a Greek play, when they ate at all, ate their children—a procedure with some point to it.

But twentieth-century audiences, having just got up from their own dinners, are expected to part with $4.80 for the privilege of watching the members of Actors Equity eat theirs, and I am not surprised that the theater has fallen upon evil days. An audience that has come glowing to the playhouse in search of mystery, adventure, romance and high passion, and that is then expected to sit quietly by while the actors pick a bite, is an audience with a justifiable dramatic complaint.

Take a look at the plays of that season I was talking about. *Point of No Return* belonged to the Hurried Breakfast school of drama, a form in which the modern suburban businessman suffers all day long from causes which he assumes are professional, financial, or amatory, but which can, in a more profound understanding of the play, be traced back to the fact that he was not allowed to have his breakfast in peace.

The Brass Ring was constructed along the same dietetic lines, and its hero might have had a far happier time of it if his wife had not been given to reciting poetry over the morning coffee. Anyway, the play opened with the morning coffee and came to its emotional peak when the middle-aged hero took his daughter out to lunch.

Enough tea and scones (I'm not sure they were scones; they may have been tarts or crumpets) were consumed during the brief run of *Lace on Her Petticoat* to fatten up the company for the winter. *Glad Tidings* went in for vast amounts of broiled lobster, the heroine of *Dinosaur Wharf* kept preparing dinner for a hero who didn't come, and the leading gentleman of *Love and Let Love* trotted out his best table linen for a lady who did.

The Grass Harp got under way with a fight over the family dinner table and resolved its problems by having everybody go on a picnic.

In *Lo and Behold* the principal character committed suicide in the only way that is acceptable nowadays—by overeating. *Legend of Lovers* took place in a restaurant—one of the characters kept stirring flyspecks into her coffee, introducing a rather sordid note into a dramatic form which is obviously concerned with the robust good health of its participants—and *Dark Legend* played a somewhat subtler game by placing its action in the back of a bakery. Even so, we were offered frequent glimpses of bread dough being shoved into an oven, and if the play had run longer the management might have worked up a tidy sideline supplying the other houses on Broadway with their nightly nourishment.

Even Socrates, at least as conceived by Maxwell Anderson, did a good deal of his thinking while strolling around the Greek festal board, and *Barefoot in Athens* left you with the decided impression that Xanthippe's principal problem with the old boy was getting him to shut up and sit down to a decent meal.

If *The Fourposter* did not belong on our season's list, it was because the author obviously lost his head in deciding to play the entire piece in a bedroom. Roger MacDougall, who wrote *To Dorothy, a Son*, behaved a great deal more shrewdly in similar circumstances. Given a pregnant heroine, confined to her bed, he was careful to move the girl (and bed) just slightly offstage, so that we might spend the evening watching the husband rush edibles across the stage and into the sanctuary. He was undoubtedly faced with a hard choice: would the audience rather see the principal female character or the line of supply? He chose according to the present rules of the game, and if his play was a failure it was surely for other reasons.

One of the year's casualties, though, may have failed because of a too insistent appetite. That would be *The Chase*. Horton Foote's melodrama was about an escaped criminal who had sworn to get the sheriff who sent him up. But for eight long scenes he didn't seem to do much of anything about it. A lot of people, including some of the critics, wondered why. I know why. That criminal was hungry. Every time you saw him he was eating.

Whenever the action shifted to the desperado's hideout, and the play began to build up a little suspense, nutrition would set in. With a crash of the cabin door, old greedyguts would burst into the room, wipe the muck of the roads from his forehead, curse the sheriff roundly three or four times, vow vengeance, and then ask his wife for something to eat. Each time his wife would reply that they didn't have nuthin' to eat—this was a brave but futile effort on her part to keep the play going—but after she'd been slapped around a bit she'd give in and manage to rustle up something for her man. If I remember correctly, he was still chawing away at a crust of bread when the sheriff surrounded the place and polished him off. There would seem to be times when too much emphasis on the staff of life tends to sap, rather than replenish, a man's vitality.

Just how the modern theater became so embroiled with table manners I don't know. The whole thing probably stems from our concern with realistic behavior, but even real people must have something more on their minds than getting their three squares a day. In any case, the protein intake is terrific.

It is also, I think, a little misguided. While no one wishes to begrudge an actor his sustenance in these parlous times, it might be interesting to see him make a gesture that did not have a knife or fork on the end of it. And I have another problem. Along about the end of the second act I get awfully hungry myself.

I will make one exception, though: Helen Hayes nibbling at a doughnut in *Mrs. McThing*. Now there was a scene.

4

THE PSYCHIATRISTS are in trouble. It's getting so that no Broadway show can afford to be without one, and at first glance you'd think that a noble profession might well feel honored at the attention dramatists have been giving it. Psychiatrists have turned up as part of the actual scenery in *The Teahouse of the August Moon, The Caine Mutiny Court-Martial, The Seven Year Itch, Oh, Men! Oh, Women!* and dozens and dozens of other highly admired plays. One highly unadmired comedy of a season or so ago based its entire plot machinery on the distressing news that the hero's favorite psychiatrist had suddenly passed on to the great big couch in the sky; and when there isn't a large-as-life practitioner in the cast of characters nowadays the figures who are present simply analyze one another.

But let's stick with the bona-fide analysts who do turn up. They're an unstable crew, the lot of them. In *The Teahouse of the August Moon,* for instance, an Army psychiatrist is dispatched to an Okinawan outfit that has gone disastrously native. The idea is that he's to straighten out whatever mental kinks have turned our occupation forces into easygoing Orientals. In a trice, though, he has gone native himself, chucked his textbooks and taken up gardening, lost himself in a passionate romance with the admirable earthworm.

In *The Seven Year Itch* there was a bumptious and fidgety analyst who knew enough about his trade to spot other people's difficulties in the twitch of an eyelid. He was, however, in a fairly alarming condition himself. As he noted in his little book, he was given to the kind of mental lapse that indicated a strong tendency to uxoricide, and we hadn't known him long before he was making plans to see his own psychiatrist.

Two professional gentlemen appeared in *The Caine Mutiny Court-Martial* as skilled witnesses in Captain Queeg's defense. They were, it developed, only a shade less distressing than the distressing Captain Queeg. One of them was splendidly insecure, the other gently verging on megalomania. Both, of course, were left in shreds by an astute, and presumably uncomplicated, trial lawyer.

Oh, Men! Oh, Women! just about finished off the youngest medical profession altogether. Here the practitioner was examined in his romantic relationships, an area in which he ought to have been informed, confident, and commanding. By the time author Edward Chodorov had put him in touch with no more than two quite normal women, he was to be seen tearing his hair, pounding the back of his neck, and quivering balefully as he collapsed onto the nearest couch (his own).

In short, the contemporary psychiatrist is a bundle of nerves who needs sympathetic attention, professional advice, and rest. That's how the theater sees him, anyway. In all the case studies lately logged on Broadway there has been only one medical character who seemed in reasonably sound shape. He was the venerable old analyst who wandered in from time to time during *Oh, Men! Oh, Women!*, and a more forlorn little figure would be hard to imagine. You felt that he knew no experienced theatergoer was going to believe in him, that he didn't really belong in this play at all, and that he had better go manufacture himself a neurosis if he wanted ever to set foot on a stage again.

If the psychiatrist has become a standard fixture in the drama of the Fifties, he has also become a standard comic fixture. Audiences may leap to the couch by day; by night they want only to laugh at it. There's probably a Freudian explanation for all this. Each of us is secretly fearful that he is due to be haled into the waiting room any minute; laughter is a kind of protective mumbo-jumbo for warding off the evil day.

And there are probably simpler explanations. The profession has, among other things, a wonderful jargon; nothing is so dear to the dramatist's heart as a jargon he can parody.

The profession also has, of necessity, a certain godlike posture. If the analyst is going to be of any use to anybody, he had better seem all-knowing and all-wise. But he has, without thinking, played right into the comedian's hands. Nothing is so tempting as a man puffed up. Give off the faintest air of infallibility and you are going to be surrounded by alert humorists, armed with pins, cheerfully prepared to let the air out.

More seriously, though, the amiable skepticism with which the craft is treated suggests to me that psychiatry has not quite established, in the popular mind, its claim to scientific stature. Our comedies aren't exactly harsh with the bumbling analysts; they seem to have a certain wry affection for them, perhaps even a hope that some day they'll amount to something. But they do seem to be saying that psychiatry, as a science, is still a little unsure of itself.

Regular medicine, in case anyone has forgotten, had to go through the same lively initiation at the hands of the theater. Time was—before medicine had quite grown up—when the presence of a doctor in the cast of characters guaranteed an evening of good, low fun. Molière rarely wrote a play without paying backhanded tribute to that band of busy gentlemen he regarded as quacks; on two or three occasions he devoted the entire evening to lambasting the tribe. Molière was, in fact, happiest when he could invent a goop of a woodcutter, have him mistaken for a medical man, and have him pass blithely through the society of the day without anyone's noticing the difference.

Medicine lived it all down, though. Hardly a play is now written in which the family practitioner, or the expensive surgeon, isn't wise, kind, and a comfort. As far as that goes, hardly a play is now written in which an ordinary doctor appears at all.

Have faith, psychiatrists. Hang on.

❧ 5 ❧

I HAVE SPENT several years pretending not to notice, but there are some ugly truths that must finally be faced and I guess this is one of them. The dramatic heroine, like the real-life woman on whom she is modeled, has got completely out of hand.

Time was when a man could twist a woman's wrist with some confidence that she would buckle prettily, breathe softly for a moment or two, and then gaze up at him with shy surrender in her eyes. Nowadays he is lucky if he gets his arm back in one piece.

Time was when a man did all the leering, stalking and sibilant whispering in a romantic encounter. Nowadays he is lucky to get out of his corner before he hits the canvas.

These things have, of course, been true in the social sense for some time, all of Mlle Simone de Beauvoir's pretty protestations to the contrary. But the theater, being a form of fiction, fancifully pretended otherwise. Since most plays are written by men, the dramatic hero tended to hold his own. The theater kept face.

No longer. The first blow was struck by the presumably fragile, superficially winsome heroine of *Dial M for Murder*. At first sight, this lady seemed a flower of some delicacy. She looked destructible. When two virile, intelligent, and resourceful men set out to destroy her, you rather imagined they would be able to do it.

One of them was an athlete, presumably still in training. The other was a remarkably sinister-looking fellow whose shoulder span could not have been entirely the creation of his tailor and who was furthermore equipped with that old-fashioned badge of ruthless male superiority—the mustache. In the old days, a man with a mustache would have made short work of the whole business.

In *Dial M*, however, the male contingent didn't have a chance. It wasn't just that those two brainy gentlemen were doomed to lose a battle of wits with the lady. One of them—the bigger and more sinister one—was foolhardy enough to engage in physical combat.

Everything was in his favor. The room was dark. The lady didn't know she was in danger. He was armed, she defenseless. You could see why the man was willing to enter such a contest, why he even conceived the possibility of his coming out of it alive. He struck.

Two minutes later, as you may or may not remember, he was shapelessly sprawled on the living-room rug, dead as chivalry. The modern odds were against him.

I am inclined to suspect, by the way, that this turn of events was one of the real reasons for the immense popularity of *Dial M for Murder*. Normally, it is the woman of the house who decides what entertainments she and her husband are going to enjoy. Women were only too happy to drop in on *Dial M* and to bring their husbands with them. Something about the play struck them as being profoundly true, profoundly admirable. Author Frederick Knott had been a canny man.

As for less murderous relationships between the sexes, both *Picnic* and *The Seven Year Itch* made it perfectly clear that a man is safe nowhere these nights—not in his own securely bolted apartment, certainly not in somebody else's back yard.

In the aforementioned play, muscular Ralph Meeker was never exactly tied to a railroad track by the passionate spinster who had a thirst for him, but he wasn't spared much, either. He was cased judiciously, ogled invitingly, all but surrounded by the pantherlike wench who paced the hot summer earth, preparing to spring.

If you thought she wasn't going to spring, you were simply out of touch with current developments. Mr. Meeker, a tower of puzzled strength, optimistically stood his ground, only to find himself clutched, clawed, and relieved of his shirt—it came away in great shreds as the lass found she could not keep her hands off him—and I must confess I felt a moment of genuine concern for Mr. Meeker's emotional future.

This sort of thing has shaken several men of my acquaintance; it has been known to set up mental blocks of one sort or another; and I was subsequently much cheered to discover Mr. Meeker, his aggressiveness restored, making off with the ingénue on his own terms.

It was once customary for notoriously forward women to drop an occasional glove by way of striking up a chance, though possibly productive, acquaintance. In *The Seven Year Itch* the up-to-date flirt dropped a thirty-pound flowerpot, narrowly missing her love-light's skull. This led to an intimate association, though not until after the hero had virtuously barred his door and the female, hammer and saw in hand, had cut a hole in the roof in order to get at him.

In *The Deep Blue Sea*, an idyll which graced our stages briefly, it took a heroic ex-aviator all of three acts to disengage himself from the octopuslike grip of a ferociously determined female who, for mysterious reasons never yet explained, was supposed to elicit our deep pity. In *Can-Can* a gentlemanly Peter Cookson worked nightly to fend off a literally irresistible blowtorch named Lilo, the while he narrowly scanned the wings to make sure that, come the worst, there was some avenue of escape.

Not that there haven't been telltale signs, over quite a long period, that this thing was coming. Bernard Shaw was under no illusions as to how matters would work out.

In *Misalliance*, which he wrote in 1910, he caused his heroine to advance frontally on a quailing male, to batter down the male's earnest protestations that he would do nothing improper, and to chase him through a greenhouse until he was suitably exhausted. For good measure, the far-seeing playwright threw in an enchantress whose stock in trade was the half-nelson: the male who crossed her was flipped to the floor with ladylike dispatch.

In 1910 all this was prophecy, and no doubt part of Shaw's shock value. In its revival in the 1950s it nestled comfortably into the contemporary scene.

The next generation? A theoretically respectable and, they tell me, quite harmless enterprise known as *Time Out for Ginger* informed us that the female adolescent was now taking up football. With this prospect in mind I hardly know what to tell my growing sons.

At the moment, the "second sex" is second to none.

TEN

Clowns

～ *1* ～

WHEN BEATRICE LILLIE isn't working in someone else's revue, which is quite often, she takes out her ballroom fan, her high-heeled boots and her favorite zither and goes romping around the country—winter and summer—in a one-woman show.

The fan is strictly for educational purposes; Miss Lillie wants us to understand its various romantic, ribald and refined uses. The boots are for an occasional clog dance, in case the urge overtakes her. The zither is meant to accompany certain not very discreet, and certainly not very authentic, folk ballads which the artiste has overheard in some decidedly shady nook.

Which of these—or a dozen other—exercises in the magnificently irrelevant is the funniest of Miss Lillie's social lapses, I shall not venture to say. You no sooner begin to feel, as you go back year after year, that Miss Lillie has surely exhausted her improbable repertory of ladylike leers and hollow, glissando laughter than she cocks what seems to be an altogether new eyebrow at you and you're off again—hurtling into the aisle.

Instead of fading with age, Miss Lillie's most familiar materials continue to seem impromptu.

I am not going to be so foolhardy as to try to explain the durability, the apparently indestructible spontaneity of the *diseuse's* severe yet graciously forgiving style. (Miss Lillie always forgives you for laughing at her; she is a genius at smoothing things over.) But there are at least two things that may be mentioned as contributing to that perennial first-time feeling.

One is the fact that the star is always at least as surprised as you are that she has said anything funny. She is not simply surprised; she is astonished. Clearly the whole thing has been a hideous mistake— nothing could have been farther from her mind than that last peculiar note that popped out of her—and you know that she goes back into a song, or a sketch, with a simple determination that no such nonsense will happen again.

Miss Lillie is past-mistress of the inadvertent, eternally convincing in her innocence. When she decides to pound her fist into her palm for emphasis, only to discover that her muff has slipped down and completely obliterated the palm, or when she proceeds to make a graceful gesture with a scarf only to discover that she is standing on it, she is honestly caught short by the bizarre mishap, appalled that such gaffs should mar the sedate, demure beauty of her present undertaking. She asks you to share her incredulity with her, and she flashes you a sweet little smile of agreement, suggesting that we all pass over the incident without comment.

There is no conscious comedy in Miss Lillie's work, no trace of calculation in that bland, bright face. Though she is a knowing comedienne, she never lets you know what she knows.

It is, of course, this spectacular ingenuousness that enables the lethal lady to indulge in occasional ribaldries without any notable lapse of taste. If you choose to extract a *double-entendre* from the cultural pursuit at hand, that, you are given to understand, is your business; Miss Lillie is occupied with more serious things.

Another of the qualities that keeps the star's work from ever running thin is its remarkable economy. Beatrice Lillie does not wear you down with a barrage of small effects. She bides everybody's time. She sings two, four, six lines of a roundelay without so much as a wayward gesture or the tiniest intimation that she may yet have trouble with her voice. Then she lets you have it. But by now there is no need for an obvious haymaker. The lightest nuance will serve to release the intense comic expectation she has built up.

Because she is never panicked into profusion, as lesser comedians often are, she is able to spread her choicest devices over a vast array of very similar songs, with a special fillip held in reserve for each. At 10:30 of an evening—or three years later—she is still inventive, and when she chooses to deal with a frenzied tenor who is swirling about the stage in a melodrama cape and bellowing "Come into the Garden, Maude" by simply standing still and staring at him in profound, silent distrust, she is as calmly and unpredictably funny as she was at her most sibilantly vocal.

Nancy Walker is another matter. Miss Walker's specialty is not grace but gloom. With increasing frequency in recent years, this contemptuous Cassandra has walked onto a stage with malice in her heart, murder in her eye, and eyelashes long enough to sweep up the debris. She never comes to praise a subject but to bury it. Nor does it in the least matter what the subject is: a wandering little revue-sketch in which she plays a matron who has just won fifty thousand dollars for a prize cupcake, or a brittle Noel Coward tea biscuit in which she has no business playing at all.

She just ambles in, her hip joints not quite comfortable in their sockets, to glance at the unfamiliar terrain and to let us know that, whatever it is, she hates it. Her relationship to any given environment may be puzzling indeed. But her attitude is clear: trust nobody, expect the worst, walk through the world with a shrug on your shoulders and a glorious despair in your heart. Because she is absolutely secure in her own misanthropy, she can never make a mistake.

She does not use a rapier. She uses the long, low moan, the expressive sag, the suggestion that life itself is much too futile for an intelligent person to be dealing with. She is willing to see the whole mess through. She is, in fact, prepared to give it the last ounce of her failing energy. But she's not going to kid anybody: no matter what you accomplish tonight, things are going to be just as rough and just as unreasonable tomorrow.

Miss Walker is not simply a skilled vaudevillian primed with artful devices for startling you into hilarity. She is a philosopher, perhaps the last of them: the whole thing, from Plato on down, is a washout.

Bert Lahr still hopes. Cast as one of the tramps in Samuel Beckett's deliberately, forlornly empty *Waiting for Godot*, he kept his trousers up with a knotted cord and his spirits up—from time to time—with sudden lyric intuitions that life might turn out to have a meaning on the day after tomorrow.

He tugged, in earnest desperation, for a very long time at a shoe that was much too tight. Eventually he got it off. When it came off, rapture itself spread over Mr. Lahr's face, over the great gray-blue background that suggested a vacant universe, and over the whole auditorium—all in a single sigh. Delight was born before our eyes, flesh became something felt absolutely, and living began.

Living began again, a few minutes later, in the clown's fierce joy in a carrot. He looked at the object lovingly, spiritually on his knees before it. When asked what it was that so dazzled him, his simple, ecstatic "It's a carrot!" spelled out in an instant his relief that miracles were going to go on happening, his deep satisfaction with a world so glorious to the touch. He ate the carrot rhapsodically, too.

Over and over again as Mr. Beckett's cerebral tennis match returned serve after serve without changing the score, this crumpled descendant of the very first goat found a bleat, a whinny, or a toss of his chin to throw into the game and give it the tang and the echo of actual, earthy experience. His anticipatory chuckle as he begged to be told a funny story he had heard before, his forcibly raised eyebrows as he positively assured himself that he was happy— these were the rhythms of an artist with an eye for God's own truth.

And all of them, I think, were the rhythms of musical comedy, of revue, of tanbark entertainment, suggesting that Mr. Lahr has, all along in his own lowbrow career, been in touch with what goes on in the minds and hearts of the folk out front. Whatever sickening void Mr. Beckett was proposing as the natural habitat of man, humanity hovered like a halo around the crossed eyes and crossed fingers of Mr. Lahr.

He did not sentimentalize the role, however. He knew what lay beneath it. Just once in the evening Mr. Lahr permitted himself to become caught in the claws of a hopelessness so sudden and so constricting that his great clown's face was wrenched and contorted into a visible cry far too intense to be made verbal: his agony, inexplicable as a baby's, was one of the most disturbing emotional images to take hold of, and shake, the contemporary theater.

But that was beneath the role. Mr. Lahr was on top of it.

Victor Borge is simply and superlatively an entertainer and I don't expect to see him playing *Othello* or even Noel Coward in the near future. I expect to see him, however.

After three full evenings spent watching him smile, mutter, fume, talk to himself, and stammer through inconclusive anecdotes about non-existent subjects the while he slashed at the keyboard, the strings, and even the lid of his piano, I am a hopeless convert. I've met people who didn't like Victor Borge, and for a while I even continued to speak to people who didn't like Victor Borge. No longer. From now on they go their way, I go Borge's.

The Danish wag with the sober face, diffident manner, and sublime distaste for half the music he plays is a specialist in the *non sequitur*. It doesn't help any to quote his jokes. He explains, for instance, that a number he is about to play was written in four flats because the composer had to move four times, and I'm sure nothing could look paler on paper. He goes on about a grandfather of his who invented a burglar alarm but unfortunately had it stolen from him, or about an aunt who invented a cure for which there was no disease—and these may read just a little bit brighter.

No, I guess they don't.

But the essential Borge is the Borge who never quite says a gag out loud, who never quite lets you get a good stern look at it, who never lets a laugh hang around long enough for it to diminish. He is, of all things, self-effacing. You can come or go as you wish; he's going to play the next concerto, anyway.

In his one-man appearances, Mr. Borge enters in evening dress, to welcome us all to New York (or whatever city he happens to be visiting and we happen to be living in). The lights dim as he turns to the piano. They dim so much, in fact, that Mr. Borge has great difficulty in seeing the keyboard. He now plays "The Blue Danube" upside down. It's almost better that way. He spends five minutes trying to drive the "Third Man Theme" out of the theater, or at least out of his instrument, with no success whatever. He poises a pencil and pad, asks for requests from the audience, and, while these are coming from all parts of the house, writes a note to his mother. He considers giving in to a shouted demand ("In spite of the many requests I have had for this number, I'm only going to play it once"). If he does oblige a patron by playing "Liebestraum," not a movement of the work escapes his infinite and very voluble loathing. ("Junk!" he snarls as he crashes out a chord, despising the whole thing with his hands, his face, his soul.) And once in a while he just plays, without comment. It's very peaceful.

Yet the artist cannot keep his mind on any one project for very long. Tiring of a concerto after something less than two bars, he will rise to read a bit of Shakespeare with all of the punctuation clearly pronounced. He will express his sorrow over the death of a composer and then, in a *sotto voce* transition, consign him to hell with a shrug. He will tell you about a friend of his who invented 4-Up, 5-Up, 6-Up, and died a discredited failure ("He never knew how close he came").

The variety of things capable of distracting Mr. Borge's attention

is inexhaustible. The fact that he can spend a whole evening inter-
rupting himself, and sustain nearly every moment of it on a level
of high hilarity, is incredible. But there it is—the incredible behaving as though it were the most offhand thing in the world. Cool,
commanding, and awash in *savoir-faire*, Mr. Borge is master in his
own asylum.

I don't see how serious playwrights could bring themselves to
write for a theater that didn't have its quota of life-giving clowns.

⌒ 2 ⌒

THIS IS a love letter, some years late. But if I don't get it off now, it
may come altogether too late to do anyone much good. The curator
of the Museum of Modern Art film library will tell you that the
print of Buster Keaton's *The Navigator* is wearing out. Unless an
additional print can be uncovered in some unlikely vault, or unless
a great deal of money is forthcoming to make possible a transfer
onto fresh stock, no one is ever again going to see one of the two
or three best films Keaton made. No one is ever again going to see
one of the funniest—albeit one of the shortest—sustained shots in
the history of the films. Keaton is the object of this love letter.

Buster Keaton is by no means forgotten. A so-so movie has
been made about his life. As I write, he still turns up at intervals
on television shows. Sometimes, as in his joint shows with Ed
Wynn, he is very funny. Rather more often he is provided with
materials so little suited to him, so little aware, even, of what his
precise talents are, that one senses only the struggle of a desperate
man to cope with a medium which he cannot command. Keaton
has also done work, from time to time, on comedy sequences for
Red Skelton films, and I suspect that he is a principal reason why
Red Skelton films, from time to time, have suddenly turned funny.

To complete the latter-day record, Keaton has appeared in Parisian circuses and the British provinces, always with some success, and in a five-minute bit toward the end of Chaplin's *Limelight*.

When you see him, or think of him nowadays, you group him with three or four other silent-film clowns who lived in the shadow of Chaplin, satellites all, second-stringers. He is lumped together with Lloyd and Langdon and even—as in a *Life* spread of several years ago—with Ben Turpin.

This was Keaton's fate even in his heyday. While there can be no doubting the genius of Chaplin and his supremacy over every other clown of his age, Keaton not only ran behind Chaplin in artistry but behind Lloyd in popularity. He always had to come in third and maybe, during that brief time when Harry Langdon seemed on the way up, fourth. As nearly as I can remember—and I *can* remember—the general critical opinion in the Twenties was that Lloyd, as a comedian, had *character*, whereas Keaton, with his frozen face, merely exploited a trick.

How time reverses the judgments of a generation, once the special interests of the generation have been washed away, is quickly seen by comparing the films of Lloyd and Keaton today. Lloyd was more nearly the trick. To a talent for sight gags and physical daredeviltry, plus an extraordinarily astute feeling for structure, he added only one "character" value: the glasses. But he was lucky. The glasses, superimposed on what was actually an aggressive personality, exactly corresponded to the mood of the moment, to the popular American notion of what a popular American was: Grandma's boy making good, Horatio Alger on the stock market, the shy kid from the backwoods making everybody sit up and take notice. America liked to think of itself, in those days, as innocent but able, young and gawky but damned successful. Lloyd was its image of itself.

Looking at a Lloyd film today, one is still impressed by the comedian as mathematician: the variety of physical gags he could wring out of a given assortment of props remains astounding. The acrobatics on window ledges have the same vitality, though it is a fundamentally characterless vitality, they always had. But whatever it was that made us idolize Lloyd, that bred affection over and above simple laughter, is hard to remember. We look at the man without very much recognition. The American image of itself has altered too profoundly in the intervening years for us to make spontaneous connection with this figure who was once so appealing, and Lloyd is somewhat trapped—as art, in its universals, is never trapped—in a passing phase. Keaton emerges the artist.

It must have been easy to underrate Keaton. He was also an acrobat, had in fact come from a family of acrobats. His frozen face—a technique we would describe, and dismiss, as "deadpan" today—may well have seemed merely circusy, unsubtle, an expressionless mask designed to remove all trace of character and to rivet attention on the broader contortions of his body. Keaton had absolute muscular control—the kind of control that permitted him to run headlong in a given direction, stop on a dime, and then run headlong in the opposite direction without ever seeming to have turned around—and this, with the face blanked out, must have seemed his chief accomplishment.

It wasn't. The mask had a meaning, it stood for something. It stood for stubbornness in the face of a tricky, hostile and oversized universe. It had something to do with the dogged determination—of all men, everywhere—that fire, flood and pestilence should never best them. This mask expects trouble. It never smiles because it knows that the universe is waiting to sneak up on it, and it cannot afford to be caught off balance. It is poised and ready to deal with an eternal, implacable and mindless enemy—the physical universe itself, whether it be represented by a recalcitrant deck chair, a locomotive out of control, or a crewless ship drifting endlessly and senselessly across an indifferent ocean.

Behind the mask is an alert mind. It is a suspicious mind which expects the worst and is constantly on the *qui vive* against the next unpredictable, but inevitable, blow. But it is not a panicky mind; it is in full control of itself, unwavering, sturdy. When the blow falls, neither the mind nor the body recoils in terror. The man stands there and waits. The universe may be crashing about him, but he is immobile, perhaps a little hurt, but not at all in a hurry. He cannot be rushed, he cannot be thrown. The face betrays no surprise, no pain, no plan. Then suddenly the body goes into action, diving at—or ingeniously around—the enemy, without warning and without apparent preparation. The mental process has been concealed from both the enemy and the audience—from the enemy so that the move cannot be anticipated and countered; from the audience so that its delight in the next piece of ingenuity shall be multiplied a thousandfold by suddenness and surprise.

Another comedian will show a gleam in his eye, put his face through a knowing, anticipatory grimace, before he acts. And he will get a certain suspense out of this, will help "build" toward the gag. Keaton stops dead, counts ten, then fuses the intellectual and the physical activity into a single explosive moment. The intellectual and physical *tenacity* of man in the face of hopeless odds is made into a universal characterization, and an unbelievably funny one.

Nothing escapes Keaton. He is not only alert to danger; he is fully aware of every conceivable departure from order and sanity. In *The General* he is in love with a conventional ingénue. There is really nothing to distinguish her from any other ingénue—she is sweet, pretty, helpful. When, in the course of her helpfulness, she sweeps out the tender of a locomotive with a broom or attempts to stop an oncoming freight train by tying a rope between trees across the tracks, she is only being helpful in a rather idiot feminine way. Keaton will do anything for her. He will steal a locomotive which is being thoroughly guarded, he will drive it behind enemy lines, he will expose himself to shellfire, he will risk his neck in a thousand ways. He adores her. Toward the close of the picture there is a pause in the action. Keaton turns toward her, the familiar uncommunicative expression on his face. Then he shakes the hell out of her. The incident is never referred to again. It alters their relationship not one bit. The picture goes on. I am not sure that I wouldn't swap the bun dance in *The Gold Rush* for this single flash of what is not slapstick at all but simple genius.

Nor are the acrobatics a mere embellishment, as they frequently are with Lloyd. Lloyd's *Safety Last* could have a dozen other climaxes appropriate to the character. Dangling from a clock many stories above a city street is not essential to Grandma's boy making good. This is a "thrill" finish to a story that might have been resolved, as *Grandma's Boy* itself is resolved, without recourse to stunting. Keaton's physical adroitness is necessary. His enemy is the physical, material universe. He must meet it on its own terms, must outwit it in direct combat. He must have a body able to do what his brain tells it to do if he is to survive a head-on clash with an adversary that is both monstrous and witless. This body is not supple for the sake of suppleness, a mere demonstration of flexibility. It is a responsive body which works with economy and precision to a purposeful end. It strikes up a tense relationship with matter—a kind of precarious dominance—which, because it is meaningful, is also in a real sense beautiful. Keaton poised in the rigging of a ship, a spyglass to his eye, tells his whole story: that foot is going to slip, the telescope is going to show him nothing; but in the present balance there is such grace, courage and ingenuity that you know the man to be indomitable. There is another characteristic Keaton shot that still turns up in film anthologies: he is standing backward on a horse, staring at the horizon, while the horse indifferently nibbles grass. I am not prepared to say exactly *what* this one means, aside from the usual coupling of steadfastness with insecurity. I only know that around our house we use this picture as a test of our friends; you either break up at the mere sight of it, or you don't get invited back.

My own rediscovery of Keaton came late, and I was dubious about it. I saw all of his films when I was a kid—I go right back to the two-reelers and a parody of Griffith called *Three Ages*—and I liked them. But they never seemed to be the smashes of their respective years. I remember the first time I saw *The General*. It was certainly a good film, but it wasn't a sensational film. It seemed to be one more or less successful comedy among a number of others that season. A few years ago, through the services of the Museum of Modern Art, I saw *The General* again. I couldn't believe my eyes. It not only hadn't dated; it was funnier than it had been the first time.

But I didn't trust myself. I figured I was succumbing to nostalgia, dating myself, yearning back to the Saturday afternoons of my youth. I was teaching in a university at the time and had a good excuse for running off a Museum of Modern Art film series for my students. I put them through it. I showed them Langdon, and they were mostly mystified: there were nice details, but had this man ever been thought a major comedian capable of sustaining a full-length film? I showed them Lloyd, and they were interested—not carried away, but interested. They jotted down a few points of gag technique in their notebooks and let it go at that. I showed them *The General*. *The General* starts slowly, and I began to think that, yes, it was a matter of nostalgia on my part. Then, after a reel or so, the notebooks were forgotten; they were, in fact, scattered all over the floor. This audience, composed of graduate students a few of whom had heard of Keaton but none of whom had actually seen him at work, was hopelessly convulsed. For an hour and thirty minutes—while Keaton passed an entire enemy army without noticing it, while Keaton struggled to maneuver a cannon silently bent on reverting in his direction, while Keaton led a battle charge with a bladeless sword—this audience forgot that it was looking at a twenty-year-old film and surrendered itself completely, even hysterically, to an authentic style and a timeless comic insight. *The General* was, quite literally, the funniest film these people weaned on talking films had ever seen.

Subsequently I tried *The Navigator* on them, with approximately the same results. *The Navigator*—in its own time perhaps the most successful of Keaton films—was made a good bit earlier than *The General*, and its relatively cruder technical quality sometimes mars the effect. There is, for instance, a nice gag inspiration in Keaton's underwater duel with a swordfish, but we have since learned to manage the mechanics of this kind of thing so much more smoothly that the sequence now seems a little effortful. On the other hand, the silent, rhythmic opening and closing of doors on a deserted and listing ship is a perfect piece of comic fantasy, and the Mack Sennett sequence in *High Button Shoes*—twenty-five years later—profited from the device without improving on it. *The Navigator* also contains what is, for me anyway, the funniest two minutes of film I have ever seen: a sustained shot in which the morose Keaton idly attempts to shuffle a deck of wet playing cards.

It is not much of a secret any more that screen comedy suffered an irremediable blow with the coming of sound. The best of the silent comedians—and Chaplin and Keaton were the best—learned how to exploit the silence imposed upon them, how to turn it into an advantage. They trained their expressive bodies to a fine point of style, made them the responsive instruments of a point of view. Much has been written about Chaplin's style, too little about Keaton's. The Museum of Modern Art, in its film footnotes, speaks of the "brilliance" of Keaton's style—an estimate it is impossible not to go along with once you have renewed acquaintance with the work —but in most quarters Chaplin is revered, Keaton forgotten. Keaton's point of view is as defined as Chaplin's, and every movement he makes, every frame of film in which he appears, belongs to it. If Chaplin was the little man doomed to be crushed, Keaton was the little man who *couldn't* be crushed. His best films have the uniform texture of Chaplin's. He was able to impress his personal outlook on those parts of the film in which he did *not* appear, to dominate and control the meaning of a film from its initial inspiration down to its tiniest detail. His imagination is everywhere stamped on the work: in the story, in the direction, even in the subtitles. The unity that followed from this practice of pursuing a single vision—the comedian's—raised the best silent comedies to a level of art no longer possible in the collaborative manufacture of the large studios. Hollywood became an assembly line, went in for piecework. Chaplin maintained his integrity, at a certain cost in technical proficiency, by holding onto his own studio and his own releasing organization. Keaton got lost in the vast shuffle of Metro-Goldwyn-Mayer.

A lot of Keaton is already gone for good. A laboratory fire wiped out his two-reelers and some of the early features, *Three Ages* among them. *The Navigator* may not be long for this world. Better hurry around next time the Museum is showing *The Navigator*, *The General*, or *Our Hospitality*. A great man is slipping away from you.

~ 3 ~

THIS IS PROBABLY nothing for a drama critic to be confessing, but I've never really been the same man since Buster Keaton stopped trying to shuffle his deck of wet playing cards, or since Harry Langdon stopped absent-mindedly holding up buildings with one hand.

I was the same man, though, the night Marcel Marceau made his first appearance in this country. The French mime walked out into a strong white light—his face and his costume a dead white, too— and began to walk up a flight of stairs that wasn't there.

Suddenly everyone who'd secretly felt that the circus clowns of his youth had been growing paler year by year, or that the dazzling magic of a curtain going up had somewhere lost a bit of its chilling suspense, saw his faith in practically everything restored. Marceau was the sort of theatrical gift that no one really deserved. To have asked for such perfection would have been presumptuous: you could only stare at it, believe it, and be thankful.

Marceau—who has since proved enormously popular in any number of return engagements—is prepared to offer you almost anything you like. He is, for instance, joyously funny—and very nearly without interruption. The first half of his solo program is usually composed of random sketches, and while it is skipping breathlessly from one to another you will find yourself unexpectedly doubling up over the image of an unlucky gambler putting a finger in his ear so that he will not hear the shot that blows his brains out, over the business of a fastidious customer wriggling his hands into a tight pair of gloves, over the tremors of a tightrope walker as he teeters his way into space.

M. Marceau acknowledges some sort of debt to Chaplin, and here and there you will discover reminiscent little grace notes: in the twitch of an upper lip, in the rapid nonsense of rubbing resin not only on a pair of skater's shoes but also into his armpits. As Marceau carries us over into the second half of the bill, though, and begins to deal exclusively with a character known as Bip, the wholly original inspiration that drives this zany becomes clear.

Bip—a wavering stalk with a long-stemmed flower soaring from the crown of his battered cap—is a careful observer of the professional world about him: he has seen painters paint, lion tamers tame, travelers hoist their baggage into narrow, jogging train compartments. He is ready to tackle each of these things with infinite grace, impeccable form; and he is due to fail so dismally that he must get down on his knees and plead with a lion to make a very small leap through a very low hoop. And nowhere is Bip more magnificent than in a non-stop, one-man contest between David and Goliath: a phantasmagoria of shepherd's pipes and gargantuan strides that turns the stage into a pinwheel of preposterous line drawings. (Good comedy is almost impossible to burlesque; this particular bit of antic brilliance, however, has been given a thoroughly successful once-over-deadly by an insufficiently appreciated comedienne named Dorothy Greener.)

The mime's talents are not confined to comedy, however. If the light tread of a balloonman is amusing in itself, there is considerable genuine beauty—of a serious kind—in the fall of this man's arm as he bestows a balloon on a child. If M. Marceau can make the embrace of two lovers a quick laughing matter, he can alter the mood in an instant by the simple tremble of an old man's chin. There is a variety, a complexity, and a richness of emotional form everywhere.

And perhaps the last and most curious thing this clown can do for his audience is to show it the whole theater standing alone on a little white box. He does it in a swirling pageant in a public garden. He does it again, most emphatically, in a very short but stunningly complete piece of visual poetry called "Youth, Maturity, Old Age, and Death." In the single, flowing rhythm with which he feels out and then finishes this imposing cycle—Death is no more than the unemotional drop of a swaying hand—M. Marceau really explains where the theater came from, why it is going to last for a very long time, and why we like it.

✎ 4 ✎

WHILE WE'RE on the subject of simple—or not so simple—fun, I'd like to say a word in defense of a fine old institution: the implausible, illogical, absolutely unintegrated musical comedy. At one recent opening I was whiling away those twenty or thirty minutes that elapse between the time Brooks Atkinson arrives at the theater and the time the management decides it has no other course but to take the curtain up, and I came across a canard, printed in the front of *The Playbill*, which aroused all my nobler, or at least my more rebellious, instincts.

Eugene Burr is the author of those chatty and comfortable essays that appear now and then in the weekly program, and I can't think he meant this one to be controversial. But there he was, picking on everything that had been perpetrated before *Oklahoma!*, undermining everything I had lived by in my formative years.

"It may be hard for modern theatergoers to realize," wrote Mr.

Burr, "but some twenty-five or thirty years ago musical productions
—even the hits—on Broadway were generally composed of tunes,
lyrics, comedy, and a set of fine performances from singers, dancers,
and clowns—and not much else." (Not much else? We want all
this and *Phèdre* too?)

Not that I mean to be the least bit captious about the later wonders wrought by Rodgers and Hammerstein—the sturdier stories
and richer lyrics and warmer backgrounds of the new dispensation.
Oklahoma! seems to me the best musical comedy I ever saw. But it
doesn't seem to me the funniest musical comedy I ever saw, and
nobody is going to make me renounce the special splendors of
watching Joe Cook stamp at a furry red animal unaccountably
traversing the stage floor, or Bobby Clark, draped in an old ban-
danna, kneading tortillas out of a wad of intractable dough.

My real objection to the rather lofty attitude now taken toward
such old-fashioned foolery is that, having happily embraced what
is new and exhilarating, we feel duty-bound to discredit what was
old and exhilarating. It wasn't enough to kill off the clowns; we
have to pretend that we never liked them much, anyway. Though
Mr. Burr is prepared to admit that these boys were "sometimes quite
funny," he goes on to insist that their zany enterprises "almost all
followed a single pattern—grimly, relentlessly and inevitably."

We are allowed no sneaking yen for the sort of plot in which
Victor Moore turned up as Public Enemy Number 13 (in case
you've forgotten, Mr. Moore was also a superstitious man, mightily
eager to dispatch one of his competitors so that he could become
Public Enemy Number 12). Instead we must swear undivided loyalty to the wholly plausible pieces which "stand as plays in their
own right," to musicals which are better because they are "believ-
able."

The trouble here is that we are busy kicking a dead old dog
because it didn't turn out to be something it never meant to be.
The kind of song-and-dance show we have come to scorn—and have
completely forgotten how to write—had a perfectly clear objective:
to be gaily, mockingly, blandly unbelievable. It wasn't trying to

wring your heart with a touching fable; it was trying to tell an out-rageous joke. It was, in fact, a form of satirical fantasy, with a cock-eyed integrity of its own, and I don't see why we had to bury it.

Maybe I've just been having too good a time with the memoirs of P. G. Wodehouse and Guy Bolton, a giddy rundown called *Bring On the Girls*.

The Messrs. Wodehouse and Bolton wrote more than their share of those idle musical inventions which distinguished, or at least characterized, the Twenties and Thirties, and they don't seem so much relics of a primitive age as reminders of a happily impudent one. Here they are planning an opening number for Fred and Adele Astaire:

> *The first scene of Act One showed the Astaires—play-ing brother and sister—thrown out with their few goods and chattels on the sidewalk. Adele, behaving as she un-questionably would have done in real life, arranged the fur-niture neatly about a lamp post, hung up a "God Bless Our Home" motto and with the help of a passing work-man—destined to become the hero—attached a percolator and fixed the hydrant so that water would be constantly available.*
>
> *After which, of course, it began to rain, and she and Fred did a number called "Hang On to Me," dancing together under a big umbrella.*

Now I don't want to swap that one for *South Pacific*. But I think I could sit through it with reasonable calm, and maybe even a secret affection. It might be that if I could catch *South Pacific* on Friday night and a bit of nonsense with the Astaires on Saturday night, I'd be a happier theatergoer today.

In any case, that home-on-the-sidewalk business comes from one sharply defined world, a world of prankish and quite deliberate im-probability. *South Pacific* comes from another. The one isn't an idiot younger brother of the other, or even a country cousin. They're simply two different species, and there's no reason under the neon why they need cancel each other out.

If the clowns and the hoofers have been summarily dismissed, it would be a mistake to view Rodgers and Hammerstein as the principal villains. Rodgers and Hammerstein write what they want to write, and there's no arguing the soundness of their private inspirations. The search for villains must center, I think, on all those other presumably creative people who might well be developing their personal bents—one of them might have a bright idea for Bobby Clark—but who feel that the only way to make money and influence audiences is to imitate the gents with the biggest hits.

Indeed, it's only when I'm drowsing through one of the drearier imitations of *Carousel* that I begin to reconstruct, most longingly, a fugitive scene in which a couple of Marx Brothers are searching for a stolen painting:

"It isn't in the house."

"Maybe it's in the house next door."

"There isn't any house next door."

"All right, we'll build one."

Whereupon we spend five excellent minutes planning the architecture for the house next door.

Anybody got a Marx Brother?

∽ ELEVEN ∾

Directors

∽ *1* ∾

SOME DAYS Shakespeare's own mother wouldn't know him. I am thinking, at the moment, of a production of *Troilus and Cressida* done up in hobble skirts and garlanded with grand pianos, elongated cigarette holders, and, for the hell of it, champagne cocktails.

As an old non-traditionalist, this sort of thing never bothers me. I could take Puck on a pogo stick if I had to, provided that the startling framework really did shock us into seeing the play itself with brand-new and wide-open eyes. There is indeed a danger in these scenic transpositions and special visions, the danger that a director's delight in repainting the superstructure will accidentally, or even wantonly, paint out something that truly belongs to the play. This did happen, in varying degrees, to a very funny light flirtation that Tyrone Guthrie once conducted with Pirandello's *Six Characters in Search of an Author* and to a beer-garden version of *Measure for Measure* that John Houseman and Jack Landau ground out for summertime consumption in Connecticut. But it's an attack that can be tolerated in the interests of freshness and simple fun.

What is much more difficult to digest, and keep down, is the sort of thing that recurs regularly in our time and has apparently been given another waltz around the floor at one of our more imposing Festivals. I've just been reading an account of a *Lear* in which the old boy was presented as something of a senile lech with an unhealthy attachment to his youngest daughter. The reason Lear gets so upset over Cordelia's refusal to say how much she loves him, and the reason he goes off his rocker shortly thereafter, is the fact that he has a secret and slightly unholy yen for the lass. That sort of thing.

We seem to be adept at spotting the embryo psychiatrist in Shakespeare, and if we aren't careful we're going to wind up *really* explaining Iago's duplicity by proving that he was passionately in love with Othello and just wanted Desdemona out of the way.*

Our new "explanations," however, create quite a few difficulties. One of them puts a strain on the actor. Since Shakespeare neglected to write our cherished implications into the passing scenes, the poor player must ogle them in, letting his eyes wander in odd directions between the inexplicit lines, huffing and puffing through specially conceived pantomime passages much as Sir Laurence Olivier was forced to do in order to demonstrate that Hamlet was Mother's boy to the end. It's a taxing procedure, and it leaves little energy for the speeches.

---

* I am behind the times. When this piece first appeared in print I was promptly informed that the contention had already been made in a reputable scholarly journal, and that—thousands of miles away—a notably cast British production had given the same thesis a thorough workout.

The new intuition also puts a certain strain on the play. There are a limited number of episodes that can be given the full off-to-Bellevue treatment, with the result that the body of the play seems to be composed of distracting, irrelevant, and positively old-fashioned straightforward emotion. It is always interesting, even fascinating, to see what a director can do to certain scenes with a little Freud at his command; the trouble with such a production is that only ten per cent of the evening is interesting.

There is, too, the little problem of stature. If Lear is sick, instead of stubborn, a bit of his majesty goes out of him. Reading a fever chart is not quite the same thing as watching the tragic downfall of a responsible man, and the scale of the enterprise tends to shrivel from a boldly pumping heart to an untidily dangling nerve end.

The business of "supplying" Shakespeare with meaning has become so troublesome of late that the distinguished and stimulating scholar Alfred Harbage has, in his *Theater for Shakespeare*, nerved himself to the point of suggesting that we stop interpreting the plays altogether and just say the lines.

While I have much more faith in directors and in directorial emphasis on a clarifying thread throughout the work than Mr. Harbage does, it may well be time for us to consider his proposal. If you can clear your head of *Hamlet* and then sit down and read *Hamlet*, a strange thing is apt to strike you. Hamlet doesn't seem quite the irredeemable invalid a hundred productions have made him. He seems rather like someone you knew at college who wanted the world to be too perfect.

Or take another case. I once knew a man who had built up a substantial business from scratch. He was an intelligent man who looked ahead and, when he was in his early seventies, he turned the business over to a group of carefully selected junior partners. The junior partners ran the business successfully, almost too successfully. The voluntarily retired older man suddenly found himself really retired, no longer consulted. His emeritus suggestions, which he found himself making more and more frequently, were listened to but not always acted on. All sorts of futile trouble followed. Our businessman had recognized the fact of change, had anticipated the need for change, but had not imagined that the change would diminish him personally. He had vacated the presidency but had expected that, spiritually, he would carry it with him. It seems to me that *Lear* is about something like that.

It may be necessary to "interpret" difficult plays. But interpretation need not be confined to our highly specialized, exceedingly contemporary, interest in abnormal psychology. There may still be such a thing as normal psychology.

～ 2 ～

W HILE WE ARE on the subject of Shakespeare, isn't it time someone drew up a little list of comic gambits that have by now done their duty in the service of Elizabethan lightheartedness and might profitably be laid to rest, or perhaps stamped on until they are good and dead?

Herewith some notes for just such a list:

Senility as a sure-fire laugh-getter. Shakespeare actually wrote a couple of doddering old goats into various of his plays, and they are—when they are not allowed to multiply too rapidly—rather charming. The mistake is to suppose that every acting company will be better for having six Justice Shallows staggering knock-kneed about the place. It's getting so that any character who isn't obviously an ingénue—you can always tell an ingénue by the fact that she is accompanied by another female who keeps saying "God ye good den, gentle coz"—is automatically thought to be funnier if he or she is played by an ague victim, palsied of hand, slavering of lip, sans eyes, sans teeth, sans everything. The reedy cackle of old-age voices is beginning to drown out the fife-and-drum music, and we can't have that.

The low-comedy servant as neglected poodle. If they don't come out of the old folks' home these days, they come out of the nearest kennel. That is to say, every character who is under one hundred and three years of age is presumed to be so full of the juices of life that he cannot stop his hair from growing. It has consequently grown right down over his eyes, his nose, and into his mouth.

This does occupy him, of course. He can spend vast amounts of time jutting out his lower lip and trying to blow the stuff out of his upper teeth, especially during those boring passages when somebody else is talking. And it leads to hilarious opportunities: since he never does succeed in clearing his line of vision, he is able to bump into another, similarly blinded, comic servant on the slightest provocation, or on no provocation at all.

He is also able to make an absolute bee-line for the nearest stage pillar and wham into it with unerring instinct, crashing into yet another one on the rebound. Between the tottering oldsters and the lurching Hairless Joneses of the current dispensation, the stage begins to resemble a game of blind-man's-buff played in the labyrinth of Minos.

The backside as art. The special delights of bumping do not end with head-on collisions. Nothing is tastier, it would seem, than the spectacle of two such clods as we have been talking about backing into a room by different doors, backing steadily toward each other on some miraculous radar beam of their own, and thumpingly ramming their rears together, whereupon they jump, scream, run in circles, and *then* collide head on.

Well, there is one bit of business that is fresher and more delectable than this. It is a law of Shakespearean comedy that the lusty hero, seeing the haughty heroine pass directly in his line of fire, must give her a hearty, playful whack on the farthingale. I have nothing against this law. I only wish that the hero might have the courage of his convictions and really clip the doll.

The way things are now he puts all his energy into the bright-eyed, toothy leer that precedes the effort, following through with a rather feeble whooshing of the general air in the vicinity and a respectful tap that no doubt keeps the actress from complaining to Equity but doesn't quite give her the cue for her leap. She leaps, as a result, either two seconds before or two seconds after the great swipe, giving the impression of having been independently stung by a bee. The lip-smacking satisfaction that the hero now takes in his accomplishment has a very hollow ring to it; he's kidding himself, that boy.

Noses. Putty noses in Shakespeare are determined by the following rule: the shorter the part, the longer the nose. There is obviously a kind of occult compensation operating here, and I hate to begrudge an actor the extra few seconds he gets onstage by having a sort of anatomical fanfare precede him, but surely the cost in make-up is a drain on this bit-player's income. Shouldn't he save up for Cyrano instead of squandering his wherewithal now?

Scrolls. I don't know who first passed the word down that any scroll of parchment used in a Shakespearean comedy must, when unleashed, be so long that it spills out over the desk and rolls endlessly across the floor. This was probably the invention of a man who was convinced (a) that not a word of the play was funny, and (b) that the only conceivable remedy was to devise a piece of distracting business so monumentally mirthless in its own right that the lines would seem bright by comparison.

As such, it was no doubt a crafty move. The only trouble is that we've caught onto it now and need a new red herring. How about having the hero put his boot to a low-comedy-servant's backside, send him bolting into the wings, turn away to pick up the conversation, and then be interrupted by a very late, very loud offstage crash? I'll bet that would be funny.

The unexpected re-entrance. This happens when a character takes his ostensible farewell, the other characters begin to go about their work, and the first joker comes back to renew the conversation. (It can, by the way, be repeated five or six times running; and it always is.) Actually—and secretly—I am a pushover for this piece of business, but for some reason or other I like it only in Molière, where it was written into the plays and may be thought of as part of the copyright. I guess the real reason I don't like it in Shakespeare is because I was honestly hoping that that fellow with one tooth missing and large black freckles on his face was never coming back.

But then I'm finicky about these things. I once saw a production of Shakespeare in which the principal comic wasn't over eighty-five, in which he didn't open his purse to let a moth fly out, in which he didn't go stamping all over the stage after the moth for a good five minutes, and it was wonderful.

~~3~~

STAGE DIRECTORS are chronically unhappy over the manner in which their work is treated by newspaper reviewers, and several have been heard to suggest that it might be better all round if the critics were simply to concentrate on the play and actors and forget about the direction altogether.

The complaint, for all its suggestion of bitterness, isn't a selfish one. Our directors aren't saying that they have been insufficiently praised, nor are they taking exception to the fact that the usual reference to their work is a cursory one embedded in the last few sentences of a review.

What gets them to biting their nails at night is the disturbing fact that the critic has no real means of knowing just how much of what he sees onstage was actually inspired by the director. His attempt to distinguish between script, star and staging is therefore bound to be a shallow bit of guesswork, if not a rude injustice to someone. Praise and blame are distributed without real knowledge of what has gone on at rehearsal, and a discreet silence might be preferable to probable error.

There is clearly a sound case to be made for this point of view.

What finally turns up in the theater is the result of an extremely complex collaboration, and—in a good production—it turns up with none of the stitches showing.

Since the reviewer has not read the manuscript in advance, he is in a poor position to say what the director has done to it. Since he has not, in fact, attended a single rehearsal, he is in no better position to know how much of an electrifying moment is the result of the actor's inspiration, how much the result of the director's guidance.

One of the most striking bits of stage business this reviewer ever saw was a flash of anger in a dowdy little play called *Harriet*. Helen Hayes had been playing Harriet Beecher Stowe all evening, and playing her gently. Suddenly, in a momentary disagreement with her beloved husband, she shot a clawlike fist toward his face, as though to rip it to shreds.

It was the only such moment in the play, it was even uncharacteristic of the general tone of the play, but, in its isolation, it was shockingly, brilliantly true. Who thought of it? The authors, who had shown no such insight elsewhere in the play? Miss Hayes, whose capacity for invention is high? Or Elia Kazan, the then young and up-and-coming director of the play? *

In *The Fourposter*, just as an anxious-father-to-be was about to run for the family doctor he paused to push a bassinet closer to his wife. Whose flair for fantastic comedy earned this laugh—author Jan de Hartog's, or director José Ferrer's? To stay with Mr. Ferrer for a moment, what about the long pantomime sequence with which he ended *The Shrike*? Was the entire passage indicated in Joseph Kramm's text, or was it richly amplified out of the actor's own intuition?

And these are only the most obvious of examples. The far more subtle and intricate processes of characterization—developed

---

* Miss Hayes tells me that it simply occurred to her during a rehearsal, and she did it. Now we know.

through untraceable labyrinths of give-and-take between performer and director—resist analysis even more strenuously. There are, I'm sure, a good many times when the director himself no longer remembers the origin of an effective line reading, a revealing gesture, an exciting emotional response.

The interplay of a dozen forces, with a good measure of happy and unhappy accident, goes into the shaping of even a few seconds' stage time. If the creative people involved can become confused about the dim beginnings of their joint work, how is an outsider to untangle these psychological crosscurrents some six weeks later—and do it without making a fool of himself?

I think these difficulties are perfectly real—up to a point. No reviewer can pretend to chart a thoroughly accurate, thoroughly knowing case history of any single production. But I am not sure that this admission necessarily closes the subject, or rules out the possibility of trying for a fair estimate of what each collaborator has contributed.

The trouble with the view outlined above is that it momentarily imagines each new theatrical venture as taking place in a vacuum, completely cut off from the past work of any of the people involved. It assumes, in effect, that the reviewer has never seen any of the performers before, that he has no knowledge of the playwright's earlier work, that the director is a total stranger—in short, that he is dealing with a bundle of utterly unknown quantities. And there are times, of course, when all of this turns out to be true; at such times the critic must tread gingerly indeed.

But most of the time—like almost any other constant theatergoer—he is busy making comparisons, adding up two and two. The constant theatergoer begins, after a while, to notice things. Having seen two or three Elia Kazan productions, let's say, he is pretty likely to notice that a certain animal vitality, an almost hysterical surface tension, and a markedly rhythmic pattern of eruption has crept into all of them.

Having been to a couple of Joshua Logan entertainments, he may begin to recognize a parlay of sustained stares, clockwork postures and delayed explosions which have a habit of turning single lines of dialogue into mushrooming two-minute laughs.

In time he may get to feeling very much at home with George Abbott's firm, emphatic, no-nonsense style, and he may eventually find himself counting the George Kaufman sight gags. If none of these gentlemen is exactly anonymous, it is because each writes his signature quite plainly across the stage—often with a flourish bold enough to invite parody.

Gradually the regular playgoer is apt to begin forming judgments as well. He may find himself thinking that Robert Lewis is happiest staging something one or two sizes larger than life, something that has been stylized well beyond genuinely realistic behavior; that Herman Shumlin has a wonderful way with a powerhouse melodrama but a heavy hand with a domestic comedy; that Harold Clurman's actors seem to have been nursed away from simple exhibitionism into complex, self-effacing, three-dimensional performance; that José Ferrer's four-line bit players are as sharply defined as his leads.

Nor is he necessarily confused about where the credit lies for an acting performance. He does not toss the whole bouquet for Lee Cobb's performance in *Death of a Salesman* at the feet of his director, because he has seen Mr. Cobb give too many first-rate performances under other auspices. Conversely, when he observes a player giving consistently dull performances under a dozen directors and then sees the same player shine briefly in the hands of Bretaigne Windust, he may feel reasonably justified in giving Mr. Windust the nod. Playwrights, too, blossom under certain directors, fade when managed by others, and the playgoer who has watched the process long enough must be forgiven if he starts figuring things out.

The reviewer, fortunately, has more than the materials of the moment to work with. He is himself engaged in a kind of collaboration with his own memories—both the vivid and the intolerable ones—and by balancing one experience against another he arrives at some sort of estimate of what has taken place. It may be necessary to keep the estimate tentative, and there is plenty of room for error; but I don't think the conclusions need be wholly unfair, nor the effort at making them abandoned.

∽ 4 ∾

THE *Herald Tribune's* Art Buchwald was interviewing Robert Morley one bilious winter's morning and Mr. Morley was having directors for breakfast. Mr. Morley, in case anyone on this side of the Atlantic has forgotten, is the enormous, pouting, and pop-eyed gentleman who has succeeded in making Oscar Wilde, Louis XVI, and various other affable monsters resemble him. He is a very good actor, of an almost extinct sort, and he has acquired the kind of behemoth stature that permits him to write, stage, and—for all I know—review the plays he appears in. As I say, he was swallowing directors whole:

> The latest danger to the theater is the new set of young American directors whose task it is to transform the theater into something of their own creation. . . . The curse of the American theater is the deference an actor pays a director. . . . Don't Americans realize a play does not need a director?

And so it went, the mincemeat dribbling all over Mr. Morley's expansive vest. (Mr. Morley does dribble; it's one of his points of style.) The odd thing about the whole headstrong pronouncement is that, in one very strict sense, it's true.

The theater got along very nicely without directors for approximately two thousand four hundred and thirty-five years. It's only in the last forty or fifty seasons, give or take a little, that we've tolerated the mastermind as an ultimate authority, and it's only in the American theater that the Kazans and Logans have become the dominant personalities that they are, putting their unmistakable seals on every aspect of production.

Poke around in the remaining records of the Elizabethan theater, for instance, and you won't find any large sums being paid off the top to a total stranger who's been asked to "shape" the proceedings. Shakespeare may have had a word or two to say to Burbage, and Burbage may have had a few more to say to the comedian who decided to scratch himself during one of the star's important speeches. But whatever got onto the stage got there by the mutual consent of the players, sans nursemaid.

Molière doesn't seem to have hired anyone to tell him what to do, and though the Greek theater undoubtedly needed a functionary to hold the chorus together, such legends as survive indicate that Sophocles himself performed the function. Somehow or other the past managed to squeak along without a succession of guiding geniuses, and the plays didn't lose much in the process.

Were the performances bad? Probably not. The directorless productions of other years were "saved" from chaos by one simple fact of theatrical life: most of the plays were performed by permanent acting companies. In a permanent acting company, temptation is at a minimum. You don't steal a scene from the leading actress if the leading actress happens to be your wife, or even the author's wife. You don't make a monkey out of a fellow performer if you're going to have to share a hotel room with him for the next six years, and you don't expand a juicy moment out of all proportion if at the very next moment the playwright himself is going to walk on to do a scene with you. You may, after a little experience at this sort of thing, learn when to give and when to take, when to listen and when to interrupt, when to make the most of a bit and when to help someone else to the dessert.

You may, in short, become quite adept at what is now called "ensemble playing," and, since your next part is probably going to come from the same hand that wrote this one, you will take some pains to see that the ensemble effect is roughly what the author had in mind. Given this dream world, who needs a director? It's a cozy picture.

The trouble—and this is what Mr. Morley has skipped—is that it no longer exists, certainly not in America. Gather thirteen actors to rehearse a new play and the chances are that eight or nine of them will never have met. Someone will have to perform the introductions, just to get the names straight. (The actors will take turns buying coffee during rehearsal breaks, in an effort to show that they are human, hospitable and bent on rapport.)

No one actor will know much about the performance habits of any other actor, and since he is quite busy with his own part he will have no time for that little life-study now. Someone will have to sit and watch and explain everybody's habits to everybody else.

No two members of the company will honestly expect to be working together again in the near future, and a throat cut along the way is simply one of those necessary exercises in professional advancement and a possible step toward the Clarence Derwent Award. (It is reported of one leading actress that she has never yet seen any part of any of her vehicles that did not call for her immediate presence onstage.) Someone will be needed to make sure that an actor does not win a prize and close the play in the same bold stroke.

And, since the playwright is now a dim and rabbity figure at the back of the auditorium who has never set foot on a stage in his life, someone will have to act as interpreter for him: explaining to him what the actors mean by "that line's a mouthful," and explaining to the actors what he means by "you can't cut those words because they're part of the rhythm."

The modern director, whatever libels may be hurled at him, has inherited a staggering series of leftover jobs. He is social director, bargaining authority, private secretary, paid informer, psychoanalyst, bodyguard, secret courier, marriage counselor, and private eye. He is the ladle that stirs a melting-pot, the Waring Blendor that reduces all those rugged individual carrots to a nice, unified pulp, and he is, in present theatrical circumstances, indispensable: he does what the actors can no longer possibly do for themselves.

Sooner or later the circumstances may change, in which case he's likely to be out of work once more. In the meantime, though, we'd better be kind to him.

I have only one other thought. The last time I was in London Mr. Morley was playing in a piece of his own partial devising, *Hippo Dancing*. In the course of this entertainment the actor was to be seen snorting, drooling, flipping, sagging, mussing his hair, disarranging his clothes, and in general behaving as though he were saying to a devoted public, "See what a mess I am—and you still love me!" I don't want to upset anybody, but I think he needs a director.

✂ TWELVE ✂

Actors

✂ *1* ✂

IT'S A COMMONPLACE to say that British acting is, on the whole, better than American acting. A couple of weeks spent strolling in and out of the London theaters—you don't have to scramble to get into a London theater, not even at the last minute—convinced me that the commonplace is true enough, provided the actor is pushing forty.

That is to say, English actors don't tumble from their cradles equipped with superb diction, faultless poise, and a flair for characterization. I think the legend supposes that they do: that just being born in Britain is a guarantee of professional competence, that the climate itself produces a steady supply of satisfactory King

Lears, that the rawest student at the Royal Academy has a kind of blood inheritance from Garrick and Betterton.

This is a pretty view of how stars are made, but it's not an accurate one. Young British actors can be quite as dull, and quite as hollow, as some of the earnest amateurs who produce plays much too big for them on the Broadway fringes. I have, for instance, seen companies at Stratford and at the Old Vic that were wondrously industrious and thoroughly uninteresting. The Memorial Theater that sits with red-brick bluntness on the bank of the Avon intermittently gives over the guest-star system and staffs its productions with ambitious newcomers. The idea is sound enough, but the results are what they must be: preparatory work, without the excitement bred of skill. Shakespeare's images rip by with no more clarity and not much more crackle than they would get from an American company working without the advantages of a Shakespearean acting tradition. The last company I saw at Stratford was, in fact, seriously inferior to the band of Canadian semi-pros appearing under Tyrone Guthrie's direction at Stratford, Ontario.

Tradition alone, then, doesn't grow geniuses. What happens to the British actor between his callow apprenticeship and his later appearances that impress us so much? I think he does one thing that we haven't yet quite seen the necessity for. He works. I don't mean that he simply applies himself in the silence of his study, or experiments in the classroom, or broods long and hard about the fundamentals of his trade. I mean that he accepts jobs. He accepts all kinds of jobs, in good plays and bad, under able direction or no direction, alongside competent fellow players or alongside amateurs. His first concern is to walk onto a stage as frequently as possible, and long after he has made his mark he will—as Gielgud, Richardson, Guinness, Evans, and Thorndike still do—keep right on appearing season after season, in play after play.

One of the first things you'll notice about a British actor is that he does not live in terror of his script. He barely seems to have asked himself whether it is any good or not. The illiteracy of his author is not his responsibility; idiocy itself may coo from the turning pages—he is undaunted. Lifeless pages and bare-bones dialogue may mean an opportunity to stand on a stage, and standing on a stage is the one thing the star desires.

He doesn't go about it tentatively, either. He doesn't read bad lines with a gingerly air, waiting for the morning notices to tell him whether the author has done right by him. He seems to say to himself, "Can I possibly *invent* a character who would say any of these things, can I become so clear a person that the words themselves will go unnoticed, can I display an attitude of mind that will in itself constitute a performance?"

He does achieve something like this. He walks in with a firm, defined, easily self-possessed air. He breathes security because he has made up his mind—his *own* mind—about what he is playing. (The character may not in every case be the author's; but it is a character.) The actor's vision of the role is intensely personal, and intensely confident. It is precise; because it is precise it may also be relaxed, and expansive. The actor has somehow or other made of the character an old familiar, and he is prepared to interpret anything from rhetoric to the weather report in the light of this special intimacy. He carries his own conviction with him, warmly. The writer may not have written anything; but the actor is going to act. (As a result, a good many so-so plays become great successes in London; but the success is valid, because the actors have made them interesting.)

We go about the process of maturing a little differently here. Our players start out with their fair share of the world's talent. As beginners, they are willing to work, dying to work. They will leap at the first part offered them with the thirst of Tantalus. They'll take the second part, too, perhaps the third.

But the moment a Broadway actor makes a distinct personal success, the roof falls in. A deep protective instinct sweeps over the performer. The next play must be *right*. It must be cautiously selected to advance his career—not his skill, mind you, but his prominence. No mistakes must be made along the way; mistakes are fatal.

Offers of work—after a distinct success—are abundant; the phone is busy and there may be thirteen scripts lying around the apartment. The actor reads each new play with a palsied hand. Is this *it*? He isn't sure; so much depends on the decision. He shows the script to his agent. He shows it to his wife. He shows it to his mother. He shows it to his psychiatrist.

All encourage him to do it. He turns it down. He decides that the quality of the writing is just this side of banal; the plotting needs seriously to be fixed; the distribution of parts doesn't quite give him the emphasis he needs at this stage of his career; the role is unsympathetic; the typing is poor.

Three years and thirty-seven scripts later—and possibly with funds running a little low—the actor puts his trembling hand to a contract. His face is ashen. Rehearsals are apt to be jumpy. Is there a chance of escaping the show out of town? The planning, the nervous patience, the anxiety and the ambition of three long years are now staked on a single venture. It must be magnificent to be worth the wait.

As things turn out, it may not be magnificent. It may fail, and the failure will be far more costly now than it would have been three years earlier.

Or then again, the play may be excellent and the player excellent in it. The lapse of time still represents a dead loss. The actor has spent three precious years standing absolutely still, and, now that his judgment has been so wonderfully borne out, he is sure to spend another three looking for the next one. Substantial careers may be built in this way; but acting itself is not improved.

Shrewdness is a professional virtue, all right. And the do-or-die tensions of the Broadway stage help make it an almost indispensable one. But caution can paralyze a talent at its earliest level; too many of our most promising beginners hustle their abilities into deep-freeze as soon as they have scored. I doubt that we can ever get the suppleness and high skill we admire in the best British performers without plunging in regularly, and getting wet recklessly.

∿ 2 ∿

BUT LET'S BE FAIR.

Agnes de Mille, in her absorbing *Dance to the Piper*, paints a dismaying picture of the contemporary dancer's life—the exhausting preparation for it, the solitary and bitter struggle for recognition, the lifelong poverty that is not even dispelled by critical success. It is impossible to read Miss de Mille without developing a tremendous respect for the men and women who have been willing to part with every kind of emotional and financial security to see to it that their particular craft, and their special vision, endures.

It occurs to me that, whatever we may say about his protective habits, nearly as much admiration is due the contemporary actor. In most seasons it is the player, rather than the playwright, who keeps the theater afloat—a Rosalind Russell who salvages an indifferent piece of writing, a Shirley Booth who fills theaters with no writing at all, a Maurice Evans who gets a revival on the boards.

Yet for all we owe our Broadway actors—a very great deal, indeed—we are paying them on the average of $790 a year, or, to budget it, $15.19 per week. The figure, released annually by the secretary of Actors Equity, varies very little from year to year.

That $790, if we may take it as representative, is, of course, an average: in such a year one fourth of Equity's membership would earn as little as $340, while the top fourth might earn better than $2,445. In the early 1950s Equity was still considering $3,500 a decent minimum—an optimistic figure if I ever heard one.

Disturbing as these revelations are, we are in the habit of not quite taking them seriously. We have a vague and somewhat more comforting image of a theater healthy enough to support its most competent people—the top stars—quite handsomely; and we are convinced in our hearts that the thousands of "unemployed" actors who drag the financial average down are really untalented hangers-on who have no business belonging to Equity.

This pleasant little daydream is easy to dispel. Of Equity's 6,000 members, 5,000 were talented enough to get jobs in one recent season. The trouble is that the jobs, on the average, blew up after ten weeks. Of the presumably well-rewarded top-bracket players who got jobs in plays that ran that season, fewer than one in eight earned $5,000, fewer than one in twenty earned $10,000. The majority of Equity members must piece out a living doing radio and television bits and taking part-time jobs in other fields.

Nor does the picture improve a great deal at the very top. Katharine Cornell, let us say, earned a good bit more than $10,000 before she was through with her successful 1951 revival of *The Constant Wife*. But in the five years after *The Constant Wife* she had no major success to repeat the coup or replenish the cashbox; a major star in a major success has no way of knowing over how long a period present winnings must be spaced.

Every actor, no matter what his competence, lives by the skin of his teeth. And even as he does, he gets very little opportunity to exercise the talent and the training for which he has made so great a sacrifice. Unlike his British brethren, he hasn't the accessible laboratories—the provincial repertories and the state-sponsored institutional theaters—in which, and pretty much at his own expense, he can improve himself or even keep his present gains from going rusty.

Equity has set up a series of "library theaters" for just such a purpose, and these are undeniably useful to a limited number of players each year. But the plays chosen are most often of a kind in which the average performer is already experienced, and the stage direction is rarely inspirational. The Actors Studio, guided by competent directors who have been most generous with their time, cannot take care of more than a carefully selected group of aspirants, and it tends to train them in a single, though virile, style.

The City Center gets a maximum of six plays on the boards each season. The fact that established performers of the caliber of Helen Hayes, Maurice Evans, Judith Anderson, and José Ferrer are willing to work for coffee and cakes, and under unfavorable production conditions, in order to experiment with unfamiliar roles is a sound indication of their anxiety to improve themselves and to serve their profession. But City Center is a dead-end proposition: each production is an isolated unit, it closes in ten days, and growth must begin all over again, somewhere else.

Off-Broadway is increasingly visited by established players— Franchot Tone and Betty Field can occasionally be seen inching about on two-by-four stages in abandoned churches—but here again the risks are at least as great as the opportunities. Rehearsals are rarely as thorough as those for Broadway productions; auditorium and stage are apt to be equally drab; failure in a role has as serious repercussions as the failure on Broadway for which the actor has been paid. Venturing off-Broadway in a "non-commercial" play may be a challenge, all right; but it is often a challenge without any discernible prize.

Each of these long-shot adventures is an heroic attempt on the part of a desperate profession to make the actor's life spiritually, if not financially, rewarding. But taken all together, they serve only a fraction of the genuinely talented, they do that only sporadically, and they nowhere offer that range and diversity of style that help an actor expand his natural equipment and prepare for the theater's most complex roles.

In short, the contemporary actor not only commits himself to a catch-as-catch-can-existence, but does so with the almost certain knowledge that he will never be permitted to mature in his work. (Small wonder that he clutches his infinitesimal gains to his breast and shudders as he reaches for a commercial script.) Nor is there much that can be promised him in the way of a really satisfying solution—until the playwrights catch hold again and win back to the theater a large and loyal audience. But if we can offer him no current solution, we can at least send up a salute.

↶ 3 ↷

THE MINUTE actors go galloping across the countryside to appear in two-week, four-week, and six-week festivals of Shakespeare, Shaw, and any other playwright whose works might conceivably constitute a "season," an old familiar passion rears its haloed head. Here these players are, jumping from role to role in a variety of masterworks, and doing it from night to night—or from week to week, anyway. The virtues of repertory become the principal topic of Coke-machine conversation during rehearsal breaks, and the insistent question returns: When we get back to New York in the fall, why can't we have repertory there?

Of course, this talk will grow fainter in August. By that time the fall will loom as a more or less practical prospect: it will be time to get a job, and such jobs as are going will be in brand-new, one-shot projects financed by unphilanthropical fellows whose sole hope is for the kind of hit that will keep an actor playing the same part forever, or at least until Brandon de Wilde is old enough to replace him. The beauties of the long-run system tend to reassert themselves as the last camp chairs, and the last paychecks, are quietly folded away.

That repertory—with its constant renewal of the creative impulse and its steady invitation to growth—makes an actor healthier and wiser is perfectly clear. Unfortunately, it has never in our time made him wealthier. Though earnest groups have banded together over the years, announced exhilarating plans, and even succeeded in raising substantial funds, the lovely daydream has always come tumbling down.

There have usually been three or four ambitious productions played to dwindling receipts, then a desperate suggestion to theatergoers that if they really care about quality they'd better hurry up and demonstrate it, then silence—and a wistful trip to the warehouse. The silence, by the way, is often an injured one: the implication is that the audience has been at fault.

I suspect one reason for such consistent failure has been the unrealistic assumption that the theater's chief business is to keep its actors happy. The theater, in its gross and ungrateful way, seems to thrive on the contrary notion that it doesn't much matter what's going on backstage so long as the audience is happy. The poor player can be as wretched as he likes in his unbearable success; if the paying customer is content, the issue is closed.

I don't imagine we're ever really going to change this state of affairs, and I feel morally certain that the next inspired company to conceive of the audience as a benevolent and protective association dedicated to the enrichment of the player's life and craft is going to stub its toe on the same old stage brace.

All of which brings up the further, and additionally dismaying, fact that—apart from outright subsidy on a national scale—no repertory scheme has ever worked unless there was a pressing economic necessity breathing down its neck. If Shakespeare's plays were presented in dizzying alteration—his actors may have had to keep some forty plots spinning in their heads each season—it wasn't because Burbage and Kemp rather fancied this method of improving themselves; it was because no one could scrape up an audience for even a quite popular play more than once or twice a week. (Burbage undoubtedly grumbled. "Why can't they support us through five or ten performances and give us all a rest?" is what he probably said, in slightly different spelling.) Like any other theatrical demand, the demand for repertory must first come from the other side of the house.

Are our long-suffering, honestly ambitious actors permanently out of luck, then? Clearly, there is no agitation at the contemporary box office for nightly changes of bill. As a matter of fact, there is a profound contemporary resentment at having to study schedules closely enough to keep from wandering witlessly into a play you've always hated. On most counts, and for most playgoers, the prospect is simply a nuisance.

I keep thinking, though, that there is one curious combination of demand and necessity that might someday bring us a partial answer. There are any number of prominent and popular actors who are no longer available for long runs in the theater: having successfully flirted with travel, television, and the movies they have become used to the excitement of real changes of pace and now frankly dread the boredom of a two-year Broadway commitment. They are constantly being invited back; but they won't come back.

They won't come back, that is, on a long-term basis. What a good many of them would do, however, is give up two or three months out of any one year to an attractive play in company with a stable, and more or less familiar, supporting cast.

Two or three months would not get a regular one-shot production off the financial hook. If the production were stored, though, against another two or three months another season and if five or six "name" players—you can name them as well as I—were to be drawn into a rotating plan involving five or six plays, some sort of shuttling year-round operation might be possible.

The ground-breaking costs would, of course, be enormous; the juggling of available free periods would test the tenacity of City Center's Jean Dalrymple. But I have a hunch that sooner or later somebody's going to try it. If and when they do, two of the preliminary conditions of repertory will have been met: the audience will have a clear reason for wanting to come, and the changes of bill will be dictated by theatrical urgencies peculiar to our time.

I'm no doubt daydreaming as lavishly as those players on the summer lawns. But we won't get repertory by mooning over Molière's wonderful working conditions; we'll get it when it's to the obvious practical advantage of everybody in sight.

᪣ 4 ᪣

EVERY SO OFTEN there's quite a whoop and holler about a new novel that dazzles us all with the discovery that beloved figures in the entertainment world can be heels at heart. There's something tasty about learning that an endearing personality has ice water coursing through every expansive vein, and we are apt to lap up each new shocking revelation with relish and a sense of surprise.

It's the surprise that surprises me. What little dreams have we been nursing all these years? How did we suppose a really emphatic entertainer got to be emphatic enough to come bursting into our living rooms, our neighborhood movie houses, or even our extremely dignified legitimate theaters—by standing hat in hand on the sidewalk until someone asked him in?

One of the sure rules of show business—you can pick your medium—is that talent is dandy, but you'd better have a little touch of the louse to go with it. "Louse" is perhaps too strong a word. A trace of get-up-and-go, a small habit of asserting oneself, a decent ability to outshout a hurricane and force it to reverse its course will do.

For the business of becoming popular, or well known, or even liked, in show business is never a business of smiling wistfully at passing employers, keeping your nails clean, and having confidence that your transparent virtues will be noised about through some sort of sympathetic magic. Much as the world loves its entertainment, the world's head still has to be bashed in before it notices that a given entertainer exists.

The process is, in most cases, a rough one. Agents everywhere are seriously hoping to discover fresh talent, but they don't quite imagine that it resides in the seedy fellow facing them across the desk;

they imagine that it is going to descend, luminous and unmistakable, from a cloud that is hovering just around the corner. Producers are avid for new faces; but it takes a lot of professional aging to make a face look that new. Audiences are literally searching for joy, but there is a sense in which every audience has to be commanded into enjoying itself.

Any entertainer who finally acquires what reviewers call "authority"—and the term is meant to be a complimentary one—is probably the possessor of talent and toughness in about equal parts. In fact, if a man were at the mercy of some tantalizing genie and could choose only one of the two on which to build his career, he'd probably be better off taking toughness. There is plenty of talent around the country that no one has ever heard of: very good actors can be found, for instance, teaching school, repairing vacuum cleaners, or doing the dinner dishes—either because they have not had the stamina to batter down doors, or because they have consciously elected the less tempestuous life.

And, conversely, there are giants in the world—no names need be mentioned—who have clambered to glory on determination alone. We're not really confused about these folk: everyone recognizes a combination of nine tenths battering ram and one tenth memory when he sees it. The funny thing is that we don't really mind these conspicuously insensitive dynamos at all. In the beginning, we are inclined to be amused by them. By mid-career, we often find ourselves respecting them for their unbelievable staying power. In the end we invariably become fond of them.

Indeed, the making of a career—and sometimes the making of a talent, too—often turns on that one moment of crisis when the spine stiffens, the jaw sets, and the vocabulary improves noticeably. The story is often told of a now well-known director who, having had some six or seven failures and finding himself at an impasse with his current leading lady, locked himself in a hotel room and faced up to the fact that if he couldn't win the fight in progress he'd never have the nerve to direct another play. The fight was a dandy, the director won it, and a very distinguished—and sensitive—career was under way. Sensitivity, it would seem, sometimes must walk on hobnailed boots.

I'm not, of course, suggesting that every successful actor need be capable of sending his aged mother scooting down a flight of stairs in a wheel chair. Nor am I suggesting—before I get a testy letter from Actors Equity—that our present stars all carry knives, despoil ingénues, and breakfast on Bloody Marys. Most of the people who have achieved security in the contemporary theater have also achieved a remarkable serenity, not to say dignity. They have long since won their fights, and once you've won a fight you can be twice as gentle as the fellow who's still afraid of one.

It's just that a judicious dash of the old Nero is as necessary as talent to the flowering of a first-rate personality, and our eyes shouldn't pop quite so wide each time the truth is breathlessly rumored.

∽ 5 ∾

As ONE who occasionally wanders onto a university campus, or takes a hesitant step into the lecture belt, I'm used to the fellow whose hand pops up during the question period and tosses what he regards as a bombshell, or at least a small needle, into the conversational haystack. The gimmick varies from year to year, of course; but the latest topic that is supposed to throw a visitor off base, and embroil him in hotheaded controversy or at least embarrassing double talk, is the Actors Studio. "What do you think of the 'method' promulgated by the Actors Studio?" this joker asks, figuring that he's now got you on a *real* spot.

Two things surprise me. One is that the Studio, which operates very quietly and with what amounts to a horror of publicity, is so widely known and discussed thousands of miles from New York

City. (The Studio lands in the newspapers only when a Marilyn Monroe decides to drop in—quite earnestly, I understand—for a bit of self-improvement; most of the time it minds its own business, works hard, and worries about quality rather than favorable quotes.)

The other surprise is that the zealous questioner somehow or other expects a practicing reviewer to be *against* the workshop that Elia Kazan helped found and that Lee Strasberg devotes all of his valuable time to directing. A caustic quip is anticipated (the questioner's fists are already clenched in preparation for a fiery reply and impassioned defense); the standard lecturer is supposed to be equipped with at least a few mild jokes about the brooding, the soul-searching, the agonized introspection that goes on wherever "method" actors gather.

I don't know exactly why all this is so, except that any up-and-coming, markedly distinctive style is apt to invite criticism, and be extraordinarily sensitive to such criticism, while it is still establishing itself. Its very distinctiveness will make it an easy mark for parody; and the intensity with which its outright partisans pursue it can't help but stir up strong response—of one kind or another—in the immediate vicinity. Everyone's heard a couple of dozen stories about the "method" actor who stops rehearsals dead because he has been given a simple cue like "Where's Julia?" and now needs three or four minutes of profound interior deliberation before he is able to "justify" his answer, "She's upstairs." Furthermore, when an Actors Studio alumnus is tossed onto a stage alongside someone who has not yet got the message, perfectly real problems—and serious clashes—are sure to develop. Directors have been led away, trembling, from such meetings.

Yet one thing seems to me to be clear. Like it or lump it, the Actors Studio has literally given birth to the clearest, most carefully defined, most virile approach to the player's craft that the American theater has produced. If it has partial roots in the Stanislavski-born, and Group Theater-nourished, techniques of the Thirties, it has gone well beyond them: from low-keyed naturalism into open fire, from prosy accuracy to ranging and even rhythmic power.

It has evolved a "right" pattern for the plays of Tennessee Williams, Arthur Miller, and William Inge—who are, after all, our best young playwrights.

Its fertility as a proving ground can no longer be questioned: Marlon Brando, Ben Gazzara, Julie Harris, Maureen Stapleton, Anthony Franciosa, Eli Wallach, Kim Stanley, Albert Salmi, Eva Marie Saint, Paul Newman, and the late James Dean have all (let's make this an understatement) been influenced by it. And its ability to set new playwrights in motion—this, by the way, is one of the tests of an acting style's validity—is demonstrated by such a venture as *A Hatful of Rain*: dramatist Michael Gazzo seems virtually to have listened his successful play into existence while catching inflections at Studio sessions.

I don't know that there's much room left for debate: the Studio simply exists as an obvious creative force, one that breathes the air of the living moment and that somehow stamps on its members a character that is peculiarly American. Together with American musical comedy, it asserts itself as an indigenous and expanding contribution to the arts of the theater that is as personal as handwriting and that cannot quite be duplicated anywhere else under the sun.

If there is any conceivable danger in admitting to a vigorous enthusiasm for the works and pomps of the "method," it lies in the possibility that—here and there and around the country—this bold and flourishing signature may come to be regarded not as one style but as all styles, as style itself. Its founders have pretended to no such universality, so far as I know; the players at the Studio are patently not preparing themselves for the richer locutions of Richard Brinsley Sheridan, or, for that matter, the lyric exercises of William Shakespeare. If they are, they do not as yet show signs of it.

And if some ardent youngster bent on deifying what is an intensely practical and intensely contemporary technique needs to carry a small antidote around with him, a pocket reminder that a single exciting style cannot hope to embrace the theater's whole range, I'd suggest that he pick up the handy collection of Stark

Young's drama criticism that has been packaged under the joint title *The Flower in Drama, and Glamour*—a small volume that can easily be carried to rehearsals. Mr. Young, who wrote most of these pieces in the 1920s, continues to be interested in mechanics as well as in truth. "There is," he points out along the way, "the American stage voice with its tone driven through the nose, its inflexible upper lip, its bad placement in the throat, and its frequent monotony." Some of the genuine stars who have come from the Studio might still look that one over.

More importantly, Mr. Young likes to remind us that the function of acting is not merely to intensify nature but to find in it some formal design ("to add to the character and event some element of abstraction that goes beyond and above them, something of that pure and separable element that arises from every artistic expression"), that there is such a thing as conscious control as well as raging inspiration ("it is better to lose the feeling and keep the gesture"), that urgency and immediacy are groundwork virtues but not the whole story ("acting is not art until it ceases to be life"). It's a good book for any actor to have at his side, preferably open.

But let's be patient. And properly grateful that we have a blazing fire to warm ourselves by while we wait for that crystalline detachment which will illuminate even as it continues to give off heat.

☙ THIRTEEN ❧

Barns

☙ *1* ❧

IT SEEMS TO ME that the pleasantest thing about summer theater—for the reviewer and paying customer alike—is that you don't have to go to it. This sounds like an insidious remark, and I hasten to add that it is intended as quite a compliment.

It just so happens that we live in an age when regular, or winter, playgoing involves a series of social, moral, and financial pressures. Our "smash hit" psychology decrees that there are a certain few shows we must see. It also decrees that we must see them while they are still suitable subject matter for cocktail conversation.

Furthermore, because seats for these lucky entertainments are in such demand, we must see them at a time determined not by our own madcap impulse for a night on the town, but by the rigorous, impartial apportionment of the box-office man who handles mail orders.

When the appointed night finally rolls around, neither rain, hail, sleet, snow nor gastrointestinal embarrassment can keep us from our clear obligation. We know what it is we must do.

Summer theater reverses all this. Should a small hurricane be blowing up, you can shut the windows and go to bed in perfect composure; you haven't been holding onto a couple of hard-won pasteboards from time immemorial. Should a covey of house guests descend suddenly upon you, you can bid them welcome with an honest nonchalance; you don't have to tear up your tickets for *My Fair Lady* right in front of them, announcing with a kind of grisly gaiety that you didn't want to see the old thing anyway.

Better still, you can achieve a remarkable coup; you can get the house guest out of the house. Clapping him on the shoulder in idiot exuberance, you can suggest: "Say, why don't we all go over to the Old Black Barn? They've got quite an interesting show this week—Elmo Lincoln in his first stage appearance." And you can march him out the front door and over to that nearest strawhat with the confident expectation that you will be able to get seats and that you will have to play the hearty host for no more than two ten-minute intermissions.

The best thing about summer theater, I think, is that it puts play-going back on a whimsical basis. All urgencies disappear. Since the chances are better than three to one that you'll be seeing an old play, you don't have to spend much time worrying about whether or not you ought to like it. Your intellectual standing in the community isn't going to depend very heavily on your decision. In fact, you are really relieved of making any decision at all.

Since the new plays you do see (summer theaters are doing more and more of them) are still in the "tryout" stage, you can look right at them without fear or favor, taking or leaving them for precisely what they are. No one has hallowed or damned them yet. (It might be argued that this constitutes the only candid and direct author-audience relationship left to the contemporary theater.)

Since you haven't poured months of planning and preparation into the event, the entertainment doesn't have to work so hard to make things up to you. Even if the show isn't very good—which, it is whispered, is sometimes the case—you don't come out feeling cheated.

You've at least had a night out on the very night you wanted out, you've been able to indulge that secret yen for soda pop that embarrasses you in more formal circumstances, you've been able to fill your lungs with cigarette smoke and fresh air simultaneously, and you may even have been casually pleased. In the summer theaters, a nice little show is a nice little show, and what'll we do tomorrow night?

It's almost relaxing. I suspect that's how the actors find it, too. There is a canard in circulation to the effect that actors go to the country to make money. My own guess is that they do it to be near the Coke machines. Drop in on a summer-theater rehearsal and you will find a thriving social life centered around the dispenser on the patio; occasionally a performer or two will, when summoned, leave the socratic gathering to rush through a scene onstage, but his real objective is to get back to the clean-living world of the porch, his real mood that of the happy inland beachcomber.

Indeed, things were so relaxed at one barn rehearsal I attended that the director was able to guide the destinies of his players while lying flat on his back in the center aisle. He was sound of mind and body, too; he was just sparing himself the usual tensions of his profession.

And it must be pleasant to play an entire season without doom hanging over one's head. Even if the show isn't quite ready, even if the star and supporting company have barely met, the venture isn't in danger of closing in Philadelphia or at the end of its first Broadway week. Salaries are pretty certain to go right on into September. If they don't much like you this week, they may find you fascinating next. You can give the ulcers a rest, and pick up a tan.

On both sides of the footlights, summer theater—in a metaphorical sense, anyway—takes the heat off. Whatever its defects, it briefly restores theater to the kind of drop-in, come-as-you-are footing it once enjoyed all the year round and then lamentably lost to the movies.

~ 2 ~

As we've been saying, everyone supposes that the reason stars who have worked all winter go traipsing off to the summer theaters is money, and it is barely possible that money has something to do with it. There may be another lure, though—apart from the Coke machines. Actors may *like* to rehearse haphazardly, open insecurely, close at the precise moment they have begun to get the hang of a role, and wake every morning to the sound of apprentices' hammers knocking next week's scenery into deceptively sturdy shape, because it's the only way they can remember what the theater once meant to them.

One of the real penalties of being a professional is loss of glamour. (The more a player acquires it for other people, the less he is able to savor it for himself.) When a young enthusiast first arrives in New York, he is still faintly drunk with the smell of paint, the wobble of scenery sliding into place, the sheer pleasure of being in the company of other people who have typewritten "sides" stuffed in their pockets.

It's an aura that is quickly dispelled, not because the commercial theater doesn't have its own kind of excitement but because the commercial theater is essentially a place of urgent, efficient, common-sense work. Almost the first thing a tyro learns is to wipe that look of enthusiasm off his face; it marks him as a beginner. He doesn't burst into a manager's office with the light of love in his eyes. He strolls in, as indifferently as possible, with a knowing calm and—if he can manage it—a suggestion that he has been painfully lured away from pursuits that interest him a great deal more.

When he gets a part, he doesn't run through the streets waving his contract. He stubs out a cigarette in Sardi's and murmurs that, well, he does have to support his family somehow. At rehearsals, he is polite but matter-of-fact, adjusting his glasses and marking up his script with the philosophical despair of one who has seen playwrights come and go and is sure that they all will. While the play is coming together, he will spend as much time as is permissible in his dressing room silently trimming mustaches.

At the out-of-town opening, he doesn't bob around backstage wishing everyone luck at the top of his lungs and behaving like a happy firecracker that is about to explode; he confesses to opening-night nerves, all right, but in a dour and impatient fashion—as though he were extremely irritated with himself for not having got past these childish extravagances. When the opening-night curtain is down, he doesn't grab the leading lady and waltz her about the stage, amid hysterical cackles from the rest of the company. He immediately becomes soberer than ever, gets paper and pencil ready, and listens to the director's notes with alarming concentration and frequent shrewd nods to show that he knew *that* problem would be coming up.

As for the odor of glue and canvas, he doesn't even see the scenery until he gets to New Haven, and the thrill of the moment is somewhat modified by the squad of armed stagehands who are standing in front of it to make sure he doesn't accidentally help lift it.

Every once in a while, though, he must yearn for a whiff of the giddy, foolishly exhilarating, somewhat slapdash but much more comradely atmosphere that once made him want to become an actor. He needs to remember what he thought the theater was going to be like when he first talked a couple of friends into renting the YMCA auditorium for two risky nights, wrote Samuel French for a copy of *Grumpy*, and saw to the printing of tickets himself. He needs to have his efficiency relaxed and his love refreshed. And this,

I think, is one reason why actors don't just lie down in an air-conditioned room and reread their notices all summer.

Not that the barns are going to let them get away with right-off-the-beach performances, or that audiences are going to invite them to turn a season's touring into something like Til Eulenspiegel's merry pranks. Standards in the country are getting higher all the time. But however professional the standards, and however cold the cash, that's still a different breeze blowing in under the rafters.

Instead of a cab ride from one city block to another, it's a walk across the lawn. Instead of a gray brick building arbitrarily set between a men's clothing store and a manufacturer of buntings, it's a theater standing all by itself. Instead of long, intense rehearsals with the death penalty waiting at the end of them, it's the best you can do in a week with a smile on your face and no great fear in your heart.

And if you'd got to feeling like a cog in a machine assembled in New Haven, you can stretch your limbs, stumble over lumber and get stuck to freshly painted fireplaces to your heart's content. You can even cheer the denim brigade on as they paint the second-act staircase during the first-act intermission.

It's like meeting a girl you haven't seen in years and discovering that your immature taste was a credit to you.

ABOUT THE AUTHOR

WALTER KERR, drama critic of the New York Herald Tribune, was born in Evanston, Illinois. He attended De Paul University for two years and completed his studies at Northwestern, where he took his B.S. in 1937, his M.S. in 1938. For eleven years he was a faculty member in the Department of Speech and Drama at Catholic University of America, Washington, D.C. He was drama critic of Commonweal for two years, then became critic for the Herald Tribune in 1950. He has directed three plays on Broadway, including King of Hearts, his wife's successful comedy of 1954. At present, he and Mrs. Kerr are preparing a musical comedy for forthcoming Broadway production.